GO
FOR THE
GREEN
TURF RACING MADE EASY

by
Bill Heller

DRF Press
NEW YORK

Published by
Daily Racing Form Press
100 Broadway, 7th Floor
New York, NY 10005

ISBN: 0-9700147-8-3
Library of Congress Control Number: 2003100925

Cover and jacket designed by Chris Donofry

Text design by Neuwirth and Associates

Printed in the United States of America

All entries, results, charts and related information provided by

821 Corporate Drive • Lexington, KY 40503-2794 Toll Free (800) 333-2211 or
(859) 224-2860; Fax (859) 224-2811 • Internet: www.equibase.com

The Thoroughbred Industry's Official Database for Racing Information

Contents

Acknowledgments

My SOON-TO-BE 15-year-old son and handicapping whiz, Benjamin (a.k.a. Bubba), came up big-time. He helped me go through stacks of *Daily Racing Form*s searching for sample races, amass mountains of statistics, which were used in the book's many tables, and, with my wife, Anna, listened to the entire manuscript and offered suggestions.

Thanks to two good friends, Dick Hamilton of the National Museum of Racing, and Bob Gersowitz, and to hard-working Joan Lawrence and Bonnie Cooper at the National Thoroughbred Racing Association.

Daily Racing Form's Debbie Hernandez and Rich Allen were extremely helpful, as were my editors at the *Form*, Dean Keppler, Robin Foster, and, of course, Steven Crist.

Special thanks to two Hall of Famers, trainer Phil Johnson and jockey Jerry Bailey, for their insights.

*To "Nights in White Satin"
and days gone by*

1

THE FINAL FRONTIER

THE TURF COURSE IS the final frontier of handicapping, the last place a well-schooled player can generate an edge. Even as rival handicappers use speed figures and pace numbers, you can still locate and cash overlays on grass if you are knowledgeable and patient enough to find them.

That's the whole idea, right, to go for the green?

Along the way, you can learn to pinpoint vulnerable grass favorites or contenders to avoid, which jockeys and trainers to bypass, and which situations lead to poor betting value. You can increase your knowledge of grass pedigrees with this book's handy alphabetical list of every dam who produced a graded grass stakes winner since 1996, as well as a few influential dams of ungraded stakes winners.

Invariably, those more than 800 dams produce subsequent quality grass horses who offer betting value when they make their initial starts on turf or when they move up in class. Other times, brothers and sisters of these stakes-producing mares win their first starts on grass.

Additional tables later in the book—more than 275 trainers' recent records with first-time turfers, nearly 100 trainers' three-year overall turf records, 35 of the nation's top jockeys' career winning percentages on dirt and grass, and lists of top grass sires—can only help your handicapping, too. All the tables and lists can be used for years.

The ticket to success in betting turf races is finding value in your bets. To determine the value of a wager, you must have a feel for the odds, or the range of odds, for the prime contenders in a race. Increasing your knowledge will make you a better handicapper or bettor.

The beauty of handicapping is that it is a skill you should improve at as you get older. But there is one caveat, and it's an important one. You can only improve your handicapping if you have an open mind and accept the reality that there is no magic formula out there, no foolproof system that continually cranks out winners.

Deal with reality. And the reality is that favorites at every racetrack win between 25 and 35 percent of the time. Year after year.

That means that 65 to 75 percent of favorites lose. Vulnerable favorites are everywhere. In grass racing, they may be the chronic losers, the ones with poor turf jockeys or trainers, or the horses with near-impossible outside post positions. By identifying vulnerable favorites, we identify races in which the horse or horses we like have fair or greater than fair betting value. In turf racing, that happens a lot.

So let's go to work.

THE GAME PLAN

How do you attack the grass game? More than 30 years of handicapping has shaped this game plan, featuring principles you can use repeatedly. Most apply to turf and dirt.

1. **Start from the bottom when reading past-performance lines (PP's).** This is a tip I got from a good friend and former newspaper handicapper, John Piesen.

   Yes, it may take you a few more minutes handicapping each race, but it's more than worth the time. Remember, in parimutuel wagering, you are literally competing with other bettors. By starting at each horse's least recent race—the bottom PP—you ensure you won't miss any useful information. Perhaps two horses in this race had already faced each other, or the horse you're considering has raced at this level previously. You will also have a better understanding of how each horse is coming into today's race.

   The bottom line on doing this is that many other bettors don't. Glancing at a horse's most recent three or four PP's will invariably lead to missing information that may be important to handicapping this race.

   Here's a telling example:

   In the Grade 2 Appleton Handicap at one mile on grass at Gulfstream Park, January 4, 2003, scratches left a field of nine. The second-longest shot in the field was Point Prince, who drew in from the also-eligibles and was dismissed at 29-1 from post 9. The two favorites were Balto Star at 9-5 and Krieger at 2-1. Krieger had won his last two starts, an allowance race and the Grade 3 Tropical Turf Handicap. Balto Star was 2 for 5 on grass, beating Krieger in one of those races.

   What about Point Prince? A glance at only his top PP (see next page), a second in an allowance race at Churchill Downs, would have suggested he didn't have a prayer. However, by starting with the bottom of his four turf PP's, there was a reason for hope. On May 30, 2002, under Pat Day, Point Prince had won his grass debut, an allowance race, by one length at 7-2 over Grammarian.

   All Grammarian had done since was win the Grade 2 Sunset Handicap, finish second in the Grade 1 Hollywood Turf

13 Point Prince
Own: Team Valor
Forest Green, Crimson Panel, Crimson Cap
CRUZ M R (—) 2002:(1489 259 .17)

Dk. b or br g. 4 (Mar)
Sire: Youmadeyourpoint (Diamond Prospect) $1,000
Dam: Princess of Note (Notebook)
Br: Stanley M Ersoff (Fla)
Tr: Romans Dale (—) 2002:(532 81 .15)

L 112

Life	7	3	1	1	$53,580	93
2002	6	2	1	1	$47,580	93
2001	1	1	0	0	$6,000	65
GP Ⓣ	0	0	0	0	$0	–

D.Fst	2	2	0	0	$21,700	78
Wet(340*)	1	0	0	1	$3,400	80
Turf(230)	4	1	1	0	$28,480	93
DstⓉ(310)	2	1	1	0	$28,480	93

24Nov02-7CD gd 1 Ⓣ :23⁴ :47³ 1:12⁴ 1:37⁴ 3↑ Alw 44120N2X **93** 9 3nk 1hd 1hd 2hd 2 3/4 McKee J5 L 109 *1.40e 82-24 Devil'sGulch120 3/4 PointPrince109 1/2 EverythingToGin118 1/2 Dueled,gamely
Previously trained by Sahadi Jenine
27Jly02-5Dmr fm 1 1/16 Ⓣ :23³ :46⁴ 1:10³ 1:40⁴ 3↑ OClm 62500N **84** 3 32 1/2 48 1/2 45 42 1/2 84 Desormeaux K J LB 116 7.50 95-04 *Zanapour*119nk Top Honours121 1 *Irish Minstrel*121nk Rail trip,outkicked
30Jun02-3Hol fm 1 1/8 Ⓣ :48² 1:12 1:35³ 1:47³+ Cinema BCH-G3 — 3 1 1/2 1 1 — — — Smith M E LB 114 18.10 — 10 *Inesperado*116no Regiment122 1/2 Johar118 3
Dueled inside, bore out badly, pulled up, vanned off Previously trained by Romans Dale
30May02-9CD fm 1 Ⓣ :23³ :47 1:11⁴ 1:35⁴ 3↑ Alw 35530N1X **88** 3 4 2 41 3/4 41 3/4 2 1/2 1 1 Day P L 110 3.80 93-07 Point Prince110 1 Grammarian120 3/4 Red Antics123 2 4w, hand urging
27Apr02-7CD sly 1 1/16 :23³ :48 1:13 1:46 Alw 43180N1X **80** 2 42 1/4 52 1/2 63 3/4 41 3/4 34 1/2 Court J K L 118 12.50 73-25 Thunderpumper118 Sarav121 3 1/2 *PointPrince*118nk Bmp start,no late gain
Previously trained by Garcia Rodolfo
20Jan02-11GP fst 6 1/2f :22⁴ :46³ 1:12³ 1:19¹ Clm 35000 (35-30) **78** 9 2 3nk 3 1 1 1/2 12 1/4 Chavez J F L 120 5.10 80-22 PointPrince120 2 1/4 FortunteRoyl120nk ExpectPc120 4 1/4 Bmpd, steadied turn
20Dec01-11Crc fst 5 1/2f :23 :47³ 1:00¹ 1:07 Md c-12500 **65** 6 6 53 1/4 32 1/2 11 1/2 110 1/2 Gonzalez C V L 120 2.40 88-15 *PointPrince*120 10 SouthernSteam120 1 1/4 ImprtilPlyer120 1 1/4 3 wide, drew off
Claimed from Ersoff Stanley M for $12,500, Ersoff Stanley M Trainer 2001(as of 12/20): (84 11 10 12 0.13)
WORKS: Dec31 **GP 4f fst :49² B** *31/71* Dec23 **GP 5f fst 1:01⁴ B** *12/39* Dec12 **GP 4f fst :49 B** *14/26* Nov14 **CD 5f fst 1:01⁴ B** *15/39* Oct30 **CD 5f sly 1:02⁴ B** *7/18* Oct15 **CD 5f fst 1:05² B** *54/60*
TRAINER: 31-60Days(133 .13 $1.44) Turf(124 .15 $1.60) GrdStk(22 .00 $0.00)

won Sunset Hcap (G2) 7/21/02
2nd by 1 length Hollywd Turf Cup (G1) to Sligo Bay 11/23/02

Cup, and win the Grade 2 San Gabriel Handicap. This was a nice horse Point Prince beat.

What had Point Prince done since? Not much. After being vanned off the track in the Grade 3 Cinema Breeders' Cup Handicap at Hollywood Park, he returned to finish eighth in an allowance/optional $62,500 claimer. Switched from Jenine Sahadi's barn to Dale Romans's, Point Prince returned after a four-month freshening to finish a game second by three-quarters of a length in an allowance race at Churchill Downs as part of the favored 7-5 entry. Point Prince was hardly a logical choice stepping up to the Grade 2 Appleton, but at least he had displayed considerable class in his very first turf race. At 29-1, he won by 1¼ lengths.

2. **Look for reasons for an improved performance.** If a horse shows sudden improvement, was it because of a change: blinkers on or off, Lasix added, a surface switch, a different jockey or a different trainer? If so, that horse is likely to perform well again.

Music's Storm had won two of four grass starts for trainer Eduardo Inda when he entered the starting gate for the Grade

1 **Music's Storm**
Red
Own:Jones Aaron U & Marie D
White; Red Cross Sashes, Red Band
DAY P (71 14 15 9 .20) 2003:(331 61 .18)

Dk. b or br c. 4 (Feb) OBSAUG00 $335,000
Sire: Storm Creek (Storm Cat) $15,000
Dam: Where Music Is(In Reality)
Br: Mockingbird Farm Inc (Fla)
Tr: Pletcher Todd A(19 5 0 2 .26) 2003:(216 49 .23)

L 123

Life	14	3	3	0	$226,170	103	D.Fst	6	1	1	0	$41,160	89
2003	2	0	1	0	$95,600	103	Wet(315)	0	0	0	0	$0	–
2002	12	3	2	0	$130,570	100	Turf(335)	8	2	2	0	$185,010	103
Kee Ⓣ	0	0	0	0	$0	–	DstⓉ(310)	5	2	1	0	$89,410	100

Previously trained by Inda Eduardo

1Mar03-8SA	gd	1	Ⓣ	:23⁴	:47²	1:11¹	1:34⁴	4↑	FKilroeMleH-G2	**98**	1	3¹	51¾	31½	3²	84¾	Desormeaux K J	LB 116	15.30	83–16	Redattore120¹ Good Journey124² Decarchy118nk	Pulled,stalked,no bid	11
25Jan03-2SA	fm	1⅛	Ⓣ	:46⁴	1:10³	1:34⁴	1:46²	4↑	ⓇSnshnMillTrf500k	**103**	5	10¹⁰	10¹⁰	9⁵	61½	2no	Desormeaux K J	LB 118	8.00	97–08	Admnnstrtr120no Msc'sStrm118¹ FrbddnAppl120¹	Off slow,rank,led late	12
26Dec02-7SA	fm	1	Ⓣ	:23³	:47²	1:11²	1:35⁴		Sir Beaufort78k	**100**	7	8¹⁰	86½	86¾	4⁵	2hd	Desormeaux K J	LB 120	13.50	83–22	Insprdo122hd Music'sStorm120½ GoldnArrow118¹	Off slw,rank,stdy6-1/2	8
1Dec02-8Hol	fm	1⅛	Ⓣ	:49³	1:13²	1:36³	1:48³	+	Hol Derby-G1	**69**	3	1¹	1¹	1hd	96½	9¹⁴	Desormeaux K J	LB 122 b	17.50	72–17	*Johar*1221½ Mananan Mclir122nk Royal Gem122½	Pulled,inside,wkened	9
6Nov02-7Hol	fm	1	Ⓣ	:23³	:46⁴	1:10¹	1:34¹		ⓇBien Bien73k	**98**	9	76¾	64¼	4¾	2hd	1hd	Desormeaux K J	LB 119 b	24.40	93–13	Musc'sStorm119hd GoldnArrow1192½ *Rshn'ToAltr*119¹	Bid 4 wide, gamely	9
16Oct02-7SA	fm	*6½f	Ⓣ	:22²	:44²	1:06⁴	1:12⁴	3↑	OClm 80000N	**84**	4	3	4²	42½	5⁴	64½	Stevens G L	LB 116 b	5.80	88–07	With Iris118½ Most Likely118¹ El Curioso118¹	Pulled,chased,wkened	7
24Jly02-8Dmr	fm	1	Ⓣ	:22³	:46	1:10¹	1:34²		ⓇOceanside84k	**77**	3	1hd	2hd	2hd	41½	78¼	Stevens G L	LB 118 b	3.30	85–05	TruPhnomnon116¹ DrmMchn114¾ DmondHop115½	Pulled,rail,weakened	8
Run in divisions																							
3Jly02-5Hol	fm	1	Ⓣ	:23²	:47²	1:11	1:34⁴		OClm 100000N	**91**	6	21½	2¹	21½	1hd	11¼	Stevens G L	LB 118 b	5.50	90–10	Music's Storm1181¼ DiamondHope120¹ SixHitter119no	Pulled,bid,led,held	7
13Jun02-6Hol	fst	7f		:22¹	:45	1:09¹	1:22¹	3↑	Alw 48000N1X	**89**	4	2	4³	4³	3⁴	2⁴	Stevens G L	LB 116 b	12.00	84–15	TmlyActon115⁴ *Msc'sStorm*116½ Dc'sAllwnc115²	3wd into lane,late 2nd	5
19May02-7Hol	fst	7f		:22¹	:45	1:09³	1:22²	3↑	Alw 48864N1X	**74**	3	4	1hd	1hd	54½	69½	Valenzuela P A	LB 115 b	7.50	78–11	Alfurune119nk Olmodavor115² *Golden Hare*116⁶	Squeezed into lane	6
31Mar02-1SA	fst	7f		:22	:44⁴	1:09⁴	1:23²		Md Sp Wt 48k	**80**	4	2	1¹	1¹	13½	13½	Valenzuela P A	LB 120 b	4.20	88–12	Music'sStorm1203½ Juststorm120⁷ OurNwRcruit1203½	Cleared 1/8, driving	6
2Mar02-1SA	fst	6f		:22	:45¹	:57³	1:10		Md Sp Wt 46k	**70**	9	2	3nk	41½	66½	69½	McCarron C J	B 120	8.70	78–12	Tough Game120³ Requesto120³ Encino Ump1201½	4 wide, weakened	9

WORKS: **Apr20 Kee 4f fst :49³ B** *25/52* ●**Apr13 Kee 5f fst 1:00¹ H** *1/26* **Apr6 Kee 4f fst :51³ B** *44/47* **Mar31 PmM 4f fst :50 B** *10/11* **Mar23 PmM 4f fst :52³ B** *11/11* ●**Feb21 SA 6f fst 1:11⁴ H** *1/13*
TRAINER: 1stW/Tm(19 .21 $0.89) 31-60Days(245 .25 $1.83) Turf(288 .19 $1.50) Alw(290 .21 $1.49)

1 Hollywood Derby, December 1, 2002. The *Daily Racing Form* comment in three of those four turf races said Music's Storm "pulled." In the Hollywood Derby, Music's Storm did it again, pulling his way to the lead and tiring badly to finish ninth by 14 lengths at 17-1.

Inda removed Music's Storm's blinkers for his next start 25 days later in a softer spot, the $78,000 Sir Beaufort Stakes. Music's Storm broke slowly, then closed powerfully, finishing second by a head at 13.50-1. Obviously, shedding blinkers made a huge difference. In his next start in the restricted $500,000 Sunshine Millions Turf at Santa Anita a month later, Music's Storm again broke slowly, and again rallied impressively, finishing second by a nose at 8-1.

Another example from California. In his grass debut at Hollywood Park, May 27, 2002, Splendid Times (see next page) was sent off at 58-1 from the brutal outside post in a field of 12. He fought his way to the lead before weakening to sixth in the 1 1/16-mile maiden race. Freshened for nearly seven weeks, Splendid Times returned in a 5 1/2-furlong maiden grass race at Hollywood with blinkers removed. Sent off at 8.30-1, he settled in sixth in the field of 11 and rallied to win by half a length. He then finished fourth by three-quarters of a length at 9.70-1 in an optional $100,000 claimer and first by a neck at 14.80-1 in an optional $80,000 claimer.

5 Splendid Times
Own:Kruse David R & Linda
Green — Shocking Pink, Green Golf Emblem On Back — **$50,000**
SMITH M E (20 4 5 0 .20) 2003:(328 52 .16)

B. g. 4 (Apr) OBSMAR01 $49,000
Sire: Gilded Time (Timeless Moment) $20,000
Dam: Venetian Red(Blushing Groom*Fr)
Br: Highland Farms Inc (Ky)
Tr: Jackson Bruce L (—) 2003:(25 2 .08)

L 118

Life	17	2	1	1	$94,700	92	D.Fst	6	0	1	1	$24,100	90
2003	4	0	0	0	$2,440	90	Wet(370)	0	0	0	0	$0	–
2002	10	2	1	0	$88,180	92	Turf(285)	11	2	0	0	$70,600	92
Hol Ⓣ	3	1	0	0	$28,560	89	DstⓉ(310)	3	1	0	0	$39,600	92

27Mar03-7SA	fm	1	Ⓣ	:23	:46^1	1:09^3	1:33^3	4↑	OClm 80000N	85	1	1^1	1½	1½	4^{1½}	5^{7¼}	Smith M E	LB 118	60.30	87-06	GoldenDrgon118^2 MrshllRooster120^{nk} VnRoug118^2	Speed,inside,wkened	8
13Mar03-3SA	fm	1	Ⓣ	:23^3	:47^1	1:10^4	1:34^1	4↑	Clm 62500 (62.5-55)	90	3	4^{2½}	4^{2½}	6^{1¾}	7^{2¾}	7^{3½}	Stevens G L	LB 118	14.50	87-11	*BitOfLuck*118½ TimberBron118½ *RodToSlw*118½	Pulling hard, weakened	7
6Feb03-7SA	fm	*6½f	Ⓣ	:21^3	:44	1:06^1	1:12^1	4↑	OClm 80000N	89	4	7	6^6	5^{4½}	6^{4½}	6^4	Nakatani C S	LB 118	32.50	92-04	*Thunder Bullet*118^1 Devil's Horn119^2 Primerica121½	4 wide into stretch	9
9Jan03-2SA	fm	1	Ⓣ	:24	:46^4	1:10^1	1:34	4↑	OClm 80000N	80	1	2^1	2^1	2^{1½}	3^2	5^7	Krone J A	LB 117	11.00	85-10	Mayakovsky117^1 *Alyzig*119^{1½} Poker Brad119^3	Stdied near 1/8,wkened	5
26Dec02-7SA	fm	1	Ⓣ	:23^3	:47^2	1:11^2	1:35^4		Sir Beaufort78k	68	2	2^{1½}	3^{1½}	3^4	7^{8½}	8^{14½}	Flores D R	LB 118	36.00	68-22	Insprdo122^{hd} Music'sStorm120½ GoldnArrow118^1	Pulled,stalked,wkened	8
27Nov02-5Hol	fm	5½f	Ⓣ	:21^1	:43^2	:55^2	1:01^4	3↑	OClm 62500N	89	6	3	6^{9½}	5^{8½}	4^{2¼}	4^{1½}	Nakatani C S	LB 117	12.20	93-05	OurNwRcrut118^{hd} Lnnyfromlb118^1 ElCroso118½	Came out,edged for 3rd	7
17Oct02-7SA	fm	*6½f	Ⓣ	:22^2	:44^4	1:07^3	1:13^2		Alw 60000NC	81	6	1	3½	2^{hd}	3½	6^6	Stevens G L	LB 119	4.40	84-10	Pxtcum119^{hd} ThundrBllt119^{2½} TrPhnomnon121^2	Pressed pace, weakened	6
28Sep02-11Fpx	fst	*1⅛		:48^4	1:14	1:37^4	1:50		Pomona Derby100k	90	5	1^1	1½	1^1	1^{2½}	2^{1¾}	Nakatani C S	LB 122	7.60	95-08	Asong For Billy116^{1¾} Splendid Times122^3 Sunkosi119^1	Clear, caught late	10
11Sep02-6Dmr	fm	1$\frac{1}{16}$	Ⓣ	:24^1	:48^1	1:12	1:41^3		OClm 80000N	92	4	1^1	1^{1½}	1^{1½}	1^{2½}	1^{nk}	Nakatani C S	LB 119	14.80	95-06	SplnddTms119^{nk} TrdtonRocks119½ LprchnKd121^{hd}	Held gamely btwn late	7
11Aug02-1Dmr	fm	1$\frac{1}{16}$	Ⓣ	:24^1	:48	1:12	1:42		OClm 100000N	86	5	5^{3½}	5^6	5^{4½}	5^{1¾}	4¾	Delahoussaye E	LB 118	9.70	92-05	LeprechunKid118½ DimondHope118^{hd} SugrBb118^{hd}	Pulled,late bid 4 wide	5
14Jly02-6Hol	fm	5½f	Ⓣ	:22^1	:44^3	:56^4	1:03	3↑	Md Sp Wt 46k	84	7	3	6^{3½}	4^2	2^1	1½	Stevens G L	LB 118	8.30	89-11	SplnddTms118½ Lnnyfromlb118^{2½} PcfcColny118^1	Stalked,rallied,gamely	11
27May02-4Hol	fm	1$\frac{1}{16}$	Ⓣ	:24	:47^4	1:12	1:42	3↑	Md Sp Wt 45k	73	12	1^{hd}	1^1	1½	4^3	6^9	Smith M E	LB 116 b	58.20	76-09	Greenland123^1 *Battler Bob*116^{nk} *Caveolin*123^{3½}	Briefly clear,wkened	12

WORKS: Apr24 **SA 5f fst 1:02^3 B** *20/31* Apr13 **SA 5f fst 1:02^3 H** *23/34* Mar21 **SA 4f fst :49 H** *21/36* Mar8 **SA 5f fst 1:00^1 H** *9/65* Mar1 **SA 5f fst 1:02^4 H** *76/86* Feb18 **SA 5f fst 1:02^3 H** *29/37*
TRAINER: 31-60Days(23 .09 $1.31) Turf(31 .06 $1.62) Routes(32 .06 $1.35) Claim(4 .00 $0.00)

3. Never take a short price on a horse doing something for the first time or on a horse with a poor turf jockey and/or trainer. Avoiding short-priced, unproven horses is a lesson taken directly from popular television personality Harvey Pack, and it rings true so many times. If a horse is stretching out for the first time or trying turf for the first time, do not settle for low odds. Discipline yourself. You are trying to find value in your wagers.

The fifth race at Santa Anita, March 8, 2003, was a 6½-furlong turf allowance for nonwinners of two (one other than maiden, claiming, or starter). One scratch reduced the field to nine. The 9-5 clear favorite was Do Whats Right, who was making his first start on grass in his fourth career start. The 4-year-old colt had raced twice on dirt the year before, finishing second and sixth. In his 4-year-old debut, he was dropped to a $50,000 maiden claimer by trainer Bob Baffert. Bet down to even money, he won by 10 lengths in a blazing 1:08⅖ and was claimed. His Beyer Speed Figure was a gigantic 106.

Good for him. That had no relevance to how he was going to perform in his first start on grass, taking on winners for new trainer Doug O'Neill. Could he have been played here? Not at 9-5. Do Whats Right did not even finish the race, getting pulled up.

In the sixth race at Belmont Park on May 9, 2003, a 1⅛-mile maiden grass race for fillies and mares, Forever Now was certain to be a heavy favorite, even though she had never raced on grass and had lost all four dirt starts, the last by a neck at odds of 1-5, which elicited the comment "Lugged in stretch." Trainer Mark Hennig was switching the daughter of top turf sire Dynaformer, out of Madame Adolphe, by Criminal Type, to grass and changing jockeys from Eibar Coa to Jerry Bailey. Hennig had won with seven of his last 40 first-time turf starters, and the dam, though 0 for 3 on grass herself, had foaled a turf winner. Forever Now was the horse to beat, but she was not the horse to bet, going off at 4-5 and finishing fifth.

4. Avoid chronic losers. This cannot be overemphasized. If a maiden has had 10 or more starts on the same surface he's racing on today without winning, avoid him. If the horse is in a nonwinners-of-two allowance race, and has had only one win from more than 10 starts, stay away. Because, time after time, these chronic losers are overbet. When they are, it inflates the value of every other horse in the race. So when you see a favorite who has a winning percentage of 10 or less, you should consider him vulnerable. Try to find a horse to beat him.

Avoid a horse like Yes We Do, who earned $116,942 in her first 25 turf starts through March 9, 2003, but won only one of them. When she entered the starting gate at Hollywood Park, December 8, 2001, her grass record was 1 for 14. Yet under Chris McCarron, she was made the 8-5 favorite in a field of seven. She almost got the job done, but was second by a neck. She was second by a neck in her next start, a stakes race at Golden Gate Fields, at 9-1. She subsequently lost in grass races at odds as low as 6-1 twice.

On April 26, 2003, Yes We Do was ambitiously placed in the $150,000 Fran's Valentine Stakes at Hollywood Park. She finished eighth in the field of nine, making her 1 for 26 lifetime on grass.

At least Yes We Do was going off at double-digit odds in her last three races—at 12-1 twice and 31-1 in the other.

Other chronic losers are more heavily bet.

Pacific Colony is a prime example. He is trained by Bob Baffert, which is an immediate indication he will be overbet because Baffert is one of the nation's best trainers on dirt. This is a son of Pleasant Colony, himself a son of the great turf influence His Majesty, out of a mare, Drifting, by the excellent grass sire Lyphard. Pacific Colony had raced exclusively on grass, and the 4-year-old colt was entered in a nonwinners-of-two allowance race at Hollywood Park, April 5, 2003. The distance was one mile for the field of 11.

Baffert had given his horse a seven-week freshening following a third-place finish by five lengths at 3-1 in a one-mile nonwinners-of-two allowance at Santa Anita.

He had a career record of one win, three seconds, and six thirds in 10 starts and was getting a modest negative grass rider switch from Laffit Pincay Jr. to Pat Valenzuela.

Pacific Colony's odds in his 10 races were 3-1, even money, 9-2, 5-2 twice, 6-5 when he won, 9-2, 9-5, 7-2, and 3-1. He had been a beaten favorite twice. Think about this: He was 1 for 10 and had never gone off at odds higher than 4.90-1.

Yet despite his record, he would go off the 2.70-1 (5-2) favorite in this race. He was a badly tiring eighth, beaten 8½ lengths.

White Chocolate showed up at Calder Race Course, September 26, 2002, in a one-mile grass allowance race for fillies and mares. Starting at the bottom PP (as it showed when she made her following start, October 19), she had won a mile maiden grass race at Calder on June 4, 2001, as the 2.40-1 favorite. At the time she had been trained by Miguel Rivera.

White Chocolate
Own:Birriel Jose A Jr
Yellow, Black Dots, Red Stripe
ARCIA J A (264 59 32 32 .22) 2002:(376 69 .18)

Gr/ro f. 4 (Apr)
Sire: With Approval (Caro*Ire)
Dam:Cee Knows(Known Fact)
Br: Live Oak Stud (Fla)
Tr: Andrade Pablo(93 14 10 8 .15) 2002:(126 19 .15)

L 119

Life	15	1	5	2	$44,531	78
2002	8	0	3	1	$23,020	78
2001	7	1	2	1	$21,511	74
Crc Ⓣ	2	1	0	0	$14,070	69
D.Fst	1	0	0	0	$195	–
Wet(345)	1	0	0	0	$170	30
Turf(305)	13	1	5	2	$44,166	78
DstⓉ(320)	5	1	1	0	$21,520	77

Sep02-5Crc fm 1 Ⓣ:24 :493 1:133 1:373 3↑ ⒻAlw 30000N1X 62 3 21½ 1½ 22 56 610 Garcia J A L 119 fb *1.50 70-20 Ariann'sSong1144¾ **Ctnbout**115hd StrshipContess115½ Brief lead, faltered 8
Previously trained by Thornbury Jeffrey D
Jly02-10AP fm 1 Ⓣ:24 :481 1:131 1:371 3↑ ⒻAlw 37800N1X 74 2 32 32 31 32½ 52½ Juarez A J Jr L 119 b 12.20 89-13 Attico116nk I Can Fan Fan1181¼ Relaunch Gal119¾ Weakened 12
Jun02-8AP fm *1 1/16 Ⓣ:232 :473 1:122 1:44 3↑ ⒻAlw 30000N1X 67 8 42½ 44 32 32½ 37¼ Juarez A J Jr L 120 b 5.30e 86-07 Red Wildcat1241¼ DynamicWay1156 WhiteChocolate1202¼ No winning bid 12
Jun02-10AP gd *1⅛ Ⓣ:494 1:161 1:423 1:552 3↑ ⒻAlw 37200N1X 66 2 57½ 59½ 54 53¾ 62½ Laviolette B S L 120 b *1.80 65-25 Suprise Me Again120hd Yalta116½ Appy Everafter120½ No factor 8
May02-10CD fm 1 Ⓣ:241 :48 1:122 1:363 3↑ ⒻAlw 44200N1X 61 1 99¼ 910 97¾ 84½ 77¾ Borel C H L 116 b 5.40 81-08 *San Dare*1181¼ Sweetmilk Creek1153½ Dixie Schic1071 No late gain 9
Mar02-10FG fm *1 1/16 Ⓣ:24 :483 1:131 1:461 4↑ ⒻAlw 30000N1X 78 8 54 53½ 54½ 43½ 2½ Albarado R J L 118 b 3.10 81-12 El Portal119½ White Chocolate118no *Bowkeen*118½ Up for second 12
Mar02-10FG fm *1 1/16 Ⓣ:244 :512 1:17 1:49 4↑ ⒻAlw 30000N1X 75 6 66¼ 54 53 24 22 Perret C L 118 b 3.60 66-30 Vauxhall1182 White Chocolate1181 Stormy Hour1182½ Best of rest 8
Jan02-6FG fm *1 Ⓣ:241 :491 1:143 1:391 4↑ ⒻAlw 32000N1X 77 2 21½ 2½ 1½ 1hd 2hd Perret C L 118 b 4.30 89-07 *Bambin*122hd WhiteChocolte1181 SkippingStone1181½ Shook clear, failed 11
Dec01-8FG fm *1 1/16 Ⓣ:242 :50 1:152 1:464 3↑ ⒻAlw 32000N1X 74 9 42½ 41½ 2hd 21½ 41½ Martinez W L 115 b 20.90 80-20 Getadderit1161 Relaunch Gal118nk Stormy Hour117nk Grudgingly 10
Previously trained by Rivera Miguel A
Jun01-5Crc fm 1 Ⓣ:233 :474 1:124 1:381 3↑ ⒻMd Sp Wt 21k 69 1 56½ 44 41½ 2hd 1½ Castillo A L 118 b *2.40 77-22 WhiteChocolate118½ *Chimaera*1222 MysticJunic1182¾ 3 wide rally, lasted 8
ORKS: Sep20 Crc 4f fst :493 B *3/16* Sep10 Crc 4f fst :503 B *18/29* Sep1 Crc 4f fst :492 B *5/31* Aug25 Crc 4f fst :50 B *6/21*
AINER: Route/Sprint(17 .29 $4.18) Turf(16 .00 $0.00) Sprint(227 .18 $1.98) Alw(9 .11 $5.76)

She didn't return to the races until December 20, 2001, for new trainer Jeffrey Thornbury, when she made the first of nine consecutive starts in nonwinners of two. She finished a close fourth at 20-1, second by a head at 4-1, second by two lengths at 7-2, and second by half a length at 3-1. Her following start was at Churchill Downs, where she was seventh at 5-1. White Chocolate made her next three starts in Chicago, finishing sixth at 9-5, third by 7¼ lengths at 5-1 as part of an entry, and fifth by 2½ lengths at 12-1.

She had been off 10 weeks when she showed up at Calder for trainer Pablo Andrade, whose turf record in the *Daily Racing Form* trainer stats was 0 for 15. This was her fourth start off a layoff in her PP's, and she had not won fresh in the first three. She had one win, five seconds, and two thirds in 12 turf starts. And she showed up wearing front bandages. In a field of eight, she was bet down to 3-2 favoritism. She led briefly before tiring to finish sixth by 10 lengths.

Mabel Kent, a 5-year-old mare, showed up in the fifth race at Santa Anita, March 13, 2003, a 6½-furlong turf allowance for nonwinners of two for California-breds. Winless in three starts on dirt, she had raced 13 times on grass, posting one win, four seconds, and four thirds. Starting at her bottom PP, she'd run second twice at 6-5 and 9-2 before running fifth at 6-5 and then winning a maiden race by 3½ lengths at 9-2. She then finished seventh at 9-2 in open allowance company before sticking to state-breds. She was third as the 2-1 favorite, fourth as the 2-1 favorite, third at 3-1 (then sixth on dirt), third at 4-1 and, in her last start, second by two lengths at 5-1. Horses like this win sometimes, but never offer value. Sent off at 8-5, she was nosed, making her 1 for 14 on grass, 1 for 17 lifetime, and still eligible for the same allowance conditions in her next start.

3 Mabel Kent
Blue — **Own: Youngman Patricia**
Yellow Black V-sash Black Sleeves
SOLIS A (349 65 51 49 .19) 2003:(334 61 .18)

Ch. m. 5
Sire: Sharp Victor (Sharpen Up*GB) $4,000
Dam: Strawberry's Best(Strawberry Road*Aus)
Br: Patricia Youngman (Cal)
Tr: Jory Ian P D(66 7 9 5 .11) 2003:(66 6 .09)

L 120

Life	17	1	5	4	$128,940	89	D.Fst	3	0	0	0	$2,820	
2003	3	0	2	1	$27,520	89	Wet(370*)	0	0	0	0	$0	
2002	6	1	0	2	$51,540	87	Turf(270)	14	1	5	4	$126,120	
SA Ⓣ	10	1	3	3	$90,500	89	DstⓉ(295)	6	0	1	3	$34,324	

13Mar03-5SA	fm	*6½f	Ⓣ	:211	:432	1:062	1:123	4↑	ⒻSAlw 52000N1X	89	5	1	42½	1hd	11½	2no	Solis A	LB 120	*1.60	94-06	Roberta's Mango118no Mabel Kent1201½ Saxony118hd	Rail, led, collared
1Feb03-8SA	fm	*6½f	Ⓣ	:214	:434	1:063	1:13	4↑	ⒻSAlw 52000N1X	87	7	5	53½	56	54½	22	Solis A	LB 121	5.70	90-07	Rough R. N.1182 Mabel Kent121½ Arms Control120hd	Came out,late 2nd
10Jan03-6SA	fm	1	Ⓣ	:232	:462	1:101	1:341	4↑	ⒻSAlw 56000N1X	87	1	44½	45½	43	42½	31¼	Solis A	LB 119	4.40	90-15	Sweet Frippery119nk *Rough R. N.*1171 Mabel Kent1193½	Altered path 1/8
7Nov02-5Hol	fst	6½f		:22	:451	1:092	1:16	3↑	ⒻSAlw 43000N1X	46	3	4	42	54½	610	623¼	Desormeaux K J	LB 120	5.70	68-19	C'sVllyGirl1181¼ JtintoHouston1188 Robrt'sMngo1172	Stalked, gave way
4Oct02-5SA	fm	1	Ⓣ	:231	:463	1:103	1:352	3↑	ⒻSAlw 49000N1X	83	8	32	32½	2hd	2hd	32¾	Smith M E	LB 118	3.20	82-14	SunsetSernd118nk *MidnitMting*1182½ MblKnt1181½	Led into lane,outkickd
12Apr02-7SA	fm	1	Ⓣ	:234	:473	1:112	1:353	3↑	ⒻSAlw 57000N1X	85	4	31½	21	2½	1½	41¼	Espinoza V	LB 120	*2.30	83-16	ProudTmmie1201 Cntloup120hd Nicol'sPursuit116hd	Pulled,bid,led,willing
21Mar02-7SA	fm	*6½f	Ⓣ	:214	:434	1:07	1:131	4↑	ⒻSAlw 53000N1X	85	6	2	21½	2hd	11½	31½	Espinoza V	LB 120	*2.40	89-09	Jeremy's Quest118no *Proud Tammie*1181½ Mabel Kent120nk	Steadied early
20Jan02-2SA	fm	*6½f	Ⓣ	:214	:441	1:073	1:14	4↑	ⒻAlw 50000N1X	73	2	5	43½	33	31½	75½	Solis A	LB 120	4.70	81-12	A Bit Special120no *Carbon Copy*1201½ Very Racy1213	Rail bid,outfinished
1Jan02-2SA	fm	*6½f	Ⓣ	:22	:443	1:084	1:151	4↑	ⒻMd Sp Wt 54k	87	5	5	31	1hd	11	13½	Espinoza V	LB 122	4.60	81-19	Mabel Kent1223½ Belle Story1172½ Brass Belt123hd	Strong handling
31Oct01-1SA	fm	1	Ⓣ	:231	:47	1:102	1:342	3↑	ⒻMd Sp Wt 40k	75	5	21	2hd	11½	11	55	Solis A	LB 119	*1.20	90-05	SalishMiracle1191 Delvllde1192½ AphobicLdy119hd	Drifted out 6-1/2,wknd
29Sep01-2SA	fm	1	Ⓣ	:224	:463	1:094	1:343	3↑	ⒻMd Sp Wt 43k	87	11	11½	11½	11½	12	2hd	Espinoza V	LB 119	4.70	94-03	Mpenzi122hd Mabel Kent1191 Evening Meeting119hd	Inside,game,caught
31Aug01-3Dmr	fm	1 1/16	Ⓣ	:232	:472	1:114	1:434	3↑	ⒻMd Sp Wt 51k	81	8	11	11	11	12½	2nk	Espinoza V	LB 118	*1.30	86-11	LJollShores118nk MbelKent118nk ThunderSerend1181	Caught final stride

WORKS: Apr8 Hol 6f fst 1:121 H *2/12* ●Apr2 Hol 6f fst 1:131 H *1/7* ●Mar27 Hol 5f fst :592 H *1/8* Mar8 Hol 4f fst :501 H *22/35* Mar2 Hol 6f fst 1:122 H *3/24* Feb23 Hol 5f fst 1:013 H *29/56*
TRAINER: Sprint/Route(38 .05 $0.65) 31-60Days(71 .13 $2.47) Turf(128 .09 $1.29) Alw(58 .09 $1.27)

5. **Expect young horses to improve.** Aztec Pearl, a beautifully bred daughter of A.P. Indy out of stakes winner Aurora, by Danzig, raced twice on dirt for trainer Shug McGaughey before making her grass debut in a 1 1/8-mile maiden race at Belmont Park, May 31, 2002. Sent off at 6.10-1 under John Velazquez, Aztec Pearl was bumped at the start, fell back to last in the field of nine, and made a modest rally to finish sixth by 9 1/4 lengths. Her next start was at a mile under Edgar Prado. This time, she rallied strongly, making up four lengths to finish fourth by two lengths at 5.40-1. She was sent to Saratoga, stretched out to 1 3/16 miles, and went off at 4-1 under Prado in a field of nine. She won by half a length despite getting bumped at the start again. A win payoff of $10 on an obviously improving Shug/Prado filly was not a bad price at all.

9 Aztec Pearl
Own:Alexander Helen C & Helen K
rpse Light Blue, Dark Blue Sash, Dark Blue
A E M (106 20 12 18 .19) 2002:(1367 287 .21)

B. f. 4 (Apr)
Sire: A.P. Indy (Seattle Slew) $300,000
Dam: Aurora(Danzig)
Br: H Alexander & H Groves (Ky)
Tr: McGaughey Claude III(9 3 2 0 .33) 2002:(288 49 .17)

L 119

Life	9	1	1	2	$53,248	85	D.Fst	0	0	0	0	$0	–
2002	8	1	1	1	$48,738	85	Wet(445)	3	0	0	1	$13,948	75
2001	1	M	0	1	$4,510	74	Turf(325)	6	1	1	1	$39,300	85
GP Ⓣ	0	0	0	0	$0	–	DstⓉ(455)	0	0	0	0	$0	–

Nov02-5Crc	gd	1 1/16	Ⓣ	:23	:471	1:112	1:421	3↑	ⒻOClm 16000(16-14)N	78	8	79	713	57	35	21¾	Coa E M	L116	*.80	83-18	*MissDixieDrem*1191¾ AztecPrl1161¼ MissBoBlush1191¼	Broke in air, rallied	10
Oct02-8Bel	my	1⅛	⊗	:471	1:12	1:37	1:493		ⒻPebbles H114k	75	5	3½	3½	2hd	46	410	Prado E S	L113	8.30	72-24	Glia1133¼ Nonsuch Bay1236 Delta Princess113¾	Vied 3 wide, tired	5
Sep02-10Bel	fm	1¼	[T]	:491	1:14	1:38	2:02	3↑	ⒻAlw 48000N1X	85	3	43	42	51¼	51¾	31¾	Prado E S	L119	13.90	80-13	CozieAdvntge1171½ WondrWomn119nk AztcPrl119½	Game finish in traffic	11
Sep02-5Bel	gd	1 1/16	[T]	:24	:47	1:122	1:43	3↑	ⒻAlw 48000N1X	67	9	812	912	75	106½	910	Prado E S	L119	13.10	81-14	Madeira Mist1171¾ Missy Kiri117no Boana1213½	Wide trip, tired	10
Aug02-5Sar	fm	1 3/16	Ⓣ	:48	1:123	1:372	1:552	3↑	ⒻMd Sp Wt 46k	85	3	51¾	62¾	73	32	1½	Prado E S	L118	4.00	81-18	Aztec Pearl118½ More Ribbons1182½ *Ziada*1182¼	Bumped after start	9
Jly02-5Bel	fm	1	Ⓣ	:24	:48	1:113	1:353	3↑	ⒻMd Sp Wt 44k	76	7	84¾	93¾	96	64¾	42	Prado E S	L120	5.40	80-12	FerventWish1201¼ BellesLettres120½ MeveThRv120hd	Good finish outside	10
May02-1Bel	fm	1⅛	[T]	:491	1:133	1:374	1:492	3↑	ⒻMd Sp Wt 44k	69	4	52½	62	95½	711	69¼	Velazquez J R	L117	6.10	73-13	Madeira Mist117½ *Wonder Again*1172¾ *Sobrina DelRey*123no	Bumped start	9
May02-6Bel	gd	7f		:221	:453	1:114	1:26	3↑	ⒻMd Sp Wt 43k	64	5	8	99¾	912	46	45	Prado E S	L116	*1.15e	68-20	Wild Punch116½ *Dignified Diva*1163 Truly ALegend1161½	Mild rally inside	10
Sep01-6Bel	gd	6f		:224	:463	:594	1:13		ⒻMd Sp Wt 41k	74	4	3	52¼	43½	37½	34	Prado E S	118	*2.25	69-24	MissingMiss113hd *AcdemicAngel*1183¾ AztecPerl1186¾	Good finish outside	7

ORKS: Jan19 GP 4f fst :50 B *25/33* Jan13 GP 3f fst :362 B *3/11* Jan6 GP 4f fst :492 B *20/40* Dec31 GP 4f fst :494 B *49/72* Dec24 GP 4f fst :49 B *24/86* Dec9 Pay 3f fst :392 B *6/6*
AINER: 61-180Days(28 .14 $0.78) Turf(50 .08 $0.91) Routes(194 .20 $1.36) Alw(116 .19 $1.29)

6. **Expect all horses, especially those showing speed and tiring, to improve greatly with first-time Lasix.** (Some horses improve the second time they're on Lasix.) The eighth race at Gulfstream Park, January 9, 2003, was a 1 1/16-mile maiden race on turf for 3-year-olds. One of the horses entered was Bon Fleur, who had raced once, was freshened, and was now adding Lasix. In his debut on October 25, 2002, at Aqueduct, Bon Fleur had gone off at 7.50-1 as part of an entry and had broken from the disadvantageous 10 post. He showed early speed, getting away third, and raced well while working his way to

the rail, finishing fourth, just a length and a half off the winner. Bon Fleur also had an exceptional Tomlinson Rating—a numerical assessment of a horse's grass breeding—much better than any of his competitors. He was also getting a good jockey switch from apprentice Luis Chavez in his debut to Eibar Coa, one of the leading riders at Gulfstream. The surprise wasn't that he won at Gulfstream, but that he paid \$13.20, winning by $2\frac{3}{4}$ lengths.

7 Bon Fleur
Own:Marablue Farm
Orange Blue, White Belt, White Band On Sleeves,
COA E M (24 4 2 2 .17) 2002:(1367 287 .21)

B. c. 3 (Apr) KEEJAN01 \$17,000
Sire: Bon Point*GB (Soviet Star)
Dam:Forgetmenot(Bering*GB)
Br: Marablue Farm (Fla)
Tr: Sciacca Gary(1 0 0 0 .00) 2002:(319 27 .08)

Ⓛ **122**

Life	**1**	**M**	**0**	**0**	**\$2,760**	**62**	**D.Fst**	**0 0 0 0**	**\$0**	**–**
2002	**1**	**M**	**0**	**0**	**\$2,760**	**62**	**Wet(280)**	**0 0 0 0**	**\$0**	**–**
2001	**0**	**M**	**0**	**0**	**\$0**	**–**	**Turf(393*)**	**1 0 0 0**	**\$2,760**	**62**
GP Ⓣ	**0**	**0**	**0**	**0**	**\$0**	**–**	**Dst**Ⓣ**(384)**	**1 0 0 0**	**\$2,760**	**62**

25Oct02-3Aqu	fm	$1\frac{1}{16}$	Ⓣ	:25	:52	$1{:}17^{3}$	$1{:}48^{1}$	Md Sp Wt 46k	**62**	10	3^{2}	4^{1}	6^{2}	$5^{\frac{3}{4}}$	$4^{1\frac{1}{2}}$	Chavez L5	114	7.50e	62-29	Elvisvader119nk Unbridled Mate1191 Manse119hd	Game finish on rail 1[illegible]

WORKS: Jan5 **GP 4f fst :48**^{3} **B** *11/39* Dec31 **GP 4f fst :49**^{2} **B** *31/71* Dec16 **GP 5f fst 1:03**^{2} **B** *12/26* Dec8 **GP 4f fst :49**^{4} **B** *17/23* Dec1 **Bel tr.t 4f fst :50 B** *43/70* Nov25 **Bel tr.t 4f fst :50 B** *28/44*
TRAINER: 61-180Days(33 .06 \$3.25) 2ndStart(25 .08 \$5.83) 1stLasix(22 .05 \$0.55) Turf(170 .11 \$3.44) Routes(229 .09 \$2.59) MdnSpWt(120 .08 \$2.01)

Another example: In Too Deep had finished fifth in a \$37,500 grass maiden claimer at Colonial Downs on August 3, 2001, at odds of 4.40-1, then raced on dirt without winning. In his first start in 2002 at Charles Town, In Too Deep was second by three-quarters of a length on dirt. He was then entered at Colonial Downs in a \$40,000 grass maiden claimer, June 22. Unlike his last turf start the year before, this time In Too Deep was racing with Lasix on the grass. Sent off at 7.10-1 at the same level at which he'd previously been fifth at 4.40-1, he won by a nose. He then won a \$20,000-\$25,000 claimer at 4.70-1 and a nonwinners-of-two allowance race at 3.20-1, all on Lasix.

8 In Too Deep
Own:Cooney Susan S
Pink Coral, Silver Bordered Dark Blue Diamond
MAWING M A (15 2 1 1 .13) 2003:(354 42 .12)

B. f. 4 (Mar)
Sire: The Deep*Ire (Shernazar*Ire)
Dam:Kissing Bridge(Linkage)
Br: Kim Condon (Va)
Tr: Cooney Susan S(2 0 0 0 .00) 2003:(26 0 .00)

L 117

Life	**11**	**3**	**2**	**1**	**\$53,067**	**77**	**D.Fst**	**4 0 1 1**	**\$6,216**
2002	**5**	**3**	**1**	**0**	**\$45,234**	**77**	**Wet(310)**	**1 0 1 0**	**\$3,600**
2001	**6**	**M**	**1**	**1**	**\$7,833**	**48**	**Turf(320)**	**6 3 0 0**	**\$43,251**
Pim Ⓣ	**0**	**0**	**0**	**0**	**\$0**	**–**	**Dst**Ⓣ**(415*)**	**5 3 0 0**	**\$42,579**

18Aug02-9Lrl	fm	$5\frac{1}{2}$f	Ⓣ	$:22^{2}$	$:45^{3}$	:58	1:04	3↑	ⒻOClm 20000 (20-18)N	**77**	3	5	4^{6}	$5^{2\frac{3}{4}}$	$3^{3\frac{1}{2}}$	$5^{1\frac{1}{2}}$	Teator P A	L 119	5.50	89-06	Wingover117¾ Silver Sequins117nk **Admiral's Pride**118½	Rail, weakened
7Aug02-8Lrl	fm	$5\frac{1}{2}$f	Ⓣ	$:22^{3}$	$:46^{1}$	$:58^{1}$	$1{:}04^{2}$	3↑	ⒻAlw 26000N1X	**70**	3	5	5^{5}	5^{4}	$2^{\frac{1}{2}}$	$1^{1\frac{1}{4}}$	Teator P A	L 114	3.20	89-12	In Too Deep1141¼ Morning High1172½ Jacquelyn T1124	Driving
12Jly02-8Cnl	fm	5f	🅃	$:22^{3}$	$:46^{3}$		$:58^{4}$	3↑	ⒻClm 25000 (25-20)N2L	**62**	4	4	$2^{\frac{1}{2}}$	$2^{\frac{1}{2}}$	$2^{\frac{1}{2}}$	$1^{1\frac{3}{4}}$	Mawing M A	L 117	4.70	88-13	*In Too Deep*1171¾ Gin Visions117no Dolce Dawn1181½	Pressed 2wd,driving
22Jun02-6Cnl	fm	5f	🅃	$:22^{1}$	:46		$:58^{1}$	3↑	ⒻMd 40000 (40-35)	**64**	7	10	$4^{3\frac{1}{2}}$	4^{3}	3^{1}	1no	Mawing M A	L 117	7.10	91-06	*In Too Deep*117no *In The Glen*1171 Say Victory115½	Rail rally, driving
9Jun02-3CT	fst	$4\frac{1}{2}$f		$:22^{2}$	$:47^{1}$		$:53^{2}$		ⒻMd Sp Wt 16k	**47**	4	4	4^{2}		$2^{2\frac{1}{2}}$	$2^{\frac{3}{4}}$	Mawing M A	L 119	4.00	83-17	Miss Hamma119¾ *In Too Deep*1191½ Dream Wedding1193¾	Finished well
16Dec01-1CT	gd	$4\frac{1}{2}$f		$:22^{1}$	$:47^{2}$		$:54^{2}$		ⒻMd Sp Wt 18k	**39**	5	3	$4^{5\frac{1}{2}}$		$4^{6\frac{1}{2}}$	2^{1}	Mawing M A	L 119	6.30	78-20	Stacys Toy1191 In Too Deep1191 Lisa's Deelites1191¼	Closed with a rush
3Nov01-1CT	fst	$4\frac{1}{2}$f		$:22^{3}$	$:48^{1}$		$:55^{1}$		ⒻMd Sp Wt 17k	**48**	2	5	$2^{\frac{1}{2}}$		3^{2}	3^{3}	Reynolds L C	L 119	14.80	72-29	Case ThePlace1192 RojoLady1191 InTooDeep119½	Lacked late response
28Oct01-4Del	fst	6f		$:22^{4}$	$:47^{3}$	1:01	$1{:}14^{3}$		Ⓕ🅁Hildene42k	**30**	1	7	$3^{\frac{1}{2}}$	3^{1}	$6^{7\frac{1}{4}}$	$5^{15\frac{1}{2}}$	Prado A J	L 115 n	41.00	54-23	Saturdy'sChild1151½ MetlChimes1159 SisGoKid1153¾	Off slow,speed,tired
13Sep01-3Pim	fst	6f		:23	$:46^{4}$	1:00	$1{:}13^{3}$		ⒻMd 35000 (40-35)	**–0**	1	4	$2^{4\frac{1}{2}}$	3^{6}	7^{10}	$9^{25\frac{3}{4}}$	Reynolds L C	115	22.50	52-20	Ravish1155 *Town Secret*119½ My Dance119nk	Rail,stopped,eased
3Aug01-3Cnl	fm	6f	Ⓣ	$:22^{4}$	$:46^{2}$	$:59^{1}$	1:12		ⒻMd 37500 (40-35)	**44**	7	1	$4^{4\frac{1}{2}}$	4^{4}	$4^{2\frac{1}{2}}$	$5^{3\frac{1}{4}}$	Verge M E	116	4.40	77-11	Carnie'sDancer118¾ EarlySignl114½ TownSecret118¾	2wd, needed more

WORKS: Apr24 **CT 4f fst :50**^{1} **B** *3/15*
TRAINER: +180Days(10 .00 \$0.00) Turf(34 .09 \$1.06) Sprint(94 .07 \$0.81) Alw(10 .10 \$0.84)

7. Expect horses to move forward off a late-tiring return race.
That sounds simplistic, but it's still worth noting. A horse off a significant layoff should get a little tired in a comeback race and move forward in his second start back.

Gasperillo Daze had been off nearly eight months when he drew the 13 post in a nonwinners-of-two allowance race at Colonial Downs, July 1, 2002. Sent off at 3-1 despite the incredibly bad post, he made a strong middle move to get a half-length lead before tiring late to finish ninth by 9½ lengths. He would almost certainly move forward off that comeback race.

Twelve days later, Gasperillo Daze drew post 2 in the same allowance class at the same distance of 1¹/₁₆ miles. He should have been a shorter price from the post-position change alone, yet went off at 4.80-1, winning by half a length.

Repository is another example. The 5-year-old mare fought for the lead, got a head in front, and weakened late to finish fourth by three lengths at 16-1 in the Grade 2 Buena Vista Handicap at one mile at Santa Anita on February 17, 2003, her first start in more than six weeks. Off two good works for trainer D. Wayne Lukas, four furlongs in 48⁴/₅ on a sloppy track and four furlongs in 48²/₅, she was entered in the ungraded Winter Solstice Stakes at Santa Anita at 6½ furlongs,

March 12, 2003. Ready to move forward in her second start back, she went wire to wire, winning by half a length and paying $12.60.

5	Cherokee's Disco							

Dk. b or br f. 3 (Feb) OBSMAR02 $210,000
Sire: Cherokee Run (Runaway Groom) $20,000
Dam: Disco Doll (Diesis*GB)
Br: London Thoroughbred Services & Mrs Anita Rothschild (Ky)
Tr: Becerra Rafael(5 0 0 1 .00) 2003:(85 15 .18)

Own: Fulton Stan E
Green Lime Green, White 'f' On Blue Ball, Lime
VALDIVIA J JR (22 4 4 1 .18) 2003:(249 24 .10)

Life 5 2 0 0 $58,739 84 / D.Fst 2 0 0 0 $2,580 62
2003 2 1 0 0 $31,200 84 / Wet(405) 1 1 0 0 $24,959 52
L 113 2002 3 1 0 0 $27,539 62 / Turf(275) 2 1 0 0 $31,200 84
Hol ① 0 0 0 0 $0 – / Dst①(325) 1 0 0 0 $0 81

6Apr03–4SA	fm *6½f ⑦ :223 :45 1:08¹ 1:14²	⑩OClm 80000N	84 2 4	3² 4² 3² 1½	Baze T C	LB 118	16.90 85–15 Cherokee'sDisco118½ DshForMony118hd Shrpbill118½	Bit tight hill,gamely 6
13Mar03–7SA	fm 1 ⑦ :23¹ :47¹ 1:11¹ 1:35	⑦SomeSenstion83k	81 1 2¹	2¹ 1hd 4½ 7³½	Baze T C	LB 116	57.70 83–11 Major Idea120½ Star Vegal161½ Favola116nk	Pressed rail, weakened 10
31Dec02–7SA	fst 6½f :22 :45¹ 1:10¹ 1:16⁴	⑩OClm 80000N	56 3 6	6½ 6⁴ 77½ 61¹½	Baze T C	LB 118	10.80 78–13 Himalayan120¹¾ HonestAnswer118² Rmisvest120½	Crowded start,3-wide 7
6Dec02–5Hol	fst 6½f :22¹ :44⁴ 1:10 1:16⁴	⑩OClm 80000N	62 2 7	73½ 64¼ 5⁶ 4¹⁰	Baze T C	LB 120	3.40 77–19 No Love Song118¹ Himalayan120⁵ Validating116⁴	Rail trip,imp position 7
	Previously trained by Jamison Johnie L							
28Jly02–5Rui	sly 6f :22³ :45⁴ :58³ 1:13	⑩Kachina49k	52 4 6	67½ 5⁶ 3⁶ 1hd	Fuentes M S	L 118	1.60e 81–17 Cherokee'sDisco118hd SMoken120¹ FrezEmOut118¹¹	Closed fast, just up 7

WORKS: Apr27 Hol ⑦ 4f fm :49 H (d)1/3 Apr20 Hol ⑦ 5f fm 1:02² H (d)4/6 Mar30 SA ⑦ 4f fm :49² H (d)6/7 Mar2 SA ⑦ 5f gd 1:02³ H (d)2/9 Feb23 SA ⑦ 4f fm :49 H (d)4/12 Feb15 SA 5f gd 1:00³ H 10/68
TRAINER: Sprint/Route(20 .15 $2.25) Turf(46 .15 $2.03) Alw(38 .11 $2.67)

Cherokee's Disco made her grass debut off a 2½-month layoff in an $83,000 stakes at Santa Anita, March 13, 2003. At odds of 57-1, she fought on the lead before tiring late, finishing seventh in the field of 10 but only beaten 3½ lengths. She shortened up to 6½ furlongs for her next grass start and dropped to an optional $80,000 claimer. In an easier spot and cutting back in distance after tiring in a longer grass debut, she won by three-quarters of a length at still healthy odds of 16.90-1.

8. **Open your thinking to consider betting your second or third choice if there is value.** Don't insist that only your first choice can win a race. Sometimes, that second or third one does come in, and when it does, you may be kicking yourself silly for not betting him.

9. **Watch as many races as you can.** If you want an edge on other handicappers, put a little more time into it. Watching the replay of a race is always preferable to just handicapping that race by reading a horse's PP's. Take notes when you watch. This isn't the SAT's. You're allowed to have a crib sheet.

10. Practice helps. By taking a few extra minutes a day, you can improve many aspects of your handicapping. If you want a better understanding of value, try this: Half an hour before each race, write down what you think the odds will be for each horse, and then write down each horse's actual odds. Doing this repeatedly can only help you realize situations that do offer value. But don't stop there. If you want to improve your knowledge of turf pedigrees, cover up a horse's turf record in the *Daily Racing Form.* Look at the horse's breeding and predict whether he's good on grass or not. Do this every day and it's almost impossible not to learn more about grass breeding. You can do the same thing with horses' records on wet tracks.

11. Pay attention! On New York Showcase Day, October 19, 2002, at Belmont Park, the third race was a one-mile maiden special weight for 2-year-old New York-breds. The 10 horse was Big Gun, a first-time starter for Christophe Clement, one of the top grass trainers in the world. Big Gun's sire was Dixie Brass, noted as an above-average turf sire in the *Daily Racing Form.* Big Gun also had the second-highest Tomlinson Rating. Even more important was that Big Gun's sister, Shopping for Love, was a multiple stakes winner and one of the seven winners that her dam, Instant Shopper, had produced from eight foals.

0	**Big Gun**	Dk. b or br c. 2 (Mar) SARAUG01 $55,000		Life	0 M 0 0	$0	–	D.Fst	0 0 0 0	$0	–
	Own:Harris Charles E & Karches Peter F	Sire: Dixie Brass (Dixieland Band) $10,000									
	Forest Green, White Dots, White Sleeves	Dam:Instant Shopper(D'Accord)		2002	0 M 0 0	$0	–	Wet(355)	0 0 0 0	$0	–
ROYO N JR (88 6 7 9 .07) 2002:(663 82 .12)		Br: Frank Mancini (NY)	120	2001	0 M 0 0	$0	–	Turf(285)	0 0 0 0	$0	–
		Tr: Clement Christophe(36 7 6 1 .19) 2002:(304 68 .22)		Bel ⑦	0 0 0 0	$0	–	Dst⑦(310)	0 0 0 0	$0	–

JRKS: Oct8 Sar tr.t 4f fst :54¹ B *10/11* Oct2 Sar tr.t⑦ 4f fm :52 B *5/7* Sep21 Sar tr.t 3f fst :38¹ Bg*5/9* Sep13 Sar tr.t 4f fst :52³ B *7/11* Sep6 Sar tr.t 4f fst :53² B *8/8* Aug28 Bel 4f fst :49⁴ B *32/57*
Aug20 Bel tr.t 4f my :50⁴ B *11/21* ●Aug13 Bel tr.t 3f fst :37 B *1/10* Jly24 Bel 3f fst :37³ B *4/8*
AINER: 1stStart(62 .05 $0.98) 1stTurf(124 .20 $1.94) 2YO(30 .10 $0.70) Turf(522 .23 $1.77) MdnSpWt(148 .19 $1.56)

By chance, Shopping for Love was racing in the eighth race, the Ticonderoga Handicap, that same day at Belmont. The *Form* displayed Shopping for Love's excellent turf record, four wins and five seconds in 15 turf starts and earnings of

11 Shopping For Love Own:D'Arcangelo Dennis & George Donald Red, White Yoke And 'djg,' Black Sleeves **BAILEY J D (80 23 12 12 .29) 2002:(748 195 .26)**	Dk. b or br m. 5 Sire: Not For Love (Mr. Prospector) $15,000 Dam: Instant Shopper(D'Accord) Br: New River Stable Partnership (NY) Tr: Nesky Kenneth A(6 0 0 0 .00) 2002:(57 4 .07)	L 122	Life 24 8 6 1 $583,669 106 2002 6 2 1 1 $128,114 102 2001 7 1 2 0 $129,069 106 Bel Ⓣ 6 2 2 0 $220,839 106 D.Fst 4 2 0 0 $56,059 80 Wet(425) 5 2 1 1 $125,056 89 Turf(285) 15 4 5 0 $402,554 106 DstⓉ(330) 9 4 2 0 $329,934 102

21Sep02-6Pim fm 1⅛ Ⓣ :472 1:114 1:361 1:483 3↑ Ⓕ[R]MdMillLadies95k 102 9 53 42½ 21 12½ 17¼ Migliore R L121 *1.30 95-06 Shopping For Love1217¼ Breezy Bri119½ *Twilights Prayer*121nk Driving 14
16Aug02-8Sar sly 1⅛ ⊗ :474 1:121 1:38 1:512 3↑ Ⓕ[S]Yaddo H84k 84 1 2½ 2½ 1½ 33½ 37¾ Bailey J D L122 *1.35 74-17 TxtbkMthd1154¼ IndyMdFrLv1133½ *ShppngFrLv*1224¼ Between rivals, tired 8
23Jun02-6Bel fm 1⅛ [T] :48 1:113 1:35 1:464 3↑ Ⓕ[S]Mt Vernon H83k 92 9 45 41 3½ 13½ 14 Bailey J D L120 *.80 95-07 ShoppngForLov1204 IndyMoodFrLv1132 Bllrs114½ 3 wide move, driving 10
Run in divisions
5May02-8Aqu gd 1 1/16 Ⓣ :241 :481 1:114 1:43 3↑ ⒻBeaugay H-G3 75 4 63 78½ 63¾ 86¾ 1013½ Arroyo N Jr L115 8.50 75-17 Voodoo Dancer1192¾ Golden Corona115no *Babae*1162¼ Bumped after start 10
18Apr02-8Aqu fm 1 Ⓣ :241 :483 1:124 1:364 4↑ ⒻAlw 55000C 94 4 43½ 62¼ 41 41 21½ Arroyo N Jr L115 1.95 91-12 GoldenCoron1161½ ShoppingForLov115hd *SilvrRil*1181¾ Game finish on rail 6
7Apr02-8Aqu fst 7f :224 :452 1:093 1:224 3↑ Ⓕ[S]Broadway H82k 80 8 2 62½ 52¾ 57 58 Arroyo N Jr L116 4.30 78-17 We'll Sea Ya1111 Maddie May1211¾ *Dat You MizBlue*1233½ 4 wide, no rally 8
28Sep01-7Med fm 1 1/16 Ⓣ :23 :464 1:114 1:432 3↑ ⒻViolet H-G3 92 3 1011 1010 92 82¾ 63½ Velazquez J R L115 5.70 79-23 Clearly A Queen115hd Queue1151½ *Paga*1171¾ Widest turn,empty 12
3Sep01-9Sar gd 1⅛ Ⓣ :47 1:102 1:343 1:46 3↑ ⒻDiana H-G2 86 9 83¾ 87¼ 93½ 84½ 511¼ Arroyo N Jr L114 21.10 88-13 Starine1145¼ Babae1143¾ Penny's Gold1201½ 4 wide trip, no rally 9
5Aug01-9Rkm gd *1⅛ Ⓣ 1:482 3↑ ⒻSpicyLivingH100k 92 4 33 32 42 12½ 1no Arroyo N Jr LB116 *.80 83-20 ShoppingForLove116no StpWithStyl1177 BigMiss115hd 3path 2nd, driving 6
24Jun01-8Bel fm 1⅛ [T] :464 1:103 1:352 1:48 3↑ Ⓕ[S]Mt Vernon H83k 85 9 52 64¼ 74 67 46¼ Arroyo N Jr L123 *1.20 83-17 Truebreadpudding1202¾ Key Oui1172½ *PollyJo*1171 Ducked out start, wide 9
9Jun01-7Bel fm 1 Ⓣ :224 :453 1:09 1:323 3↑ ⒻJstAGameBCH-G3 106 8 57½ 65¼ 31 1hd 2nk Arroyo N Jr L114 15.30 95-09 LicnsF118nk ShoppingForLov114½ *VlOfAvlon*1151½ Gamely between rivals 11
23May01-8Bel sly 1 ⊗ :231 :462 1:102 1:362 4↑ ⒻAlw 52380N$YmT 89 1 31½ 31 3nk 2hd 21½ Arroyo N Jr L120 2.20 83-25 A.O.L.Hys1161½ ShppngFrLv120nk BfflBrdWmn1169¼ Stayed gamely inside 4
WORKS: Oct15 Bel tr.t 4f fst :491 B *34/179* Oct2 Bel tr.t 3f fst :371 B *5/14* Sep17 Bel tr.t 5f my 1:042 B *4/4* Sep9 Bel tr.t 5f fst 1:01 B *1/3* Sep1 Bel tr.t 3f fst :394 B *5/7* Aug7 Bel tr.t 6f fst 1:111 B *1/3*
TRAINER: Turf(42 .07 $0.28) Routes(75 .07 $0.78) Stakes(6 .50 $1.97)

$402,554, which included a second by a neck in an open Grade 3 stakes the year before. Big Gun was an easy pick and won at 9-2.

Say you don't have stats to check out a dam's proven success with grass horses, an item usually carried in the *Form*'s invaluable horse-by-horse race analysis, "A Closer Look". Say you're betting at Fair Grounds on January 9, 2003. In the eighth race, the first division of a 5½-furlong maiden grass race for 3-year-olds, a first-time starter by Indian Charlie named Running Charlie wins and pays $37.60. In the 10th race, the other division of that maiden race, there's a son of Indian Charlie named Justalittlemagic, who is making his first start on grass. He wins and pays $18.60. Apparently, Indian Charlie can sire grass winners.

5 Running Charlie Green Own:Philip Ewbank Forest Green Yellow Cross Sashes **LOVATO F JR (86 11 9 15 .13) 2002:(707 83 .12)**	Dk. b or br c. 3 (Apr) KEESEP01 $77,000 Sire: Indian Charlie (In Excess*Ire) $10,000 Dam: Two Fer(Olden Times) Br: Hargus Sexton & Sandra Sexton (Ky) Tr: Cohn Alice G(9 1 2 0 .11) 2002:(51 8 .16)	Ⓛ 119	Life 0 M 0 0 $0 – 2003 0 M 0 0 $0 – 2002 0 M 0 0 $0 – FG Ⓣ 0 0 0 0 $0 – D.Fst 0 0 0 0 $0 – Wet(308*) 0 0 0 0 $0 – Turf(292) 0 0 0 0 $0 – DstⓉ(361) 0 0 0 0 $0 –

WORKS: Dec23 FG 4f fst :50 B *19/48* Dec4 FG TR 2 5f fst 1:03 Hg*6/9* Nov13 FG 3f fst :364 Bg*6/11*
TRAINER: 1stStart(6 .00 $0.00) 1stTurf(7 .00 $0.00) Turf(20 .00 $0.00) Sprint(35 .20 $4.97) MdnSpWt(10 .10 $0.86)

When Trekking and Sunstone both scratched from the fifth race at Belmont Park on June 29, 2003, my top selection was Cozie Advantage, who had been off since October 23, 2002. Could Cozie Advantage fire fresh? The answers was in her

5 **Justalittlemagic**
Own:Donver Stable & Carroll Josie
White, Red And Black Yoke, Red Sleeves
BARADO R J (132 24 35 18 .18) 2002:(1374 270 .20)

B. c. 3 (Jan) KEENOV00 $31,000
Sire: Indian Charlie (In Excess*Ire) $10,000
Dam:Magic Bear(Doonesbury)
Br: Pat Holden & Drumkenny Farm (Ky)
Tr: Carroll Josie(23 3 2 2 .13) 2002:(229 36 .16)

Blinkers ON | Life 2 M 0 0 $1,818 54 | D.Fst 1 0 0 0 $1,818 54
2002 2 M 0 0 $1,818 54 | Wet(298*) 1 0 0 0 $0 42
L 119 2001 0 M 0 0 $0 – | Turf(272) 0 0 0 0 $0 –
FG ① 0 0 0 0 $0 – | Dst①(366) 0 0 0 0 $0 –

Dec02-10FG sly 6f :22 :454 :574 1:103 Md Sp Wt 28k 42 8 9 109¼ 1113 111² 111½ Albarado R J L 119 34.40 73 – 14 Oak Hill119⁵¾ Classic Band119no Mt Pro119¼ Always back 12
Jly02-7WO fst 5f :21² :444 :584 Md Sp Wt 60k 54 2 3 3³ 47½ 410 55¼ Clark D 119 3.65 80 – 14 Red Satan109³¼ Shipman114¾ Makin Headlines119¼ Weakened stretch 10
WORKS: ●Jan3 FG 4f fst :48³ B 1/54 Dec15 FG 4f fst :514 B 63/77 Dec6 FG 5f fst 1:02³ B 21/32 Nov29 FG 6f fst 1:16³ B 2/3 Nov15 WO tr.t 5f gd 1:01⁴ Hg3/6 ●Nov9 WO 4f fst :48 H 1/19
TRAINER: 1stTurf(24 .08 $0.41) 1stBlink(21 .10 $0.34) Turf(83 .13 $1.38) Sprint(129 .16 $1.08) MdnSpWt(76 .14 $1.46)

PP's. She'd raced fresh four times in her 10-race career and finished second, fifth in a stakes, second by a head, and first by 1½ lengths. Her trainer, John Kimmel, was winning with 18 percent of his layoff horses who had been out of action longer than 180 days. Cozie Advantage won and paid $10.80.

12. Always check the dam of first-time turf performers with the list of graded-stakes-winning dams in this book.

13. Understanding shippers is a must to succeeding at Saratoga. This annual six-week meet is simulcast all over the continent and produced North American records in handle in 2001 and 2002. It is nothing short of remarkable how popular Saratoga has become, attracting horses from all over the country. In the sixth race, Sunday, August 4, 2002, the fifth day of the meet, a field of nine grass horses contested a $35,000 claimer. Those horses' last starts had been at Belmont Park, Colonial Downs, Churchill Downs, Aqueduct, Philadelphia Park, and Calder.

Now look at a race a few days later in the 2002 meet, Saturday, August 10. The last starts of the nine grass horses contesting an allowance race in the seventh had been made at Saratoga, Monmouth Park, Rockingham Park, Churchill Downs, Aqueduct, Gulfstream Park, and Belmont Park. The lone main-track-only horse's last start was at Delaware Park. In the 10th race that day, a $35,000 grass claimer, the last starts of the 15 horses entered had been made at Saratoga, Belmont Park, Colonial Downs, Monmouth Park, Delaware Park, Laurel, and Penn National.

When evaluating shippers, don't get suckered into the following rationale for betting one of them when your buddy next to you argues, "They didn't ship this horse here for nothing," or, "They shipped here for a reason." Everybody ships into Saratoga for the same reason: to win a race at the best meeting in the world. Evaluate horses, not motives.

A note about the race examples used in this book: All Saratoga races offering horse-by-horse analysis feature winners who were selected that day by the author, who handicaps Saratoga, Belmont Park, and Aqueduct for the *Daily Gazette* in Schenectady, New York.

2

THE BASICS

AS SOPHISTICATED AS HANDICAPPING has become, the basics will never change. The basics are speed, class, and form. Speed asks: How fast is the horse? Class asks: How good is the horse? Form asks: How well is the horse likely to run today?

Handicappers have been arguing over the relative significance of speed, class, and form for decades, and the debate will likely continue for many more.

How do those three major schools of handicapping affect grass racing? On turf, speed may not be quite as important as it is on dirt. Speed takes on its greatest significance in sprints, and there are far fewer sprints contested on grass than on dirt.

Plus, you don't need a personal guru or pace figures to understand that 22 seconds is fast for an opening quarter, as is 45 for a half and 1:09 for three-quarters of a mile.

What's most important about speed in grass racing is relative: How many speed horses are there in a given race, and, is one faster than the others? Most important of all is determining whether or not there is a lone speed horse in a race. As fundamental as that sounds, it cannot be overstated.

Check out the eighth running of the $100,000 Mac Diarmida Handicap (Grade 3) at Gulfstream Park, January 19, 2003 (pages 21-24). Two scratches left a field of 12 in the 1⅜-mile stakes.

Now try and find the speed in this race. There is but one horse with proven speed, Riddlesdown. In fact, of all the 115 North American turf past-performance lines of the other 11, only four showed that horse in front at the first call of his race. On a yielding course at Aqueduct, Quiet Ruler had been first in an allowance race through an opening half in an incredibly slow 54⅖. Marquette had been first in three races off moderate fractions. But he had not been even near the lead in his three most recent grass starts.

Did Riddlesdown have a legitimate shot if Marquette didn't push him early?

Riddlesdown had been given a freshening following his hard-fought, front-running second by half a length to Tap the Admiral in the $100,000 John Henry Handicap at Arlington Park the day before the Breeders' Cup, October 25, 2002. In an extremely poor ruling—at least it seemed that way, since I had bet Tap the Admiral to win—Tap the Admiral was disqualified for brushing lightly with Riddlesdown, who was placed first. If anything, it looked as if Riddlesdown had caused the slight contact. Regardless, the disqualification stood.

Trainer Niall O'Callaghan gave Riddlesdown a two-month freshening, and he returned to action in the 1½-mile W. L. McKnight Handicap (Grade 2) at Calder Race Course. Sent off at 16-1 in the field of 12 under Roger Velez, Riddlesdown tried going wire to wire, was second by half a length at the next-to-last point of call, and tired to 11th. But he was only beaten 4¼ lengths in a race he may have needed after the time off.

10

Gulfstream Park

MacDiarmdaH–G3

1⅜ MILES. (Turf). (2:10³) 8th Running of THE MAC DIARMIDA HANDICAP. Grade III. Purse $100,000 Guaranteed. FOR THREE YEAR OLDS AND UPWARD. By subscription of $100 each, which shall accompany the nomination, $1,000 to pass the entry box and $1,000 additional to start, with $100,000 guaranteed. The owner of the winner to receive $60,000; $20,000 to second, $11,000 to third, $6,000 to fourth and $3,000 to fifth. Trophy to winning owner. This race will be limited to 12 Starters, with Also Eligibles. (High Weights on the scale Preferred.) In the event this stake is taken off the turf, it may be subject to downgrading upon review of the Graded Stakes Committee. Closed Wednesday, January 8, 2003 with 31 Nominations. (Rail at 0 feet.)

---

1 Whitmore's Conn
Own: Shanley Michael & Lynn
Red — Yellow, Purple S, Yellow Cap
PRADO E S (57 6 7 11 .11) 2002:(1527 289 .19)

Dk. b or br h. 5
Sire: Kris S. (Roberto) $150,000
Dam: Albonita (Deputed Testamony)
Br: Bud Wolf & Joe D'Agostino (NY)
Tr: Schulhofer Randy(2 0 0 1 .00) 2002:(151 33 .22)

L 114

Life 25 5 4 4 $336,190 103
2002 9 3 2 0 $210,100 103
GP ⊕ 1 1 0 0 $21,600 96

D.Fst 5 0 0 2 $23,490 89
Wet(375) 1 1 0 0 $25,200 78
Turf(300) 16 4 4 2 $287,500 103
Dst⊕(400) 1 1 0 0 $90,000 103

WORKS: Jan16 GP 4f fst :494 B 14/22 Jan6 GP 4f fst :483 B 9/40 Dec19 GP 4f fst :503 B 19/23 Nov29 Bel tr.t 4f fst :503 B 29/56 Nov24 Bel 5f fst 1:03 B 14/17 Nov16 Bel 4f fst :52 B 34/37
TRAINER: Turf(83 .27 $2.84) Routes(122 .24 $2.20) GrdStk(24 .21 $2.93)

---

2 Mr. Pleasentfar (Brz)
Own: Raising Dust Stable
White — Gold, Orange Rds & Triangle, Purple
MARTIN C W (9 1 1 0 .11) 2002:(454 54 .12)

B. h. 6
Sire: Emmson*Ire (Ela–Mana–Mou*Ire)
Dam: Pleasant Tale (Pleasant Colony)
Br: Haras Garcez Castellano (Brz)
Tr: Malek Raja(1 0 1 0 .00) 2002:(25 2 .08)

L 113

Life 19 5 1 2 $185,807 101
2002 4 0 0 0 $269 51
2001 8 3 0 1 $168,350 101
GP ⊕ 1 0 0 0 $0 74

D.Fst 3 0 0 0 $269 51
Wet(327*) 5 2 0 0 $15,909 –
Turf(311*) 11 3 1 2 $169,629 101
Dst⊕(398) 3 2 0 0 $150,000 101

WORKS: Dec22 Crc 4f fst :49 B 3/25 Nov11 Crc ⊕ 5f fm 1:001 H (d) 1/2 Nov4 Crc 4f fst :494 B 12/38
TRAINER: Turf(8 .00 $0.00) Routes(7 .00 $0.00) GrdStk(1 .00 $0.00)

---

3 Macaw (Ire)
Own: Melillo George & Sandra
Blue — Royal Blue, Hot Pink Diamond Belt, Hot
SANTOS J A (60 12 10 6 .20) 2002:(1160 176 .15)

B. c. 4 (Jan)
Sire: Bluebird (Storm Bird)
Dam: No Quest*Ire (Rainbow Quest)
Br: Denis Brosnan & Joan Brosnan (Ire)
Tr: Tagg Barclay(8 1 2 2 .13) 2002:(222 32 .14)

L 114

Life 15 3 3 2 $136,418 96
2002 3 1 2 $132,336 96
2001 3 M 2 0 $4,082 –
GP ⊕ 0 0 0 0 $0 –

D.Fst 0 0 0 0 $0 –
Wet(293*) 0 0 0 0 $0 –
Turf(350*) 15 3 3 2 $136,418 96
Dst⊕(470) 0 0 0 0 $0 –

WORKS: Jan13 PmM 4f fst :502 B 7/14 Jan7 PmM 4f fst :501 B 11/23 Dec18 PmM 5f fst 1:043 B 1/1 Dec5 Bel tr.t 7f fst 1:30 B 1/1 Nov30 Bel tr.t 4f fst :50 B 49/88 Nov25 Bel 5f fst 1:022 B 7/17
TRAINER: Turf(101 .11 $0.95) Routes(127 .11 $0.87) GrdStk(4 .00 $0.00)

4 Riddlesdown (Ire)
Own:Tanaka Gary A
Yellow Emerald Green Gold Trim On White Sash
VELEZ R I (10 0 0 0 .00) 2002:(253 32 .13)

Ch. h. 6
Sire: Common Grounds (Kris)
Dam: Neat Dish(Stalwart)
Br: McLoughlin John (Ire)
Tr: O'Callaghan Niall M(8 3 1 0 .38) 2002:(284 39 .14)

L 113

Life	25	7	3	1	$204,954	99		D.Fst		0	0	0	0	$0 –
2002	7	2	0	0	$107,262	99		Wet(250*)		0	0	0	0	$0 –
2001	6	0	0	0	$6,054	97		Turf(181*)		25	7	3	1	$204,954 99
GP ⓣ	1	0	0	0	$0	81		Dst ⓣ(270)		3	1	0	0	$38,015 99

28Dec02-11Crc fm 1½ ⓣ:50 1:152 2:043 2:28 3↑ WLMcKnightH-G2 94 4 12 11 1hd 2½ 114¼ Velez R I L113 16.60 87-10 Man From Wicklow1181 Serial Bride1141¼ Rochester117hd On hedge, tired 12
25Oct02-7AP yl 1⅛ ⓣ:511 1:161 1:412 1:594 3↑ John Henry H100k 97 1 11½ 11½ 1½ 1hd 2½ Chavez J F L116 3.60 77-24 DTpThAdmrl114½ Rddlsdn1162 NtnlAnthm1152 Bumped-offstrided str 7
Placed first through disqualification.
21Sep02-14KD gd 1½ ⓣ:531 1:223 2:124 2:381 3↑ KyCupH-G3 65 10 11 11½ 1½ 41½ 724¼ Melancon L L114 22.10 — 46 Rochester1152¼ Nowrass1124¼ Continental Red1172 Pace,gave way 10
6Jly02-8AP fm 1½ ⓣ:482 1:123 2:022 2:272 3↑ StrsStrpBCH-G3 98 2 11 11½ 13 12 42 Sibille R L116 7.50 100 — Cetewayo118nk Private Son115¾ Pisces1171 Weakened a bid 9
1Jun02-9CD fm 1⅜ ⓣ:494 1:15 1:383 2:154 3↑ Louisville HG3 99 8 12 11½ 11 21 51¾ Perret C L115 5.20 84-14 DTwo PointTwoMill112½DHPisces116DHClassicPar114no Pace,faltered 9
Placed 4th through disqualification.
11May02-4CD fm 1⅜ ⓣ:502 1:153 1:401 2:161 3↑ Alw 57460NC 97 6 12 13½ 13 11½ 11¾ Perret C L116 5.60 84-09 Riddlsdown1161¾ RdMountin1161 EvnThScor118no Controlled pace,drivg 6
16Feb02-8GP yl 1⅜ ⓣ:502 1:152 1:40 2:172 3↑ GP BC H-G1 81 5 85¾ 87½ 97¾ 129¾ 1115¼ Decarlo C P L113 13.60 51-34 Cetewayo1153¼ BndIsPssing117¾ ProfitOption1152¾ Steadied into 1st turn 12
Previously trained by Demercastel Philippe
29Dec01-11Crc fm 1½ ⓣ:513 1:162 2:043 2:274 3↑ WLMcKnght H-G2 97 10 63½ 63½ 72¾ 84¾ 62¾ Prado E S 114 36.10 89-09 ProfitOption115½ DeelitefulIrving1131¼ Eltwsul114½ 3 wide, lacked a rally 12
2Nov01♦ M-Laffitte(Fr) hy *1⅛ⓣ RH 3:312 3↑ Prix Scaramouche (Listed) 54¾ Junk A 129 16.00 Bosham Mill1242 Torrealta126hd Odessa1182½ 13
Timeform rating: 101 Stk 35700 Cloes up.outpaced 2f out,came again on rail
21Oct01♦ Longchamp(Fr) hy *1½ⓣ RH 2:442 3↑ Prix du Conseil de Paris-G2 1018¼ Doleuze O 128 64.00 Yavana's Pace130½ Epitre1281 Foundation Spirit1215 11
Timeform rating: 91 Stk 73400 Tracked clear leader in 3rd,weakened 1-1/2f out.Maille Pistol11th
9Sep01♦ Longchamp(Fr) yl *1⅛ⓣ RH 3:252 4↑ Prix Gladiateur-G3 43¼ Mosse G 126 9.90 Yavana's Pace1262½ Woodford Reserve123¾ Generic130hd 10
Timeform rating: 113 Stk 58500 Trackled in 3rd,lost 3rd on line
19Aug01♦ Deauville(Fr) sf *1⅞ⓣ RH 3:202 3↑ Prix Kergolay-G2 54¾ Mosse G 130 6.20 Generic132nk Samsaam1304 Speedmaster132½ 6
Timeform rating: 108 Stk 75200 Trailed to over 1f out,evenly late

WORKS: Dec3 CD 5f fst 1:044 B 8/8 Nov27 CD 4f fst :50 B 18/26 Nov20 CD 3f fst :39 B 11/12 Nov15 CD 5f fst 1:021 B 14/28 Oct22 CD 4f fst :533 B 72/74
TRAINER: Turf(104 .11 $1.43) Routes(224 .16 $1.50) GrdStk(43 .14 $1.13)

5 Whata Brainstorm
Own:Eaton John & Laymon Steve
Green Sky Blue, Yellow Diamonds, Yellow
CHAVEZ J F (59 8 7 6 .14) 2002:(1196 223 .19)

Dk. b or br h. 6
Sire: Honor Grades (Danzig) $15,000
Dam: What a Future(Roberto)
Br: Hooper Fred W (Fla)
Tr: Picou James E(1 0 0 0 .00) 2002:(90 5 .06)

L 114

Life	27	6	6	1	$607,190	107		D.Fst		5	1	1	0	$33,790 79
2002	4	0	1	0	$17,240	101		Wet(345)		1	0	0	0	$3,000 78
2001	3	1	1	0	$226,000	107		Turf(300)		21	5	5	1	$570,400 107
GP ⓣ	4	1	2	0	$210,740	107		Dst ⓣ(405)		3	0	1	0	$49,000 104

28Dec02-11Crc fm 1½ ⓣ:50 1:152 2:043 2:28 3↑ WLMcKnightH-G2 97 2 32½ 44 42½ 32 72¾ Velasquez C L114 10.00 88-10 MnFromWicklow1181 SerilBride1141¼ Rochstr117hd On hedge, weakened 12
7Dec02-7Hou fm 1⅛ ⓣ:494 1:141 1:384 1:513 3↑ GS Chal Turf259k 94 4 53 55 52¾ 64¾ 54½ Valenzuela P A L126 9.30 76-20 LRein'sTrms126½ MystryGivr1261½ ForbiddnAppl1261¾ Inside, no menace 9
8Nov02-8Aqu yl 1⅜ ⓣ:542 1:211 1:463 2:243 3↑ Alw 58000C 79 1 52½ 62¾ 52 77½ 89½ Carrero V L117b 3.65 40-51 QuietRuler1202½ GrittySndie123nk PerfctStrngr1171½ Rank under restraint 8
21Feb02-9GP fm *1⅛ ⓣ:501 1:132 1:382 1:501+ 4↑ Alw 46000N$mY 101 4 31 41¾ 31 31 2no Chavez J F L116b *2.60 87-18 Stoksky116no WhtBrnstrm116¾ Mr.Lvngstn120nk Bumped stretch, missed 7
25Mar01-8FG fm *1⅛ ⓣ:484 1:131 1:38 1:503 4↑ ExplsveBidH-G2 102 6 43 44 42½ 43½ 42½ Chavez J F L116b 3.80 88-12 Tijiyr110nk Northcote Road115½ King Cugat1211¾ Prominent, lacked kick 13
11Mar01-10GP fm 1¼ ⓣ:481 1:122 2:00 2:233 3↑ PanAmericnH-G2 107 2 31½ 32 32 1hd 12½ Velazquez J R L114b 4.30 97-03 WhatBrinstorm1142½ SubtlePower1152½ Crigsteel114hd Drew clear, driving 7
10Feb01-10GP fm 1⅜ ⓣ:48 1:13 1:362 2:132 3↑ GP BC H-G1 104 5 87½ 99½ 84½ 63½ 2nk Chavez J F L113b 8.80 86-10 SbtlPowr113nk WhtBrnstorm113hd Stokosky1141¾ Swung out, closed well 9
30Dec00-11Crc fm 1½ ⓣ:503 1:153 2:06 2:29 3↑ WLMcKnght H-G2 95 11 107 94½ 73 34 32½ Chavez J F L113b *2.00 83-08 A LittleLuck1141 Stokosky1151½ WhataBrainstorm1131 Rallied five wide 12
18Nov00-8Aqu gd 1⅜ ⓣ:484 1:14 1:392 2:174 3↑ Red Smith H-G2 99 8 68½ 711 61 3½ 42¾ Gryder A T L114b 8.20 80-17 Cetewayo114nk Understood113¾ Val's Prince1181¾ Game finish inside 13
28Oct00-10Crc fm 1⅛ ⓣ:483 1:113 1:354 1:474 CalderDerby-G3 98 6 106 104 74½ 2hd 11¾ Homeister R B Jr L122b 4.50 90-16 Whata Brainstorm1221¾ Muntej1221¼ Womble117¾ Circled, edged away 12
15Oct00-8Bel fm 1⅛ Ⓣ:514 1:154 1:381 1:493 Jamaica H-G2 86 4 63½ 72½ 84½ 76 64 Samyn J L L117b 7.80 76-18 KingCugat123no MandarinMarsh1141½ PardeLeder1152 Wide trip, no rally 8
24Sep00-9Bel gd 1½ ⓣ:501 1:153 2:063 2:312 LRealizatnH-G3 102 2 105 92½ 2hd 2hd 22½ Chavez J F L115b 10.20 69-28 Ciro1232½ Whata Brainstorm1158¾ Lodge Hill1151¼ Led between calls 10

WORKS: ●Jan15 GP ⓣ 4f gd :483 H (d) 1/7 Jan7 GP 1f fst 1:53 B 1/1 Dec23 Crc ⓣ 4f fm :48 H (d) 3/5 Dec18 GP 5f fst 1:021 B 11/13 ●Nov30 Bel tr.t 6f fst 1:15 B 1/5 Nov24 Bel 6f fst 1:151 B 2/2
TRAINER: Turf(26 .04 $1.01) Routes(42 .05 $1.04) GrdStk(1 .00 $0.00)

6 Quiet Ruler
Own:Sarf Randy J & Old Brookside Farm
Black Silver, Black Sash, Black Bars On Silver
VELAZQUEZ J R (57 10 6 6 .18) 2002:(1394 289 .21)

Ch. h. 5
Sire: Woodman (Mr. Prospector) $40,000
Dam: Rivermorn(Riverman)
Br: Gallagher's Stud (NY)
Tr: Bates Larry(1 0 0 0 .00) 2002:(178 18 .10)

L 113

Life	31	6	4	2	$280,470	96		D.Fst		4	0	0	1	$6,060 68
2002	10	3	1	0	$165,540	96		Wet(310)		2	0	0	0	$1,230 18
2001	12	3	3	1	$106,560	86		Turf(305)		25	6	4	1	$273,180 96
GP ⓣ	0	0	0	0	$0	–		Dst ⓣ(355)		1	1	0	0	$34,800 96

Previously trained by Mueller Russell
7Dec02-7Hou fm 1⅛ ⓣ:494 1:141 1:384 1:513 3↑ GS Chal Turf259k 89 6 87½ 811 88½ 86½ 66½ Prado E S L126 4.80 73-20 LRin'sTrms126½ MystryGivr1261½ ForbiddnAppl1261¾ Rank stretch, 3w bid 9
8Nov02-8Aqu yl 1⅜ ⓣ:542 1:211 1:463 2:243 3↑ Alw 58000C 96 3 11 1½ 1½ 12½ 12½ Velazquez J R L120 3.45 49-51 QuietRuler1202½ GrittySndie123nk PerfectStrngr1171½ Pace, clear, driving 8
19Oct02-9Bel sf 1⅛ Ⓣ:531 1:183 1:43 1:55 3↑ ⓈMohawk H150k 94 10 42½ 41½ 32 1½ 11¾ Velazquez J R L113 45.50 54-42 QutRulr1131¾ Whtmor'sConn124nk Chsn'Wmmn114nk 3 wide move, driving 11
21Sep02-7Bel fm 1⅛ Ⓣ:492 1:133 1:371 1:49 3↑ ⓈAshleyColeH83k 86 7 53½ 43 52 75½ 84 Velazquez J R L113 15.90 80-13 I'm All Yours122nk Haggs Castle113hd CelticSky120½ Between rivals, tired 9
31Aug02-5Sar gd 1⅛ ⓣ:232 :464 1:104 1:414 3↑ ⓈAlw 46000N2x 90 2 89 810 74½ 21½ 1½ Velazquez J R L121 3.25 87-20 Quiet Ruler121½ Platinum Setting121nk Motives1192 Svd grd, split rivals 10
12Aug02-6Sar fm 1⅜ ⓣ:501 1:141 1:382 1:56 3↑ ⓈAlw 46000N2x 87 7 73¾ 52 65½ 41½ 21½ Velazquez J R L121 7.00 77-16 IrishColonial1171½ QuietRuler121nk BestShotYet1211¾ Game finish outside 9
3Aug02-7Sar fst 1⅛ ⊗:482 1:124 1:381 1:512 3↑ Alw 48000N1x 68 2 64½ 73½ 63¾ 45½ 57 Velazquez J R L118 4.30 75-07 Connie'sMgic1212½ AboveJustic116¾ LordBurligh1112½ Wide trip, no rally 7
10Jly02-4Bel gd 1⅛ Ⓣ:511 1:15 1:384 1:502 3↑ ⓈAlw 46000N1x 80 6 52½ 53 43 61 62½ Velazquez J R L118 7.10 75-16 Touch'Clss1181 HmSndwich118hd BestShotYt118no Buried inside stretch 9
26May02-8Bel fm 1⅛ Ⓣ:474 1:113 1:351 1:47 3↑ ⓈKingston H85k 79 4 84½ 85½ 74¾ 89½ 87½ Velazquez J R L114 28.75 87-08 CelticSky117¾ ReluctntGroom116hd I'mAllYours1241¼ Inside, no response 10
10May02-6Bel fm 1⅛ Ⓣ:482 1:122 1:364 1:482 3↑ ⓈAlw 46000N2x 72 5 43½ 52½ 61½ 63½ 65¾ Carrero V5 L116 8.40 81-13 NoWhtFlgs1211 Robb'sRockn1162½ Hrstofors1211¼ Between rivals, no bid 9
Previously trained by Vasquez Jacinto
22Dec01-7Crc fm 7½f ⓣ:232 :462 1:10 1:28 PeteAxthelm100k 76 2 3 1112 1212 119 119 Santos J A L119 13.60e 87-04 One Eyed Joker122½ Tour Of The Cat1191½ Boastful119nk Outrun 12
Previously trained by Mueller Russell
24Nov01-3Aqu fm 1⅛ ⓣ:484 1:134 1:382 1:504 3↑ ⓈAlw 44000N1x 86 6 66 66 74½ 42½ 11½ Prado E S L116 *2.75 84-12 QuietRuler1161½ Winloc'sNelson116¾ LittlMToo116no Split rivals, driving 12

WORKS: Jan15 Crc 5f fst 1:032 B 8/18 Dec23 Crc ⓣ 5f fm 1:032 B (d) 2/2 Nov30 Bel tr.t 4f fst :494 B 40/88 Oct29 Bel tr.t 4f fst :53 B 69/70
TRAINER: 1stW/Trn(13 .08 $0.46) 31-60Days(20 .10 $1.64) Turf(51 .06 $0.49) Routes(80 .10 $0.99) GrdStk(1 .00 $0.00)

7 Just Listen
Own:Guez Marie Romaine & Guez D
Orange Royal Blue, Brown Dots, Brown Cap
HOMEISTER R B JR (35 3 1 4 .09) 2002:(871 112 .13)

B. g. 7
Sire: Local Talent (Northern Dancer)
Dam: Avanti Sassa*Ger(Sassafras*Fr)
Br: Old Mill Farm (Ky)
Tr: Catanese Joseph C III(6 2 0 0 .33) 2002:(102 9 .09)

L 113

Life	31	3	7	3	$125,931	100		D.Fst		5	2	2	0	$26,680 91
2002	3	0	0	0	$4,250	97		Wet(310)		2	0	1	0	$7,030 90
2001	7	0	2	1	$29,731	98		Turf(300)		24	1	4	3	$92,221 100
GP ⓣ	1	0	0	0	$3,000	97		Dst ⓣ(465)		7	0	2	1	$46,140 99

28Dec02-11Crc fm 1½ ⓣ:50 1:152 2:043 2:28 3↑ WLMcKnightH-G2 97 12 42½ 32½ 32 52½ 83 Homeister R B Jr L112b 43.70 88-10 MnFromWicklow1181 SerilBride1141¼ Rochstr117hd Lacked late response 12
5Dec02-5Crc fm 1 ⓣ:231 :471 1:112 1:35 3↑ OClm 40000 (40-35)N 91 3 89½ 74¾ 3½ 3½ 4½ Homeister R B Jr L117b 5.60 92-07 FirstSpear117hd HndsomeGeorge116nk Dillonmyboy117nk 3 wide, bid, hung 10
Previously trained by Soyer Guillaume
20Jan02-10GP fm 1⅜ ⓣ:521 1:174 1:411 2:161 3↑ MacDiarmdaH-G3 97 11 95½ 95½ 83 95½ 53½ Velasquez C L114b 58.70 69-25 CrashCourse114½ Unite'sBigRed112no Eltawaasul1131½ Improved position 12
29Dec01-11Crc fm 1½ ⓣ:513 1:162 2:043 2:274 3↑ WLMcKnght H-G2 96 9 116½127½ 105¾ 105¾ 73½ Velasquez C L114 45.60 89-09 ProfitOption115½ DeelitefulIrving1131¼ Eltawasul114½ Failed to menace 12
7Dec01-1Crc fst 1⅛ ⊗:494 1:142 1:401 1:533 3↑ OClm 40000 (40-35)N 88 1 3½ 32 42 23 24 Douglas R R L117b 1.30 82-14 Kassar1204 Just Listen1174¼ Stauch1146½ Inside, 2nd best 5
17Nov01-8Aqu fm 1⅜ ⓣ:501 1:161 1:403 2:164 3↑ Red Smith H-G2 95 10 31 32 3½ 52 73½ Espinoza J L L113b 32.75 85-14 Mr.Pleasentfar115¾ Eltawasul114no ReglDynsty1131 Chased 3 wide, tired 12
13Oct01-5Crc fm 1⅜ ⓣ:493 1:154 1:394 2:161 3↑ FlyngPdgeonH100k 97 8 73½ 84¾ 73½ 42 2nk Castellano A Jr L114b *2.50e 84-16 Mr. Pleasentfar114nk Just Listen114½ Kassar1141½ Angled out, edged 9
8Sep01-8Bel fm 1⅜ ⓣ:50 1:15 1:393 2:15 3↑ Man O'War-G1 98 7 711 76¾ 73½ 68½ 67½ Migliore R L126b 94.25 82-15 With Anticipation1262½ Silvano126nk Ela Athena1232½ Steadied first turn 8
18Aug01-8Crc fm 1⅛ ⓣ:231 :471 1:102 1:403 3↑ Ensign Ray H30k 94 3 73½ 86½ 76¾ 43 31½ Toribio A R L113b 12.20 92-13 Mr. Livingston114¾ Special Coach114½ Just Listen113¾ Closed willingly 10
31Jly01-8Crc fm 1⅛ ⓣ:231 :473 1:111 1:422 3↑ OClm 40000 (40-35)N 87 8 75 52¾ 41½ 31½ 42½ Castellano A Jr L117b 12.60 82-16 Brassy Fred117½ Atiba117hd Pisces1191¾ Inside, flattened out 9
Previously trained by Cruguet Jean
30Dec00-11Crc fm 1½ ⓣ:503 1:153 2:06 2:29 3↑ WLMcKnght H-G2 79 10 96 83¾ 115¾ 1111 1111½ Coa E M L113b 10.40 74-08 A Little Luck1141 Stokosky1151½ Whata Brainstorm1131 No factor, wide 12
23Nov00-11Crc fm 1⅜ ⓣ:483 1:14 1:374 2:144 3↑ FlagDownH28k 95 5 66½ 67½ 52 41¾ 31½ Douglas R R L116b *1.70 90-16 Brassy Fred1151 Stokosky116nk Just Listen116nk Closed willingly 8

WORKS: Jan15 GP ⓣ 4f gd :50 B (d) 4/7 Dec23 Crc ⓣ 5f fm 1:013 H (d) 1/2 Dec16 Crc ⓣ 4f fm :482 H (d) 2/4 ●Nov25 Crc ⓣ 4f fm :473 H (d) 1/5 Nov19 Crc 4f fst :50 B 19/42 ●Nov2 LMB 3f fst :40 B 1/8
TRAINER: Turf(18 .06 $9.58) Routes(29 .07 $6.18) GrdStk(1 .00 $0.00)

8 Marquette

Pink

Own:Cavanaugh J R & Early Morning Farm
Lime Green, Pink Sleeves, Pink Cap
JRNER T G (9 0 2 0 .00) 2002:(456 67 .15)

B. h. 7
Sire: Spectacular Bid (Bold Bidder) $3,500
Dam: Wicklow Royalty(Simply Majestic)
Br: Cavanaugh J R (Fla)
Tr: Root Richard R(4 0 0 0 .00) 2002:(138 17 .12)

L 113

Life	20	5	2	2	$317,178	103	D.Fst	3	0	0	0	$7,179	99
2003	1	0	0	0	$4,500	90	Wet(310)	0	0	0	0	$0	–
2002	9	1	0	1	$57,236	103	Turf(315)	17	5	2	2	$309,999	103
GP Ⓣ	3	1	1	0	$38,700	92	DstⓉ(315)	0	0	0	0	$0	–

Jan03-10GP gd 1 Ⓣ :232 :472 1:121 1:374 3↑ Appleton H-G2 **90** 5 811 89¼ 85¾ 44½ 54½ Turner T G L 115 f 39.90 72–24 Point Prince1151¼ Krieger115nk Red Sea1141¾ Improved position 9
Previously trained by Mora Myra
Nov02-9Crc gd 1⅛ Ⓣ :492 1:122 1:362 1:481 3↑ [S]B HeathTurfH150k **90** 5 43 43½ 33½ 42½ 42½ Cabassa A Jr L 113 f 18.80 86–14 Misqu'sApprovl116hd SirBrin'sSword1161 StyForvr1141½ No late response 7
Oct02-8Crc fm 1⅛ Ⓣ :501 1:141 1:374 1:492 3↑ FlyngPdgeonH100k **88** 4 74¼ 78 75½ 33 34½ Cabassa A Jr L 114 f 13.20 78–18 Band IsPassing1194¼ *LinkToJimmy*112nk Marquette114½ No late response 9
Sep02-3Crc fst 5f ⊗ :22 :46 :584 3↑ Wayme H44k **71** 4 7 713 77 75½ 56½ Cabassa A Jr L 114 f 7.50 88–15 StrightA113nk PleseMDoc1163¾ TrmintionDust1122¼ Checked start, outrun 7
Sep02-5Crc gd 1 Ⓣ :234 :481 1:123 1:373 3↑ Miami BCH-G3 **65** 6 1½ 11 3½ 57½ 818¼ Cabassa A Jr L 115 f 8.00 62–20 *Band Is Passing*1172 Pisces1161½ Doowaley1132¾ Off hedge, faded 8
Aug02-7Del hd 1 1/16 Ⓣ :251 :491 1:124 1:42 3↑ Sussex H100k **85** 3 1hd 2hd 11 1hd 55 Cabassa A Jr L 115 f 6.80 92 — Syncline115no Dr. Kashnikow117½ Sardaukar115nk Set pace, steadied 7
Jly02-5Crc fst 1⅛ ⊗ :481 1:124 1:383 1:521 3↑ Americana H100k **99** 7 21 1hd 11½ 1hd 44¼ Homeister R B Jr L 113 f 4.30 89–17 Dancing Guy1153¼ Sir Bear1211 Wertz119no Inside, gave way 7
Jun02-1Crc gd 1⅛ Ⓣ :474 1:111 1:37 1:50 3↑ KissinKris38k **103** 4 21½ 33½ 33 15 14¼ Cabassa A Jr L 115 f 13.10 80–20 Marquette1154¼ **Zloty**115¾ Dillonmyboy117½ 3 wide, drew away 8
Previously trained by Parody Albert
May02-4Mnr fm 7½f Ⓣ :231 :454 1:084 1:272 3↑ MemorialDayH79k **67** 7 8 88¾ 77½ 1112 1111½ Nuesch D LB 115 f 10.00 90–02 MagicalMdness1151½ *IrishSilence*1131¼ Tlkmeister122hd Outrun early, tired 11
Previously trained by Waunsch Joseph J
3Apr02-8Crc fm 1 Ⓣ :223 :461 1:101 1:342 3↑ JackieWackiH33k **87** 3 45 52½ 53½ 44 47½ Ferrer J C L 116 f 4.10 88–04 Mr.Livingston1153 TourOfThCt1161½ Unit'sBigRd1193 Failed to menace 5
Previously trained by Violette Richard A Jr
5May00-7CD fm 1⅛ Ⓣ :483 1:122 1:354 1:474 3↑ Woodford-G1 **83** 1 11 11 1½ 45 79 Chavez J F L 118 6.00 88 — *Manndar*1141½ Falcon Flight1181 Yagli1201 Used in pace 8
Apr00-8Kee fm 1 Ⓣ :234 :471 1:112 1:35 4↑ MakrsMarkMl-G2 **101** 5 42 52 21½ 21 2nk Bailey J D L 120 3.40 97–09 *Conserve*116nk Marquette120nk *Inkatha*1161½ 5wide bid, hung 9
WORKS: **Nov11 Crc Ⓣ 5f fm 1:022 B (d)** *2/2* **Nov5 Crc 4f fst :502 B** *12/22*
TRAINER: Turf(13 .00 $0.00) Routes(40 .10 $2.62) GrdStk(1 .00 $0.00)

9 Rochester

Turqse

Own:Augustin Stable
White & Green Halves White Sleeves
AY P (48 8 5 7 .17) 2002:(1155 258 .22)

B. g. 7
Sire: Green Dancer (Nijinsky II) $15,000
Dam: Central City*GB(Midyan)
Br: Strawbridge George Jr (Pa)
Tr: Sheppard Jonathan E(7 0 1 1 .00) 2002:(421 51 .12)

L 117

Life	23	9	4	1	$673,133	109	D.Fst	1	0	0	0	$360	63
2002	10	3	3	1	$443,124	109	Wet(310)	0	0	0	0	$0	–
2001	10	5	1	0	$208,846	98	Turf(310)	22	9	4	1	$672,773	109
GP Ⓣ	1	0	0	0	$330	85	DstⓉ(360)	2	0	1	0	$2,376	92

Dec02-11Crc fm 1½ Ⓣ :50 1:152 2:043 2:28 3↑ WLMcKnightH-G2 **98** 1 106¾ 98 94½ 84½ 32¼ Day P L 117 *2.10 89–10 MnFromWicklow1181 **SerilBrid**1141¼ Rochstr117hd Angled wide, up for 3d 12
Previously trained by Drysdale Neil
Nov02-8Hol fm 1½ Ⓣ :482 1:13 2:024 2:271 3↑ HolTurfCup-G1 **100** 11 511 75 43 44½ 44 Martin E M Jr L 126 4.80 81–17 Sligo Bay1261 *Grammarian*1262½ Delta Form126½ Split foes,outkicked 11
Previously trained by Sheppard Jonathan E
6Oct02-4Kee fm 1½ Ⓣ :494 1:153 2:062 2:302 3↑ Sycamore BC154k **101** 5 66½ 55 52¾ 31 11 Day P L 125 2.60 85–13 Rochester1251 Roxinho1202¼ Lord Flasheart1201¾ Rallied 5w,stiff drive 7
Sep02-14KD gd 1½ Ⓣ :531 1:223 2:124 2:381 3↑ KyCupH-G3 **109** 3 77 64¼ 54½ 1½ 12½ Martin E M Jr L 115 11.30 47–46 *Rochester*1152½ Nowrass1124½ Continental Red1172 Under brisk urging 11
Aug02-8Del gd 1⅛ Ⓣ :474 1:121 1:381 1:51 3↑ CaesrRodneyH200k **95** 2 811 810 62¾ 3nk 24½ Bartram B E L 115 8.30 81–14 Revved Up1154½ *Rochester*115nk Spruce Run113nk 5 wide bid, no match 8
Jly02-4Del fm 1½ Ⓣ :482 1:123 2:05 2:294 3↑ Cape Henlope60k **91** 2 616 49 32½ 2hd 11½ Day P L 116 *1.20 91–04 Rochstr1161½ DwnOfThCondor1161 PhiBtDoc116nk Quick mve,ridden out 9
Run in divisions
2Jun02-9Rkm gd *1⅛ Ⓣ 1:472 3↑ NH SweepsH-G3 **97** 8 88 88½ 83¾ 65½ 43¾ Martin C W L 114 18.30 84–12 *DelMarShow*1201¾ Mus-if116½ Dr.Kshnikow1151½ Swung wide top stretch 9
1Jun02-9CD fm 1⅜ Ⓣ :494 1:15 1:383 2:154 3↑ Louisville HG3 **92** 2 66½ 77 53½ 85½ 85½ Day P L 116 5.30 80–14 [D]TwoPointTwoMill112½ [DH]Pisces116 [DH]ClssicPr114no Clip heels 3/16s 9
Placed 7th through disqualification.
4Apr02-8Kee fm 1½ Ⓣ :514 1:181 2:091 2:322 4↑ Elkhorn-G3 **94** 9 78½ 31½ 42¼ 22 22 Day P L 116 5.10 73–22 KimLovesBucky1162 Rochester116¾ *Cetewyo*118½ Stalk,5w,no late gain 10
0Mar02-10Tam gd *1⅜ Ⓣ :524 1:201 1:451 2:24 4↑ Alw 14700NC **90** 10 97¾ 88¾ 87¾ 43½ 2nk Martin C W L 118 *.70 — — FunN'Gun118nk Rochester118hd *Guardianofthegte*1184¾ Closed fast 5 wide 10
6Oct01-9Bel fm 1¼ [T] :511 1:154 1:392 2:022 3↑ Knickerbckr-G2 **96** 2 43½ 33 52½ 64¾ 83¾ Day P L 115 8.50 75–15 Sumitas115nk Manndar116nk Crash Course115nk Traffic inside stretch 11
7Oct01-4Kee fm 1½ Ⓣ :513 1:162 2:064 2:311 3↑ SycamoreBC166k **98** 1 67 67 63¼ 41 1no Day P L 119 5.20 81–15 Rochester119no Chorwon1251 Regal Dynasty1191½ Move to rail 1/8 p,drv 7
WORKS: **Jan16 GP 5f fst 1:024 B** *16/22* **Dec18 Cam 6f fst 1:15 B** *1/2* **●Nov19 Ash 5f fst 1:03 B** *1/4*
TRAINER: Turf(243 .12 $1.26) Routes(328 .13 $1.01) GrdStk(27 .22 $2.23)

10 Serial Bride

Purple

Own:Runnin Horse Farm Inc
Hunter Green, Hunter Green Rhf On White
COA E M (72 15 8 13 .21) 2002:(1367 287 .21)

Ch. h. 6
Sire: Stuka (Jade Hunter) $1,500
Dam: Risky Bride(Blushing Groom*Fr)
Br: Allen E Paulson (Ky)
Tr: Pointer Norman R(5 1 1 0 .20) 2002:(287 50 .17)

L 115

Life	30	6	7	5	$254,600	100	D.Fst	7	1	2	2	$28,300	83
2002	13	3	4	1	$181,920	100	Wet(310)	2	0	1	0	$7,280	82
2001	7	2	0	1	$34,240	89	Turf(255)	21	5	4	3	$219,020	100
GP Ⓣ	7	1	1	1	$32,650	93	DstⓉ(352)	1	1	0	0	$30,000	95

28Dec02-11Crc fm 1½ Ⓣ :50 1:152 2:043 2:28 3↑ WLMcKnightH-G2 **100** 3 22 21 2hd 1½ 21 Decarlo C P L 114 b 15.20 90–10 MnFromWicklow1181 SerilBride1141¼ **Rochstr**117hd Outfinished, held 2nd 12
7Dec02-11Crc fm 1⅛ Ⓣ :484 1:12 1:352 1:47 3↑ Trop Turf H-G3 **97** 6 65½ 65¾ 64¾ 44 31¾ Decarlo C P L 114 b 13.80 93–11 Krieger1131 Stokosky113¾ Serial Bride114nk Saved grd, willingly 12
2Nov02-9Aqu yl 1⅛ Ⓣ :504 1:154 1:402 1:522 3↑ KnickerbkrH-G2 **94** 4 33½ 42½ 32 31 22 Decarlo C P L 114 b 17.80 74–23 DwnOfTheCondor1142 SerilBrid114nk PolishMinr114½ Game finish inside 9
4Oct02-9Med gd 1⅜ Ⓣ :494 1:15 1:392 2:182 3↑ Manila50k **95** 10 73¾ 75 42 41½ 1nk Coa E M L 114 b 11.10 78–20 Serial Bride114nk Punkin Head114nk Stokosky114nk Rallied four wide 10
4Aug02-7Mth sf 1⅛ Ⓣ :483 1:131 1:381 1:503 3↑ Battlefield65k **95** 7 85¾ 85¼ 83¾ 63¼ 42¼ Espinoza V L 113 b 24.70 76–21 Autonomy115¾ *Revved Up*1151 Spruce Run113½ Outside bid, gaining 9
8Jun02-10Pha fm 1½ Ⓣ :531 1:194 2:101 2:35 3↑ GreenwoodCpH100k **94** 3 32½ 43 41½ 41½ 2¾ Elliott S L 114 b 17.40 65–30 *Cetewayo*122¾ SerialBride1141¾ DwnOfTheCondor116½ Eased out, rallied 8
27May02-7Mth fm 1⅛ Ⓣ :51 1:15 1:382 1:494 3↑ Alw 45000N$mY **92** 7 65 63¼ 53¼ 42½ 43½ Boulanger G L 115 b 19.50 78–12 Revved Up1151½ *Eltawaasul*115nk First Spear1151¾ Lacked late response 8
5May02-7Pim fm 1 1/16 Ⓣ :241 :492 1:14 1:444 3↑ OClm 30000 (30-25)N **92** 7 67½ 65½ 53½ 21 11½ Ferrer J C L 119 b *1.40 79–21 Serial Bride1191½ Purple Sand115¾ Adjust117no Wide, driving 9
18Apr02-7GP fm *1⅛ Ⓣ :484 1:12 1:36 1:483+ 4↑ Alw 36000N2X **93** 4 35 36½ 36 11 14 Coa E M L 118 b *1.30 95–13 *Serial Bride*1184 **Zloty**118nk Oklahoma Hello1182¾ Drew clear, ridden out 8
23Mar02-10GP fm 1 Ⓣ :234 :473 1:11 1:343 4↑ Clm 62500 (62.5-57.5) **86** 6 98¾ 911 75¼ 62¼ 84¼ Decarlo C P L 120 b 11.50 89–06 Scagnelli1201 Slowhand120¾ Glick120¾ No late response 12
2Mar02-5GP fm 1 1/16 Ⓣ :24 :481 1:121 1:422+ 4↑ Clm 57500 (62.5-57.5) **91** 3 33 32½ 41½ 32½ 23¼ Decarlo C P L 118 b 51.50 80–23 InFrnk'sHonor1203¼ SrlBrd1181¼ RolldStckng120hd Clipped heels far turn 10
8Feb02-6GP fm *1 Ⓣ :232 :471 1:112 1:352 4↑ Alw 36000N2X **89** 9 910 911 79½ 85¾ 54½ Decarlo C P L 118 b 30.70 92–06 Backatitagain122½ RideoutsPtton1183 Conormr118hd Passed tired rivals 10
WORKS: **Dec4 GP 4f fst :50 B** *16/21* **Nov30 GP 5f fst 1:034 B** *9/10* **Oct29 Mth 5f fst 1:014 B** *5/11* **Oct25 Mth 7f fst 1:293 B** *1/1*
TRAINER: Turf(73 .11 $1.03) Routes(140 .18 $1.42) GrdStk(5 .00 $0.00)

11 Gritty Sandie

Gray

Own:Kimmel Caesar P & Nicholson Ronald A
Orange, Black Cross Sashes, Black
BAILEY J D (23 5 6 3 .22) 2002:(832 213 .26)

Ch. g. 7
Sire: Manila (Lyphard) $4,000
Dam: Madam Sandie(Our Native)
Br: Kimmel Caesar P & Kimran Stables (Ky)
Tr: Toner James J(1 0 0 0 .00) 2002:(135 19 .14)

L 114

Life	39	5	5	9	$470,695	103	D.Fst	0	0	0	0	$0	–
2002	8	1	1	0	$78,125	100	Wet(325)	1	0	0	1	$4,510	71
2001	8	0	1	2	$112,670	102	Turf(315)	38	5	5	8	$466,185	103
GP Ⓣ	1	0	0	1	$3,740	85	DstⓉ(420)	15	2	1	6	$191,735	100

28Dec02-11Crc fm 1½ Ⓣ :50 1:152 2:043 2:28 3↑ WLMcKnightH-G2 **98** 10 127½ 109 104½ 105 42½ Samyn J L L 113 fb 25.10 89–10 MnFromWicklow1181 **SerilBrid**1141¼ **Rochstr**117hd Swung wide, belatedly 12
8Nov02-8Aqu yl 1⅜ Ⓣ :542 1:211 1:463 2:243 3↑ Alw 58000C **92** 6 74½ 83¾ 75 64½ 22¼ Samyn J L L 123 fb *3.30 47–51 **QuietRuler**1202¼ GrittySndie123nk PerfectStrngr1171½ Game finish outside 8
27Oct02-6WO sf 1⅜ Ⓣ :511 1:153 1:404 2:191 3↑ SkyClasscH-G2 **96** 9 33 43 41 66½ 54 Ramsammy E L 116 fb 20.85 65–31 Strut TheStage119¾ Cetewayo118nk *ManFromWicklow*1191¾ Finished well 9
5Oct02-5Bel fm 1¼ [T] :512 1:16 1:392 2:023 4↑ Alw 58000C **100** 4 42 41 43 41½ 11 Samyn J L L 116 fb 5.00 79–19 GrittySndie1161 [DH]DputyStrik120 [DH]ClssicPr123½ Came wide, driving 5
13Sep02-8Bel fm 1⅜ Ⓣ :532 1:191 1:433 2:18 4↑ Alw 58000C **94** 3 55 55½ 53 43½ 41½ Samyn J L L 117 fb 2.60 73–19 DwnOfTheCondor119no DputyStrik121no Eltwsul1211¼ Good finish outside 5
21Aug02-7Sar fm 1½ [T] :501 1:151 2:05 2:282 4↑ Alw 58000C **93** 7 21 21½ 2½ 2½ 62 Prado E S L 117 fb *1.40 88–10 ReglDynsty117½ DeputyStrike121½ *PlesntBrz*116nk With pace, weakened 8
13Jly02-8Bel fm 1⅜ [T] :49 1:133 1:371 2:132 3↑ BowlingGrnH-G2 **99** 2 913 917 913 82¾ 52¼ Davis R G L 114 fb 5.50e 84–13 **Whitmor'sConn**1121¾ StgingPost115hd MoonSoltr116nk Going well outside 9
21Jun02-8Bel fm 1¼ [T] :503 1:142 1:374 2:013 4↑ Alw 56000C **95** 4 1111 1110 117½ 93½ 41½ Davis R G L 116 fb 9.60 82–15 Eltawaasul1201 ***Whitmore'sConn***113½ *Crigsteel*116hd Rough trip, gamely 12
17Nov01-8Aqu fm 1⅜ Ⓣ :501 1:161 1:403 2:164 3↑ Red Smith H-G2 **91** 11 106¼ 105¾ 104½ 104¾ 105½ Davis R G L 116 fb 8.00 83–14 **Mr.Pleasentfr**115¾ Eltwsul114no ReglDynsty1131 Wide throughout, tired 12
26Oct01-9Bel fm 1¼ [T] :511 1:154 1:392 2:022 3↑ Knickerbckr-G2 **98** 4 95½ 105½ 96¾ 86¼ 62½ Nakatani C S L 116 fb 10.70 76–15 Sumitas115nk Manndar116nk Crash Course115nk Between foes, no rally 11
23Sep01-14KD fm 1½ Ⓣ :49 1:174 2:06 2:283 3↑ KyCup Turf HG3 **93** 1 58 64 73½ 54 56¼ Samyn J L L 115 fb *1.00 89–17 Chorwon1135 ThKnightSky1141 MnFromWcklow114nk 7w lane,no threat 7
11Aug01-9Sar gd 1½ [T] :474 1:124 2:021 2:262 3↑ SwordDancrH-G1 **102** 3 76 95 75½ 77¼ 53¾ Prado E S L 114 fb 24.25 100–11 *WithAnticiption*114¾ KingCugt1201¼ SlewVlley114¾ 4 wide run third turn 9
WORKS: **Jan13 Pay 4f fst :51 B** *9/22* **Dec24 Pay 3f fst :39 B** *15/20* **Dec16 Pay 5f fst 1:032 B** *1/1* **Dec7 Pay 4f fst :511 B** *7/11*
TRAINER: Turf(75 .19 $2.89) Routes(109 .17 $2.24) GrdStk(13 .15 $1.26)

12 Williams News — Lime
Own:On Target Racing Stable
Orchid, Black 'gp', Black Cap
HUSBANDS P (5 3 0 0 .60) 2002:(856 169 .20)

B. g. 8
Sire: Alleged (Hoist the Flag)
Dam: Wooden Crown(His Majesty)
Br: Willmott Stable (Ky)
Tr: Vivian David A(1 1 0 0 1.00) 2002:(184 22 .12)

114

Life	40	6	10	7	$948,681	106	D.Fst	5	0	0	1	$5,430	70
2002	3	0	0	1	$12,800	98	Wet(300)	0	0	0	0	$0	–
2001	8	1	1	1	$157,610	104	Turf(300)	35	6	10	6	$943,251	106
GP Ⓣ	0	0	0	0	$0	–	DstⓉ(375)	6	1	2	1	$116,882	104

Previously trained by Sahadi Jenine

28Dec02-11Crc	fm	1½	Ⓣ	:50 1:152 2:043 2:28	3↑ WLMcKnightH-G2	**97**	8	65	76	84	73½	62¾	Douglas R R	L 115	7.00	88-10	MnFromWicklow1181 **SerilBrid**1141¼ **Rochstr**117hd	Saved ground, no rally	12
23Nov02-8Hol	fm	1½	Ⓣ	:482 1:13 2:024 2:271	3↑ HolTurfCup-G1	**97**	7	712	64½	53¼	34½	55½	Solis A	LB 126	10.00	79-17	Sligo Bay1261 *Grammarian*1262½ Delta Form126½	3wd 3rd turn,no bid	11
19Oct02-4SA	fm	1⅛	Ⓣ	:48 1:121 1:36 1:474	3↑ Alw 65000N$mY	**98**	2	54½	59½	47½	31½	31½	Solis A	LB 118	2.50	88-10	DevineWind118½ Sigfreto1181 WilliamsNews1184½	Came out str,late 3wd	5
1Dec01-6Hol	gd	1½	Ⓣ	:491 1:144 2:053 2:294	3↑ Hol TurfCup-G1	**100**	2	814	77½	41½	72½	42½	Smith M E	LB 126	11.10	69-28	*SuperQuercus*1262 Bonaprtiste126½ BlzingFury122hd	4wd 3rd turn,rallied	9

Previously trained by Amoss Thomas

17Nov01-8Aqu	fm	1⅜	Ⓣ	:501 1:161 1:403 2:164	3↑ Red Smith H-G2	**97**	6	85½	85¼	83¾	72¾	52¼	Prado E S	L 117	3.80	86-14	**Mr.Pleasentfar**115¾ Eltawsul114no RegIDynsty1131	Came wide, no punch	12
30Sep01-8WO	gd	1½	Ⓣ	:502 1:151 2:034 2:282	3↑ CanIntrntl-G1	**91**	9	95¼	106½	115	117½	119	Clark D	L 126	9.10	87-08	Mutamam126½ Paolini126¾ [D]Zindabad126½	No rally	12
11Aug01-9Sar	gd	1½	[T]	:474 1:124 2:021 2:262	3↑ SwordDancrH-G1	**104**	6	99	62¾	42½	33	42¾	Albarado R J	L 114	22.00	101-11	*WithAnticiption*114¾ KingCugt1201¼ SlewVlley114¾	Inside run third turn	9
1Jly01-7AP	fm	1½	Ⓣ	:50 1:15 2:043 2:274	3↑ StrsStrpBCH-G3	**93**	7	911	85¾	66	45	36¼	Guidry M	L 116	*2.00	111 —	Falcon Flight1142¾ *Langston*1143½ Williams News116½	Belatedly	11
2Jun01-9CD	fm	1⅜	Ⓣ	:504 1:161 1:402 2:161	3↑ Louisville H109k	**93**	2	22	2½	22½	34½	58¾	Albarado R J	L 117	*1.50	75-14	WithAntcpton1126 ProftOpton112½ **GrttySnd**1151	Flattened out stretch	6
25Apr01-8Kee	fm	1½	Ⓣ	:502 1:143 2:042 2:29	4↑ Elkhorn-G3	**102**	9	76	64¼	2hd	11½	1½	Albarado R J	L 116	2.90	92-14	WilliamsNews116½ **GrittySandie**116½ Craigsteel1164½	5-6w trip,stiff drive	9
25Mar01-9FG	fm	*1 1/16	Ⓣ	:25 :493 1:134 1:452	4↑ Alw 43000N2Y	**98**	3	33½	33½	34	34	22	Albarado R J	L 117	1.90	87-12	Kris's Sleigh1222 *Williams News*1173 Pleasant King1171½	Game try	6
4Nov00-9CD	fm	1½	Ⓣ	:501 1:151 2:033 2:264	3↑ BC Turf-G1	**89**	13	85½	85½	84½	1212	1311½	Husbands P	L 126	38.10	98 —	Kalanisi126½ Quiet Resolve126no *John's Call*126hd	Wide trip, no threat	13

WORKS: ●Jan13 **Crc 6f fst 1:153 H** *1/6* Dec19 **SA 5f fst 1:002 H** *36/127* Dec12 **SA 5f fst 1:022 B** *37/49* Dec6 **SA 4f fst :492 H** *25/36* Nov19 **SA 4f fst :481 H** *9/25* Nov13 **SA 7f fst 1:27 H** *6/13*
TRAINER: 1stW/Trn(13 .08 $2.08) Turf(16 .00 $0.00) Routes(59 .12 $1.03) GrdStk(1 .00 $0.00)

The Mac Diarmida was an eighth of a mile shorter, and while there were nine other horses in it who had contested the McKnight, the one-length winner, Man From Wicklow, was not among them. Rochester, who'd finished third in the McKnight, would go off the 3-1 second choice in the Mac Diarmida behind Whitmore's Conn at 5-2.

What would have been a reasonable price on Riddlesdown? We'll never know. Although he had every right to move forward off his return race, and seemed to have an excellent chance of getting loose on the lead, he was sent off at 29.80-1.

Riddlesdown sprinted clear easily, as Marquette chased him in second before tiring badly and finishing last. Under clever rating by Velez, Riddlesdown got away with plodding fractions of 25⅕, 49⅘, 1:14⅘, 1:39, and 2:03. He sprinted his last eighth in 11⅗ and won by 1½ lengths, paying $61.60. The exacta came back $607.80, the trifecta $10,515, and the $1 superfecta—with 8-1 Macaw, 37-1 Just Listen, and 16-1 Williams News finishing second, third, and fourth—paid $69,375.

Here's another interesting example of lone speed. Timber Cruiser (see page 26) made his grass debut at Santa Anita, February 2, 2003, in a 1⅛-mile maiden race with blinkers removed. Though he hadn't raced on the lead in three prior dirt starts, he did with blinkers removed in his grass debut. Usually, the addition of

TENTH RACE
Gulfstream
JANUARY 19, 2003

1⅜ MILES. (Turf)(2.10^{3}) 8th Running of THE MAC DIARMIDA HANDICAP. Grade III. Purse $100,000 Guaranteed. FOR THREE YEAR OLDS AND UPWARD. By subscription of $100 each, which shall accompany the nomination, $1,000 to pass the entry box and $1,000 additional to start, with $100,000 guaranteed. The owner of the winner to receive $60,000; $20,000 to second, $11,000 to third, $6,000 to fourth and $3,000 to fifth. Trophy to winning owner. This race will be limited to 12 Starters, with Also Eligibles. (High Weights on the scale Preferred.) In the event this stake is taken off the turf, it may be subject to downgrading upon review of the Graded Stakes Committee. Closed Wednesday, January 8, 2003 with 31 Nominations. (Rail at 0 feet).

Value of Race: $100,000 Winner $60,000; second $20,000; third $11,000; fourth $6,000; fifth $3,000. Mutuel Pool $442,522.00 Exacta Pool $326,400.00 Trifecta Pool $259,372.00 Superfecta Pool $92,500.00

Last Raced	Horse	M/Eqt.	A.Wt	PP	¼	½	¾	1	Str	Fin	Jockey	Odds $1
28Dec02 ^{11}Crc^{11}	Riddlesdown-IRE	L	6 113	4	$1^{1\frac{1}{2}}$	1^{2}	1^{4}	1^{3}	$1^{2\frac{1}{2}}$	$1^{1\frac{1}{2}}$	Velez R I	29.80
28Dec02 ^{11}Crc^{9}	Macaw-IR	L	4 114	3	6^{1}	$6^{\frac{1}{2}}$	$7^{\frac{1}{2}}$	$6^{1\frac{1}{2}}$	2^{hd}	$2^{1\frac{3}{4}}$	Santos J A	8.10
28Dec02 ^{11}Crc^{8}	Just Listen	Lb	7 113	7	3^{2}	3^{1}	$5^{1\frac{1}{2}}$	5^{hd}	$4^{1\frac{1}{2}}$	3^{nk}	Homeister R B Jr	37.90
28Dec02 ^{11}Crc^{6}	Williams News	L	8 118	12	$10^{1\frac{1}{2}}$	$9^{1\frac{1}{2}}$	$9^{1\frac{1}{2}}$	$7^{\frac{1}{2}}$	5^{2}	4^{nk}	Husbands P	16.00
28Dec02 ^{11}Crc^{4}	Gritty Sandie	Lbf	7 114	11	12	11^{1}	11^{2}	9^{1}	6^{1}	5^{nk}	Bailey J D	7.50
28Dec02 ^{11}Crc^{3}	Rochester	L	7 117	9	$4^{\frac{1}{2}}$	$4^{\frac{1}{2}}$	$3^{\frac{1}{2}}$	2^{hd}	$3^{1\frac{1}{2}}$	$6^{1\frac{3}{4}}$	Day P	3.00
28Dec02 ^{11}Crc^{7}	Whata Brainstorm	L	6 114	5	$5^{\frac{1}{2}}$	$10^{\frac{1}{2}}$	10^{hd}	12	$8^{1\frac{1}{2}}$	$7^{1\frac{1}{4}}$	Chavez J F	9.50
28Dec02 ^{11}Crc^{5}	DH Whitmore's Conn	Lb	5 114	1	8^{hd}	5^{hd}	$4^{\frac{1}{2}}$	$8^{1\frac{1}{2}}$	7^{hd}	8	Prado E S	2.70
28Dec02 ^{11}Crc^{12}	DH Mr. Pleasentfar-BRZ	L	6 114	2	11^{1}	12	12	$11^{\frac{1}{2}}$	9^{2}	$8^{2\frac{1}{2}}$	Martin C W	93.00
7Dec02 ^{7}Hou^{6}	Quiet Ruler	L	5 113	6	9^{2}	$8^{1\frac{1}{2}}$	$8^{1\frac{1}{2}}$	10^{1}	$10^{\frac{1}{2}}$	10^{1}	Velazquez J R	12.70
28Dec02 ^{11}Crc^{2}	Serial Bride	Lb	6 115	10	7^{1}	7^{1}	6^{hd}	$4^{\frac{1}{2}}$	11^{2}	$11^{5\frac{3}{4}}$	Coa E M	6.80
4Jan03 ^{10}GP^{5}	Marquette	Lf	7 114	8	$2^{\frac{1}{2}}$	$2^{\frac{1}{2}}$	2^{1}	3^{1}	12	12	Turner T G	52.00

DH—Dead Heat.

OFF AT 5:09 Start Good. Won driving. Course firm.
TIME :25^{1}, :49^{4}, 1:14^{4}, 1:39, 2:03, 2:14^{3} (:25.31, :49.80, 1:14.98, 1:39.07, 2:03.08, 2:14.75)

$2 Mutuel Prices:				
	4–RIDDLESDOWN–IRE	61.60	32.00	22.40
	3–MACAW–IR		10.80	8.60
	7–JUST LISTEN			21.80

$2 EXACTA 4–3 PAID $607.80 $2 TRIFECTA 4–3–7 PAID $10,515.00 $1 SUPERFECTA 4–3–7–12 PAID $69,375.00

Ch. h, by Common Grounds–Neat Dish, by Stalwart. Trainer O'Callaghan Niall M. Bred by McLoughlin John (Ire).

RIDDLESDOWN (IRE) sprinted clear in the early stages, set a moderate pace while racing uncontested on the lead for a mile, maintained a clear advantage into midstretch then held off the runner-up under brisk urging. MACAW (IRE) raced in good position along the inside for a good part of the way, angled between horses leaving the turn and finished willingly for the place. JUST LISTEN raced up close along the inside for a mile, was shuffled back a bit on the turn then finished willingly along the rail. WILLIAMS NEWS raced well back to the turn, advanced four wide into the stretch then closed late in the middle of the track. GRITTY SANDIE was outrun to the turn then rallied belatedly. ROCHESTER chased the leaders while three wide to the top of the stretch and weakened. WHATA BRAINSTORM checked in tight during the early stages, raced in traffic while well back on the turn then failed to threaten while improving his position. WHITMORE'S CONN failed to mount a serious rally. MR. PLEASENTFAR (BRZ) was never a factor. QUIET RULER raced in traffic on the turn then lacked a strong closing bid. SERIAL BRIDE raced wide and tired. MARQUETTE raced up close between horses to the turn then gave way.

Owners— 1, Tanaka Gary A; 2, Melillo George & Sandra; 3, Guez Marie Romaine & Guez D; 4, On Target Racing Stable; 5, Kimmel Caesar P & Nicholson Ronald; 6, Augustin Stable; 7, Eaton John & Laymon Steve; 8, Shanley Michael & Lynn; 9, Raising Dust Stable; 10, Sarf Randy J & Old Brookside Farm; 11, Runnin Horse Farm Inc; 12, Cavanaugh J R & Early Morning Farm

Trainers— 1, O'Callaghan Niall M; 2, Tagg Barclay; 3, Catanese Joseph C III; 4, Vivian David A; 5, Toner James J; 6, Sheppard Jonathan E; 7, Picou James E; 8, Schulhofer Randy; 9, Malek Raja; 10, Bates Larry; 11, Pointer Norman R; 12, Root Richard R

Scratched— Maumee (5Jan03 ^{7}GP^{1}), Zloty (8Jan03 ^{9}GP^{3})

$2 Pick Three (1–3–4) Paid $2,717.20; Pick Three Pool $40,758.

blinkers causes a horse to show more early speed. Regardless, he won wire-to-wire at 29-1 by 1½ lengths.

Exactly three weeks later, Timber Cruiser moved up to allowance company in a 1½-mile optional $40,000 claimer. The scratch of Theatre Script left a field of eight. In all the PP's of the other horses in the race, there was only one showing a horse on the lead at the

5 Timber Cruiser
Own:Jones Aaron U & Marie D
Green White, Red Cross Sashes, Red Diamond
GARCIA M S (65 8 4 6 .12) 2002:(546 66 .12)

Dk. b or br g. 4 (Apr) KEEJUL00 $575,000
Sire: Saint Ballado (Halo) $125,000
Dam:River of Stars(Riverman)
Br: Pollock Farms & Coker C & R & Taylor Made Farm (Ky)
Tr: Barrera Larry(3 1 0 0 .33) 2002:(2 0 .00)

L 119

Life	4	1	0	0	$30,000	83	D.Fst	3	0	0	0	$0	66
2003	2	1	0	0	$30,000	83	Wet(320)	0	0	0	0	$0	–
2002	2	M	0	0	$0	66	Turf(305)	1	1	0	0	$30,000	83
SA Ⓣ	1	1	0	0	$30,000	83	DstⓉ(235*)	0	0	0	0	$0	–

2Feb03-3SA fm 1⅛ Ⓣ :49 1:133 1:37 1:49 4↑ Md Sp Wt 50k 83 1 11 11½ 1½ 11 11½ Garcia M S LB 121 29.30 84-16 TimberCruiser1211½ CasulThunder1212 Mirific121hd Drifted bit,held game 6
4Jan03-4SA fst 6½f :211 :434 1:094 1:164 4↑ Md Sp Wt 48k 12 10 3 85 109 1013 1030½ Krone J A LB 122 b 4.10e 58-11 *C.J.'sHonour*1222½ Sequoian122½ ThrowinHeat123½ Wide,gave way,eased 10
Previously trained by Inda Eduardo
14Apr02-2SA fst 7f :22 :443 1:103 1:232 3↑ Md Sp Wt 48k 66 7 1 21 31½ 65 68 Valenzuela P A LB 117 b 7.30 80-14 Olmodvor1131½ StpPymnt124nk PrfssrHggns117hd Stalked pace, weakened 8
18Feb02-8SA fst 6½f :221 :453 1:103 1:171 Md Sp Wt 46k 39 1 9 73½ 1010 1117 1122¾ Smith M E B 120 24.60 64-19 RelentlessSeller120hd *LikAHro*1201 MyCptin1202½ Saved ground,gave way 11
WORKS: ●Feb19 Hol 5f fst 1:002 H *1/14* Jan25 Hol 5f fst 1:002 H *6/52* Jan18 Hol 5f fst 1:011 H *15/51* Dec30 Hol 5f fst 1:003 H *7/14* Dec24 Hol 6f fst 1:134 H *8/15* Dec6 Hol 5f fst 1:023 H *15/19*
TRAINER: Turf(1 1.00 $60.60) Routes(2 .50 $30.30) Alw(2 .00 $0.00)

first point of call. In a mile race three starts back, On My Honour was first by a head, then first by half a length through fractions of 23 and 46⅖, before tiring to sixth. In two subsequent longer turf tries, he had raced close to a slow pace, behind halves of 47⅖ and 48⅖.

In Timber Cruiser's win on grass, he'd gotten away with a half in 49. However, he had shown speed in a dirt sprint, only 1½ lengths off a half in 44⅗ in one of them. If Timber Cruiser could beat On My Honour to the lead, he'd have a legitimate shot. Sent off at 10-1, he did exactly that, winning wire to wire again by 3½ lengths.

The flip side of a lone speed in a race is a race with either several speed horses or two or more extremely fast front-runners who will hook up.

In the seventh race at Santa Anita, January 11, 2003, a 6½-furlong allowance/optional claimer, a field of 10 included two extemely fast horses. Though he'd been off nine months, Devil's

3 Devil's Horn
Own:Circle B Ranch
Blue White Royal Blue Circle B On Back
BAZE T C (49 7 3 6 .14) 2002:(916 95 .10)

Dk. b or br g. 6
Sire: Skywalker (Relaunch) $7,500
Dam:Social Pretense(Tri Jet)
Br: Eugene G Burnison (Cal)
Tr: Burnison E G(1 1 0 0 1.00) 2002:(25 6 .24)

L 119

Life	9	3	2	1	$130,064	99	D.Fst	6	0	2	1	$22,844	8
2002	4	3	0	1	$113,220	99	Wet(355)	0	0	0	0	$0	-
2001	5	M	2	0	$16,844	89	Turf(335)	3	3	0	0	$107,220	9
SA Ⓣ	3	3	0	0	$107,220	99	DstⓉ(345)	3	3	0	0	$107,220	9

14Apr02-6SA fm *6½f Ⓣ :212 :432 1:06 1:12 4↑ Alw 63494N1X 99 8 1 12 13½ 14½ 13 Baze T C LB 122 f *1.40 97-06 Devil's Horn1223 *With Iris*1201 Solitario1201 Steady handling
28Feb02-7SA fm *6½f Ⓣ :22 :442 1:07 1:124 4↑ ⓈAlw 50000N1X 97 2 3 11 12½ 12½ 14 Baze T C LB 121 f *1.00 93-07 *Devil'sHorn*1214 PintedAvnu1201½ RidAndShin119nk Speed,inside,driving
10Feb02-3SA fst 6½f :213 :443 1:093 1:16 4↑ ⓈAlw 50000N1X 88 6 2 41¼ 3½ 2hd 33¼ Baze T C LB 121 f 8.90 90-10 EddieEddie120¾ PintedAvenu1202½ *Dvil'sHorn*1211 3wd bid turn,held 3rd
19Jan02-9SA fm *6½f Ⓣ :214 :434 1:064 1:13 4↑ Md Sp Wt 54k 96 11 1 11½ 1½ 13 12 Baze T C LB 123 f 14.30 92-09 Devil's Horn1232 Valid Redress1223 ***Primerica***1223 Drifted in,clear,held 1
Previously trained by Lage Armando
8Jly01-5Pln fst 6f :213 :45 :572 1:094 3↑ Md Sp Wt 28k 52 1 3 31 21 56 413 Baze R A LB 121 b *.70 82-06 Spanish Eyes1167 Bastian Lane1162½ *Dixie Valley*1163½ Erratic late
Previously trained by Burnison E G
24Jun01-7Hol fst 6f :214 :451 :571 1:092 3↑ ⓈMd Sp Wt 42k 67 5 3 22½ 31½ 34 611 Desormeaux K J LB 123 fb 3.20 82-15 *BringThHt*1172½ *GnrlStor*1173½ Jcqui'sDlight117½ Stalked pace, weakened
Previously trained by Lage Armando
28May01-1BM fst 6f :223 :454 :574 1:10 3↑ Md Sp Wt 29k 81 6 1 22½ 2hd 22½ 22½ Lumpkins J LB 123 f *.80 88-12 SilverPrince1232½ Devil'sHorn123½ *TrickyTrvis*1174 Bid turn, outfinished
3May01-6BM fst 6f :223 :45 :57 1:093 3↑ Md Sp Wt 29k 89 2 5 11½ 12½ 14 21 Lumpkins J LB 123 f 3.00 92-10 Menhal1231 Devil's Horn1232 *Silver Prince*1232 Long lead, caught
Previously trained by Burnison E G
14Apr01-4SA fst 6½f :213 :442 1:092 1:16 3↑ Md Sp Wt 46k 71 4 8 84½ 88 89 79½ Desormeaux K J LB 124 f 17.10 79-18 Lytle Creek1242 Alotta Numbers117¾ *Barron H*117hd Steadied past 1/2
WORKS: Jan4 SA 6f fst 1:13 H *4/16* Dec6 SA 6f fst 1:131 H *7/18* Nov29 SA 5f fst :592 H *7/36* Nov23 SA 4f fst :484 H *14/29* Nov15 SA 3f fst :353 H *3/13*
TRAINER: +180Days(2 .50 $15.30) Turf(7 .43 $5.63) Sprint(19 .37 $4.18) Alw(3 .67 $2.93)

Horn had won off a six-month layoff previously. In his last race, also at 6½ furlongs, he'd won wire to wire by three lengths at 7-5, setting fractions of $21^2/5$ for the quarter and $43^2/5$ for the half.

But Devil's Horn had another speedster to contend with today, Teebar. His last start had been on dirt, but the one before was on grass at Hollywood Park. In a 5½-furlong allowance/optional claimer, he opened up a four-length lead by running a quarter in $21^1/5$ and a half in $43^2/5$. He then tired to seventh.

How could either horse win unless the other scratched? The betting public didn't seem to agree, sending off Devil's Horn as the 5-2 favorite and Teebar at 19-1.

They staged a sizzling pace duel, with Devil's Horn half a length in front after a 21-second quarter, and Teebar a head in front after a half-mile in 42. It's hard to imagine a faster half-mile. Devil's Horn came back and put Teebar away, only to weaken late to fifth. R. Baggio, who'd been second at 8-5 in his previous race, won by three-quarters of a length and paid $18.40.

Let's talk about class. Dr. Kashnikow had made a favorable impression in the first two starts of his career, both at Saratoga, for trainer John Kimmel and jockey Richard Migliore. As a 3-year-old in a 1¹/₁₆-mile maiden grass race during the summer of 2000, Dr. Kashnikow staged a three-wide rally, fought hard to the wire, and finished second by three-quarters of a length at 5.90-1, a promising debut to say the least. He then won a maiden race by half a length and did not race again at three.

Dr. Kashnikow traveled to Gulfstream Park to make his 4-year-old debut and won by three-quarters of a length, despite a layoff of more than five months, as the 2-1 favorite. Returning to New York after another freshening, he won a nonwinners of three (two other than maiden, claiming, or starter) at Aqueduct by 2½ lengths at 4.50-1. Kimmel left Dr. Kashnikow in an off-the-turf race at Belmont Park on a fast track, and he finished a distant fourth in the four-horse field. You should not only dismiss the race, but you could even cross the whole line out in *Daily Racing Form* as you handicap.

Returned to grass, Dr. Kashnikow won an allowance race by 1¾ lengths at 2-1.

Dr. Kashnikow made his stakes debut in his next start, and it was an imposing challenge: the Grade 2 Bernard Baruch Handicap at Saratoga at 1⅛ miles. This ambitious placing by Kimmel pitted Dr. Kashnikow against Bill Mott's 5-year-old grass star, Hap, ridden by Jerry Bailey. At 1⅛ miles, Hap had been literally unbeatable, winning all six of his starts including the 2000 Bernard Baruch, the Grade 2 Dixie Stakes, and, in his last start, the Grade 3 New Hampshire Sweepstakes Handicap by seven lengths at Rockingham Park at odds of 3-10.

Dr. Kashnikow would be getting seven pounds from Hap (121 to 114), but it was hard to envision him threatening Hap, especially at

Hap's best distance. Sent off at 11.90-1, Dr. Kashnikow moved up on the inside into second and held well for third in the seven-horse field, only beaten 3¾ lengths by Hap. The conclusion? Dr. Kashnikow had demonstrated considerable class running that close to Hap at nine furlongs.

I was thrilled when Dr. Kashnikow showed up four weeks later at Saratoga in the 1¹⁄₁₆-mile, Grade 2 Fourstardave Handicap, named for the brilliant New York-bred who won at least one race at Saratoga for eight consecutive years.

In the interim between starts, Dr. Kashnikow had one sharp work, four furlongs in 49 breezing—the fifth fastest of 28 at that distance at the Oklahoma training track—and a maintenance work, five furlongs in 1:03. The 49 on Oklahoma translates to a 48 or faster on the main track, an indication that Dr. Kashnikow had maintained his edge after his good performance in the Bernard Baruch.

Migliore was out of town, and Kimmel put up an even better grass jockey, John Velazquez, on Dr. Kashnikow.

I was hoping for 4-1 in the field of 12 and got 6-1 instead. Under a flawless ride by Velazquez, Dr. Kashnikow split horses late and beat Tubrok by three-quarters of a length, paying $15.40. Now everyone knew he had class.

Understanding form entails understanding that Thoroughbreds are equine athletes, not machines. Like human athletes, they are good some of the time and not so good other times.

Like humans, only the greatest Thoroughbreds can stay in top form for an extended period of time. That's why there are so few horses who remain undefeated for a season, let alone a career.

You'll frequently hear or read about form cycles, which simply means horses are either improving from start to start or going in the opposite direction. Working that into the handicapping equation, where the horse may be moving up or down in class, racing at a different distance or on a different surface, shipping to another track and/or changing jockeys, trainers, and/or equipment, is a challenge, one met best by tenets you consider valid.

In Chapter 1, we already mentioned two of these: A horse should get a little tired in a comeback race and move forward in his next start; and, adding Lasix can trigger significant improvement in a horse. There are other widely accepted tenets. For example, a horse should do okay stretching out to a route off two sprints.

Here's another: Workouts are significant in almost every situation.

Their importance may vary directly with the trainer using them, but the point of view here is that a horse showing a good race followed by a really good work or works is likely to race well or even better in his next start.

That's the conclusion I made when Phi Beta Doc showed up at Saratoga for the Grade 3 Saranac Handicap at 1³/₁₆ miles, September 1, 1999.

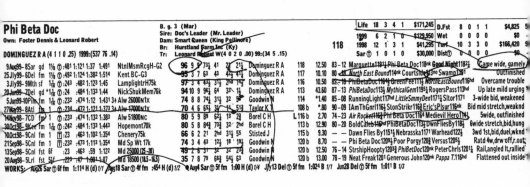

Co-owned and trained by Bob Leonard, Phi Beta Doc was stakes placed as a 2-year-old in 1998 and had blossomed at three. He won the $76,000 Nick Shuk Memorial Stakes at Delaware and the $75,000 Lamplighter Handicap at Monmouth Park. He then finished fourth by 1¼ lengths to a top turf horse, North East Bound, in the Grade 3 Kent Breeders' Cup Stakes at Delaware.

Phi Beta Doc made his Saratoga debut on August 9, in the Grade 2 National Museum of Racing and Hall of Fame Stakes. Breaking from post 9 in a field of 13, Phi Beta Doc was a solid second by $1\frac{1}{4}$ lengths to Marquette under regular rider Ramon Dominguez in the $1\frac{1}{8}$-mile stakes.

Leonard kept Phi Beta Doc at Saratoga and pointed him to the Saranac. In between starts, Phi Beta Doc had worked twice on turf, going four furlongs in $45\frac{4}{5}$ around the dogs, pylons placed near the inner rail on the turf course to protect the grass, and six furlongs in $1:11\frac{4}{5}$ around the dogs. In races, Phi Beta Doc was a stalker, not a crazed front-runner. It didn't take Columbo to deduce that Phi Beta Doc was sitting on a strong performance from a better post (2) than he had in his previous Saratoga stakes try.

The 6-5 favorite in the field of eight would be Monarch's Maze, ridden by Jerry Bailey. Monarch's Maze had finished third and first in maiden races and then won an allowance race by $5\frac{1}{2}$ lengths at 10.70-1. Phi Beta Doc went off at 4-1 and won by $2\frac{1}{4}$ lengths, setting a course record of 1:51.61.

Let's examine both class and form in a more recent, higher-profile stakes race at Saratoga, the Grade 1, $500,000 Sword Dancer Invitational Handicap, August 10, 2002, at $1\frac{1}{2}$ miles. Eleven horses went to the post. Each horse's weight is in parentheses. In post-position order, they were:

1. **Denon (118)** Trained by Bobby Frankel, Denon began racing in France, winning two of six starts there, an allowance race and the Group 3 Prix de Fontainebleau at one mile by $1\frac{1}{2}$ lengths at 7.70-1 (see next page for PP's). Sent off at 2-1 in both of his last two starts abroad, he was third by a neck in the Group 1 Prix Jean Prat at $1\frac{1}{8}$ miles and fourth by three lengths in the Group 2 Prix Guillaume d'Ornano.

   Denon began racing for Frankel in the U.S. on November 25, 2001, and made quite an initial impression, winning the Grade 1 Hollywood Derby at $1\frac{1}{8}$ miles by a length. Subsequently, he

1 Denon
Own:Flaxman Stable
Dark Blue, Light Blue Cross Sashes, Dark
PRADO E S (91 16 13 12 .18) 2002:(951 177 .19)

B. c. 4
Sire: Pleasant Colony (His Majesty) $75,000
Dam: Aviance*Ire(Northfields)
Br: Flaxman Holdings Ltd (Ky)
Tr: Frankel Robert(10 0 1 1 .38) 2002:(299 76 .25)

L 118

Life	11	4	2	2	$707,637	110	D.Fst	0	0	0	0	$0	–
2002	4	1	1	0	$319,000	110	Wet(330)	0	0	0	0	$0	–
2001	5	2	0	2	$374,872	109	Turf(305)	11	4	2	2	$707,637	110
Sar Ⓣ	0	0	0	0	$0	–	DstⓉ(350)	2	0	0	0	$9,000	95

6Jly02-10Mth fm 1⅜ Ⓣ :48¹ 1:13² 1:37 2:12⁴ 3↑ UntdNationH-G1 110 5 33½ 32½ 32 3nk 2nk Gomez G K L 118 2.90 103-05 **With Anticipation**119nk Denon118½ *Sarafan*1173¼ Brushed between 3/16 7
15Jun02-6Hol fm 1¼ Ⓣ :50¹ 1:15³ 1:38³ 2:01² 3↑ CWhittinghmHG1 109 8 53½ 32 42½ 21½ 11¼ Gomez G K LB 116 7.40 87-07 Denon1161¼ Night Patrol114hd Skipping1171¼ Came out,rallied,game 9
16Mar02-8SA fm 1½ Ⓣ :49² 1:14¹ 2:03¹ 2:26⁴ 4↑ SanLuisReyH-G2 95 7 64 75 66 67 54¼ McCarron C J LB 118 *1.00 88-11 ContinentlRed116no Keemoon115hd SpeedyPick112nk 5wd into lane,no bid 8
16Feb02-8SA fm 1½ Ⓣ :47² 1:12 2:02¹ 2:26 4↑ SanLuisObsH-G2 90 1 46½ 44½ 57 610 58½ McCarron C J LB 119 *.60 87-11 Nazirali112nk *ContinentalRed*116nk Bonprtiste1142 Blcked fin turn,stdied 7
25Nov01-7Hol yl 1⅛ Ⓣ :47³ 1:12² 1:36⁴ 1:49¹+ Hol Derby-G1 109 2 54 67¼ 41½ 31½ 11 McCarron C J LB 122 *1.10e 83-19 Denon122¹ Sligo Bay122³ *Aldebaran*122hd Tight early,rallied 12
Previously trained by Jonathan Pease
15Aug01♦ Deauville(Fr) sf *1¼ Ⓣ RH 2:07⁴ Prix Guillaume d'Ornano-G2 4³ Jarnet T 123 *2.00 Masterful123¹ Chancellor123hd Sagacity123² 9
Timeform rating: 113+ Stk 75100 *Rated in 7th or 8th,progress 2f out,up for 4th*
3Jun01♦ Chantilly(Fr) gd *1⅛ Ⓣ RH 1:48 Prix Jean Prat-G1 3nk Jarnet T 128 *2.00 Olden Times128hd King Of Tara128hd Denon128⁵ 5
Timeform rating: 116 Stk 112000 *Trailed to 3f out,wide bid,gaining late*
13May01♦ Longchamp(Fr) gd *1 Ⓣ RH 1:35² Poule d'Essai des Poulains-G1 41¾ Jarnet T 128 4.50 DNoverre128hd Vahorimix128hd Clearing1281½ 12
Timeform rating: 115 Stk 233000 *Trckd ldrs,outfnshd.Placed 3rd via DQ.Black Minnaloushe plcd 6th*
15Apr01♦ Longchamp(Fr) hy *1 Ⓣ RH 1:50¹ Prix de Fontainebleau-G3 11½ Jarnet T 128 7.70 Denon1281½ Tarzan Cry128³ Okawango128⁸ 6
Timeform rating: 116 Stk 56700 *Well placed in 3rd,dueled 1-1/2f out,led 100y out*
17Nov00♦ Saint-Cloud(Fr) hy *1 Ⓣ LH 1:53² Prix Thomas Bryon-G3 2½ Jarnet T 128 6.50 Chichicastenango128½ Denon128⁵ Champetre128² 7
Timeform rating: 105+ Stk 47100 *Unhurried in 5th,led 2f out,headed near line*
26Oct00♦ Longchamp(Fr) hy *1⅛ Ⓣ RH 2:04 Prix des Feuillants-EBF 12½ Asmussen C B 121 5.70 Denon1212½ Poussin121nk Nolt118⁴ 6
Timeform rating: 93 Alw 22700 *Tracked leader,led over 2f out,drew clear*
WORKS: Aug7 Sar 4f fst :49⁴ B *27/45* ● Aug1 Sar tr.tⓉ 6f fm 1:12⁴ B *1/5* Jly25 Sar tr.tⓉ 5f fm 1:00¹ H *4/11* Jly2 Hol 4f fst :50⁴ H *22/24* Jun26 Hol 4f fst :48² H *6/31* Jun13 Hol 3f fst :36³ H *7/30*
TRAINER: 31-60Days(215 .28 $2.21) Turf(506 .25 $1.83) Routes(537 .26 $1.85) GrdStk(228 .28 $2.07)

was freshened and finished fifth in a pair of Grade 2 Santa Anita stakes, both at 1½ miles, at odds of 3-5 and even money. Frankel freshened him again, and the 4-year-old colt by Pleasant Colony won the Grade 1 Charlie Whittingham Handicap at 1¼ miles by 1¼ lengths at 7.40-1, then finished second by a neck to With Anticipation in the 1⅜-mile, Grade 1 United Nations Handicap at Monmouth Park at 2.90-1, while carrying one pound less. In the Sword Dancer he would carry two pounds less than With Anticipation.

Since the United Nations, Denon had worked five furlongs in 1:00⅕ and six furlongs in a bullet 1:12⅘ on grass at Saratoga. Edgar Prado was aboard for the first time.

2. **Man From Wicklow (114)** He had won just two of his previous 12 starts, both allowance races. His last start was against softer in the 1½-mile, $62,000 Cape Henlopen Stakes at Delaware when he finished second by 1¼ lengths. The race before, he had finished a close 10th between two other starters in the Sword Dancer, Eltawaasul and Whitmore's Conn.
3. **Volponi (115)** This versatile 4-year-old colt, trained by Hall of Famer Phil "P.G." Johnson, was stretching out off two super efforts. He won the Grade 3 Poker Handicap at Belmont Park

2 Man From Wicklow No
Own: Violette Richard A
Black/sky Blue Diamonds, Black
CASTELLANO J J (55 6 4 10 .11) 2002:(688 109 .16)

Dk. b or br g. 5
Sire: Turkoman (Alydar) $3,500
Dam: Star of Wicklow(Fast Play)
Br: Cavanaugh J R (Fla)
Tr: Violette Richard A Jr(6 3 0 1 .50) 2002:(88 11 .13)

L 114

Life	21	4	2	3	$183,650	102	D.Fst	2	0	0	0	$1,290	28
2002	2	0	1	0	$12,120	97	Wet(330)	0	0	0	0	$0	–
2001	8	2	0	3	$109,200	102	Turf(280)	19	4	2	3	$182,360	102
Sar (T)	2	1	0	0	$28,800	96	Dst(T)(340*)	2	0	1	1	$42,120	97

21Jly02-8Del fm 1½ (T) :491 1:133 2:04 2:281 3↑ Cape Henlope62k 97 10 46 33 2hd 1½ 21¼ Luzzi M J L116 b 7.80 98-04 Crigsteel1161¼ MnFromWicklow116nk RglDynsty116nk Led,hung,saved 2nd 10
Run in divisions Previously trained by Hickling Nancy
21Jun02-8Bel fm 1¼ [T] :503 1:142 1:374 2:013 4↑ Alw 56000C 91 12 107¾105½ 95½ 72 103½ Luzzi M J L116 b 29.00 80-15 Eltawaasul1201 *Whitmore's Conn*113½ *Craigsteel*116hd Had no rally 12
Previously trained by Violette Richard A Jr
17Nov01-8Aqu fm 1⅜ (T) :501 1:161 1:403 2:164 3↑ Red Smith H-G2 92 12 53 53¾ 62¼ 93¾ 95 Luzzi M J L113 b 18.50 83-14 Mr.Pleasentfar115¾ **Eltawsul**114no ReglDynsty1131 Close up, no response 12
26Oct01-9Bel fm 1¼ [T] :511 1:154 1:392 2:022 3↑ Knickerbckr-G2 91 10 107 94¾ 106¾ 107½ 115¾ Migliore R L114 b 9.60 73-15 Sumitas115nk Manndar116nk Crash Course115nk Wide trip, tired 11
23Sep01-14KD fm 1½ (T) :49 1:174 2:06 2:283 3↑ KyCup Turf HG3 93 5 33 32 63½ 64½ 36 Deegan J C L114 b 6.30 89-17 Chorwon1135 ThKnghtSky1141 MnFromWcklw114nk 5-6w trip,no threat 7
6Aug01-7Sar fm 1⅜ [T] :493 1:144 1:382 2:151 3↑ Alw 48000N3X 96 2 41 41 42½ 1hd 1½ Migliore R L120 b *1.95 88-13 MnFromWicklow120½ Berchtesgdn1161 ComtKris120½ Bumped stretch 7
7Jly01-8Bel fm 1⅜ [T] :472 1:104 1:342 2:103 3↑ BowlingGrnH-G2 102 5 52¾ 54½ 31½ 45¼ 36½ Luzzi M J L112 b 15.10 95-12 KingCugt119½ SlwVlly1126 *MnFromWcklow*112no 4 wide run second turn 7
9Jun01-4Bel fm 1⅛ [T] :464 1:11 1:351 1:47 3↑ Alw 46000N2X 100 4 810 810 53¼ 3nk 11¼ Luzzi M J L121 b 10.70 94-09 MnFromWicklow1211¼ *MelNDve*123no *PrimPin*121¾ Wide move, clear late 11
3May01-8Aqu fm 1⅛ (T) :491 1:131 1:372 1:491 3↑ Alw 46000N2X 89 3 85¾ 86½ 74 65¾ 54 Arroyo N Jr L121 b 5.80 88-08 Dr. Kashnikow1212½ Abuzaid121¾ Prime Pine123nk Good finish outside 9
2Mar01-7GP fm 1⅜ (T) :462 1:12 1:361 2:134 4↑ Alw 41000N2X 92 1 58 611 3½ 42 3¾ Migliore R L118 b 4.10 83-12 LovShffl118nk MstInnvtv118½ MnFrmWcklw118hd Ckecked turn,stdy late 9
22Nov00-4Aqu fm 1⅛ (T) :493 1:14 1:391 1:512 3↑ Alw 46000N2X 89 1 83¼ 74 74¼ 44 21¾ Arroyo N Jr L120 b 4.30 79-18 Slowhnd1201¾ MnFromWicklow120no CochRily1231 Game finish for place 10
7Nov00-8Lrl fm 1¼ (T) :49 1:133 1:373 2:01 JapanRcgAssn50k 88 3 2hd 2hd 2hd 31½ 71¾ Dunkelberger T L L117 b 2.60 86-16 *DawnOfTheCondor*117hd Hotspur117no Certntee115½ Vied 2wd,wkned late 8
14Oct00-5Bel fm 1¼ [T] :481 1:121 1:37 2:003 3↑ Alw 44000N1X 94 5 75 75¾ 51¾ 1½ 13½ Arroyo N Jr L120 b 34.00 88-12 ManFromWicklow1203½ RateBase120nk *Slowhand*1172¼ Got through inside 11
6Oct00-9Bel gd 1¼ [T] :513 1:161 1:404 2:05 3↑ Md Sp Wt 42k 87 9 41½ 2hd 12½ 13½ 1¾ Rosario H L5 L113 b 45.50 66-37 *Man From Wicklow*113¾ Cypress1224½ Vegas1222 Clear, dug in, held on 11
7Sep00-4Med fm 170 (T) :223 :47 1:112 1:403 3↑ Md Sp Wt 24k 62 3 87½ 87¾ 94 810 56¼ Rosario H L Jr L117 b 23.00 81-15 Swamp Wolf117no Whirley1171¾ *Thorn Cat*1174 Well back,no rally 9
19Aug00-10Sar gd 1 3/16 (T) :49 1:131 1:382 1:573 3↑ Md Sp Wt 42k 44 11 41½ 41¾ 78 118½ 1117½ Luzzi M J L117 32.00 52-23 Newspeak117¾ Papa's Boy1171½ Leady1172½ Chased outside, tired 12
22Jly00-2Bel fm 1⅛ [T] :49 1:14 1:382 1:50 3↑ Md Sp Wt 42k 55 3 1210 1211 1212 1213 1113½ St Julien M L116 30.00 64-20 PolshTms1162¾ MovDrctor116nk BrodwySnowmn1163 Bumped after start 12
28Jun00-9Bel fm 1 1/16 (T) :231 :463 1:104 1:402 3↑ Md Sp Wt 42k 62 4 66¼ 74¾ 54 68½ 710¾ Luzzi M J L116 10.80 79-10 Quiet Quest1161½ *Roundstone*116no Soldotna116½ No response 10
15Oct99-6Bel sf 1 1/16 (T) :243 :492 1:143 1:48 Md Sp Wt 42k 53 1 61½ 61½ 74¼ 74¼ 75 Luzzi M J 118 3.65 47-44 DelMarShow118nk SintJoseph1181½ RedGmbler118nk Inside trip, no punch 10
1Oct99-5Bel fst 1 1/16 ⊗ :23 :462 1:121 1:461 Md Sp Wt 42k 28 10 1310 1322 1319 1222 1128¼ Luzzi M J 118 25.75 38-32 MndrinMrsh1183¾ TwigN'Brris1184 SturdyPlyr118hd Hustled, no response 14

WORKS: Aug4 Sar 5f fst 1:014 B *31/54* Jly11 Aqu (T) 5f fm 1:034 B (d) *3/3* Jun9 Aqu 6f fst 1:152 H *2/3* Jun2 Aqu 5f fst 1:02 B *7/16* May23 Aqu 4f fst :531 B *14/14* May16 Aqu (T) 4f fm :501 B (d) *1/1*
TRAINER: Turf(88 .06 $0.90) Routes(173 .14 $1.50) GrdStk(21 .10 $0.91)

by 2¼ lengths at 9.30-1, getting a mile in 1:32⅕, then finished second by a neck at 3.25-1 in the 1⅛-mile, Grade 2 Bernard Baruch Handicap at Saratoga to Del Mar Show, beating multiple stakes winner Forbidden Apple by a nose. He had never raced at 1½ miles, but P.G. had won the Sword Dancer at that distance with Kiri's Clown in 1995.

3 Volponi
Own: Amherst Stable & Spruce Pond Stable
Blue, Pink Yoke, Pink Blocks On Sleeves,
SANTOS J A (66 10 12 9 .15) 2002:(674 98 .15)

B. c. 4
Sire: Cryptoclearance (Fappiano) $20,000
Dam: Prom Knight(Sir Harry Lewis)
Br: Amherst Stable (Ky)
Tr: Johnson Philip G(12 1 2 1 .08) 2002:(120 18 .15)

L 115

Life	19	6	5	2	$492,256	113	D.Fst	12	4	4	1	$299,670	113
2002	4	2	1	0	$132,480	110	Wet(335)	0	0	0	0	$0	–
2001	10	3	2	0	$266,176	113	Turf(225)	7	2	1	1	$192,586	110
Sar (T)	1	0	1	0	$30,000	109	Dst(T)(205)	0	0	0	0	$0	–

26Jly02-8Sar fm 1⅛ [T] :484 1:124 1:362 1:482 3↑ B Baruch H-G2 109 1 11 1½ 1½ 2½ 2nk Bridgmohan S X L116 3.25 96-17 DelMrShow120nk Volponi116no ForbiddenApple1212 Set pace, gamely rail 7
5Jly02-8Bel fm 1 (T) :224 :451 1:081 1:321 3↑ Poker H-G3 110 4 32½ 31½ 3½ 2hd 12¼ Bridgmohan S X L115 9.30 99-05 Volponi1152¼ Saint Verre112nk Navesink117¾ Speed 3 wide, driving 7
30May02-8Bel fst 1 :224 :451 1:091 1:343 4↑ Alw 56000N$mY 95 2 42 42½ 42¾ 47½ 47 Bridgmohan S X L123 b *.40 89-18 OpenSesm116½ WildSummr1163¾ CountryBGold1162¾ 4 wide, no response 7
8May02-6Bel fst 7f :23 :452 1:093 1:222 4↑ Alw 54000C 105 5 3 2½ 2½ 12½ 11 Bridgmohan S X L121 b *.85 91-15 Volponi1211 Cherokee Beau1173½ *Tarek*1155 Speed outside, driving 5
24Nov01-8Aqu fst 1 :232 :453 1:092 1:331 3↑ Cigar MileH-G1 108 8 5¾ 41¾ 52½ 54 45 Bridgmohan S X L115 b 5.60 96-16 *Left Bank*1203¼ Graeme Hall118hd Red Bullet1181¾ Bumped start, chased 9
19Oct01-8Med fst 1⅛ :451 1:084 1:34 1:462 Pegasus H-G2 113 2 42¼ 42 41½ 2hd 12¾ Bridgmohan S X L114 b 4.10 95-14 Volponi1142¾ BurningRoma119½ GiantGentlemn1169½ Duel,clear final 1/16 6
6Oct01-2Bel fst 1 :234 :463 1:11 1:361 3↑ Alw 46000N2X 108 4 2½ 2½ 2½ 1½ 13¾ Bridgmohan S X L116 fb 1.50 86-21 *Volponi*1163¾ Pure Prize1202¼ Harley Quinn11911 Bumped start, driving 5
8Sep01-5Bel fst 1 1/16 :23 :451 1:094 1:431 3↑ Alw 46000N2X 93 6 53¼ 42 4¾ 2hd 2no Migliore R L118 b *.80 81-14 *Dayton Flyer*116no *Volponi*1185 Even TheScore118¾ Bumped start, 4 wide 7
25Aug01-10Sar fst 1¼ :473 1:111 1:354 2:012 Travers-G1 93 2 84 87 76½ 715 716½ Migliore R L126 b 13.70 81-02 Point Given1263½ E Dubai1261¼ *Dollar Bill*126¾ Wide, no response 9
30Jly01-9Sar fst 1⅛ :472 1:114 1:354 1:482 3↑ Alw 44000N1X 110 3 52 41½ 3nk 110 113¼ Migliore R L116 b *2.70 99-01 Volponi11613 Personable Pete1161¼ Carefree1203 Quick 3 wide move 12
15Jly01-8Bel fm 1¼ [T] :473 1:111 1:343 1:584 Lexington-G3 88 2 44½ 57 64¾ 67¾ 45¾ Samyn J L L118 7.50 91-12 ShrpPrfrmnc1141 PckgStr1144¼ **Whtmr'sCnn**114¼ Between rivals stretch 8
16Jun01-7Bel fm 1⅛ [T] :474 1:113 1:354 1:481 Hill Prince-G3 92 2 66 75 85½ 44 43 Samyn J L L120 6.60 86-18 Proud Man122nk Package Store114no *Navesink*1181¾ Shuffl back far turn 10
12May01-8Haw fm 1⅛ (T) :503 1:151 1:39 1:502 Haw Derby-G3 84 4 21 21 21 43½ 54½ Velazquez J R L113 2.30 79-15 Kalu119¾ *Proud Man*1191 Rahy's Secret1151½ Tired 7
14Apr01-7Aqu fst 6½f :223 :454 1:094 1:16 3↑ Alw 43000N1X 83 6 5 55 54 26 25¼ Samyn J L L115 7.90 91-09 Stake Runner1155¼ Volponi1152¾ Home Silver121¾ Game finish for place 8
22Oct00-9Bel fm 1⅛ [T] :464 1:114 1:36 1:48 Pilgrim-G3 90 7 78 74¾ 61¾ 1½ 12 Velazquez J R L115 9.90 88-16 Volponi1152 Baptize1224¼ Strategic Partner1151¼ Quick outside move 10
1Oct00-6Bel fst 6f :223 :453 :57 1:102 Md Sp Wt 41k 74 7 6 84¾ 73½ 45½ 34¼ Samyn J L L118 b *1.65 82-17 LittlBoldSwp1183½ TurnBckThTim118¾ *Volpon*1183¼ Inside move, gamely 9
9Sep00-3Bel fst 1 :224 :462 1:113 1:371 Md Sp Wt 42k 69 4 52 41½ 43 39 29 Samyn J L L120 *1.55 70-19 Dayton Flyer1209 Volponi1206½ Broad Initiative120½ Second best 9
19Aug00-2Sar fst 7f :221 :452 1:114 1:252 Md Sp Wt 41k 73 8 2 66 55¾ 22½ 22 Samyn J L L118 *2.70 76-19 Hero'sTribute1182 Volponi1184¾ BroadInititive1183¾ Game finish outside 9
14Jly00-2Bel fm 6f (T) :22 :453 :574 1:102 Md Sp Wt 41k 59 2 7 78 86¾ 54½ 31 Velazquez J R L117 *1.15 91-06 *Baptize*117no Heroic Sight1171 Volponi1171¼ Came wide, game finish 12

WORKS: ●Jly14 Bel tr.t 5f fst :59 H *1/11* Jun30 Bel 6f fst 1:12 H *2/3* Jun25 Bel 7f fst 1:264 B *2/2* Jun18 Bel 5f fst :593 H *2/36* ●Jun9 Bel tr.t 4f fst :47 H *1/33* ●May28 Bel 3f fst :353 B *1/8*
TRAINER: Turf(134 .14 $1.94) Routes(197 .13 $1.63) GrdStk(11 .18 $2.80)

4. **Hawkeye (118)** He shipped in from Great Britain off seven straight losses and was a distant third in his lone try at 1½ miles. Blinkers had been added in his last start when he was second in a listed stakes. He would have the services of Jean-Luc Samyn and an awful lot to prove.

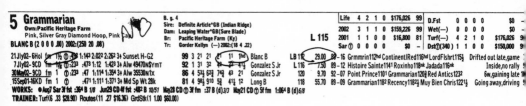

4 Hawkeye (Ire)
Own:Tanaka Gary A
Emerald Green, White Sash, Gold Blocks
SAMYN J L (22 3 4 1 .14) 2002:(301 40 .13)

B. c. 4 TATFOA98 $786,382
Sire: Danehill (Danzig) $79,700
Dam: Tea House*Ire(Sassafras*Fr)
Br: Norelands Bloodstock (Ire)
Tr: Jarvis Michael A (—) (—)

118

Life	12	3	1	4	$399,596	–	D.Fst	0	0	0	0	$0	–
2002	3	0	1	1	$92,724	–	Wet(325)	0	0	0	0	$0	–
2001	8	3	0	2	$306,192	–	Turf(360*)	12	3	1	4	$399,596	–
Sar Ⓣ	0	0	0	0	$0	–	DstⓉ(415)	1	0	0	1	$54,889	–

5Jly02♦Sandown(GB)	yl	1¼Ⓣ RH 2:132	3↑ Gala Stakes (Listed)	21¼	Robinson P	131 b	*1.10	Izdiham1201¼ Hawkeye1311¾ Cape Town1311¼	5
Timeform rating: 111			Stk 43600					Tracked in 3rd,dueled 4f to 2f out,held by winner.Border Arrow4th	
16Jun02♦San Siro(Ity)	fm	1½Ⓣ RH 2:244	3↑ Gran Premio di Milano-G1	310	Robinson P	132	6.00	Falbrav1323 Narrative1327 Hawkeye1321½	7
Timeform rating: 110			Stk 359000					Trckd in 3rd,outpaced over 3f out,regained 3rd 1f out.Sabiango5th	
11May02♦Kranji(Sin)	gd	*1¼Ⓣ LH 2:011	3↑ Singapore Airlines Intl Cup-G1	58	Stevens G L	124	4.90	Grandera1242 Paolini1262½ Indigenous1262¼	13
Timeform rating: 109			Stk 1663000					Rated in 10th,late gain into 5th.Western Pride 11th	
16Dec01♦Sha Tin(HK)	gd	*1¼Ⓣ RH 2:024	3↑ Hong Kong Cup-G1	4¾	Stevens G L	123	16.00	Agnes Digital126hd Tobougg123nk Terre a Terre123½	14
Timeform rating: 122			Stk 2307000					Tracked ldrs,fnshd gamely.Jim and Tonic5th,ChocIce9th,Silvano11th	
Previously trained by Aidan O'Brien									
20Oct01♦Newmarket(GB)	yl	1¼Ⓣ Str 2:074	3↑ Champion Stakes-G1	45	Kinane M J	123	7.00	Nayef123¾ Tobougg1234 Indian Creek123nk	12
Timeform rating: 116			Stk 569000					Tracked leaders,lacked rally.Rebelline 8th	
29Sep01♦Ascot(GB)	sf	1 Ⓣ RH 1:443	3↑ Queen Elizabeth II Stakes-G1	33	Kinane M J	123	6.50	Summoner1271½ Noverre1231½ Hawkeye1231½	8
Timeform rating: 112			Stk 480000					Rated in 5th,brief bid 2f out,one- paced late.Bach4th,Vahorimix5th	
9Sep01♦Longchamp(Fr)	yl	*1 Ⓣ RH 1:39	3↑ Prix du Moulin de Longchamp-G1	34½	Kinane M J	123	11.00	Slickly1283 Banks Hill1201½ Hawkeye123½	8
Timeform rating: 118+			Stk 219000					Trailed,rail move to gain 3rd 100y out.OldenTimes4th,Vahorimix6th	
19Aug01♦Curragh(Ire)	sf	1 Ⓣ Str 1:451	3↑ Desmond Stakes-G3	11	Kinane M J	123	2.25	Hawkeye1231 Pebble Island1231 Maumee1231	6
Timeform rating: 112+			Stk 69600					Trckd in 4th,2nd over 1f out,led 200y out,handily.Dr Brendler 4th	
28Jly01♦Curragh(Ire)	gd	1 Ⓣ Str 1:412	Connell Race	1½	O'Donoghue C3	124	1.25	Hawkeye124½ Maumee1274 Whisper Ridge1231½	5
Timeform rating: 103+			Alw 17600					Tracked leader,bid over 1f out,drifted left,led near line	
30Jun01♦Curragh(Ire)	yl	1 Ⓣ Str 1:423	Derby Festival Maiden	12½	Kinane M J	128	2.50	Hawkeye1282½ Scarlet Velvet1233 San Marco128no	10
Timeform rating: 91+			Maiden 16100					Tracked in 4th,led 170y out,drew clear	
17Apr01♦Leopardstwn(Ire)	sf	1 Ⓣ LH 1:514	Foxrock Maiden	48½	Kinane M J	126	*.80	Exaltation1261½ Business Elite1265½ Lunardi1261½	9
Timeform rating: 74			Maiden 15100					Led,met challenge 2f out,headed 1-1/2f out,weakened 1f out	
31Aug00♦Gowran Park(Ire)	yl	1 Ⓣ RH 1:393	Bagenalstown EBF Maiden	313¼	Kinane M J	128	*1.00	Siringas12313 Elbader128nk Hawkeye1282	16
Timeform rating: 89p			Maiden 9300					Tracked in 6th,4th 1f out,failed to take 2nd	

TRAINER: 1stNA(1 .00 $0.00) 1stW/Tm(0 .00 $0.00) 31-60Days(0 .00 $0.00) Turf(2 .00 $0.00) Routes(2 .00 $0.00) GrdStk(2 .00 $0.00)

5. **Grammarian (115)** In only his fourth lifetime start, Grammarian had won the 1½-mile, Grade 2 Sunset Handicap at Hollywood Park by a head at 29-1 while racing on phenylbutazone, an analgesic that is legal in California and illegal in New York. The race before, in allowance company at Churchill Downs, he was fourth by 1½ lengths at 7.50-1. The jockey

5 Grammarian
Own:Pacific Heritage Farm
Pink, Silver Gray Diamond Hoop, Pink Cap
BLANC B (2 0 0 0 .00) 2002:(250 20 .08)

B. g. 4
Sire: Definite Article*GB (Indian Ridge)
Dam: Leaping Water*GB(Sure Blade)
Br: Pacific Heritage Farm (Ky)
Tr: Gorder Kellyn (—) 2002:(18 4 .22)

L 115

Life	4	2	1	0	$176,026	99	D.Fst	0	0	0	0	$0	–
2002	3	1	1	0	$159,226	99	Wet(—)	0	0	0	0	$0	–
2001	1	1	0	0	$16,800	81	Turf(—)	4	2	1	0	$176,026	9
Sar Ⓣ	0	0	0	0	$0	–	DstⓉ(340)	1	1	0	0	$150,000	9

21Jly02-6Hol	fm	1½ Ⓣ	:48[illegible] 1:143 2:022 2:262	3↑ Sunset H-G2	99	3	21	21	21	11	1hd	Blanc B	LB 112	29.00	89-16	Grmmrin112hd ContinentlRed116hd LordFlshrt115½	Drifted out late,game	
7Jly02-9CD	fm	1 1/16 Ⓣ	:233 :473 1:12 1:423	3↑ Alw 49470N$YmT	92	1	31	32	[illegible]	[illegible]	41½	Gonzalez S Jr	L 116	7.50	89-12	Histoire Sainte1141 Roxinho118nk Jadada116nk	Inside,no rally	
30May02-9CD	fm	1 Ⓣ	:233 :47 1:114 1:354	3↑ Alw 35530N1X	86	4	53½	62¾	74¾	43	21	Gonzalez S Jr	120	9.70	92-07	Point Prince1101 Grammarian120¾ Red Antics1232	6w,gaining late	1
15Sep01-16KD	fm	1 Ⓣ	:471 1:111 1:371	3↑ Md Sp Wt 28k	81	4	98½	910	5¾	41¼	12	Long B	118	55.70	89-09	Grammarian1182 Recency1182½ Muy Bien Chris1221½	Going away,driving	

WORKS: ●Aug7 Sar 3f fst :364 B 1/8 Jun29 CD 4f fst :482 B 10/51 May28 CD Ⓣ 3f fm :37 B (d)3/3 May21 CD Ⓣ 5f fm 1:064 B (d)6/8
TRAINER: Turf(6 .33 $28.90) Routes(11 .27 $16.36) GrdStk(1 1.00 $60.00)

from his upset win, Brice Blanc, made the trip to New York with Grammarian, but Blanc seldom rides at Saratoga.

6. **Eltawaasul (114)** He had only won one of his last 10 starts, an allowance race at Belmont Park two starts back. In his last race, he'd been eighth at 8.90-1 to Whitmore's Conn when he was taken up in the stretch in the $1\frac{3}{8}$-mile, Grade 2 Bowling Green Handicap at Belmont, though he had beaten him by a length in that allowance win at $1\frac{1}{4}$ miles. Eltawaasul had one third to show for two starts at 12 furlongs.

Eltawaasul			
Own:Connors Christopher G			
Dark Blue, Gold Emblem, Blue/white			

Ch. h. 6
Sire: Nureyev (Northern Dancer) $100,000
Dam: Grand Falls (Ogygian)
Br: John T L Jones Jr & Roncon (Ky)
Tr: Reynolds Patrick L(7 1 0 2 .14) 2002:(112 20 .18)

L 114

Life	33	8	3	6	$285,662	102
2002	6	1	1	1	$65,600	102
2001	14	4	2	1	$175,440	102
Sar ⊕	3	0	0	0	$2,280	86

D.Fst	0 0 0 0	$0 –
Wet(340)	0 0 0 0	$0 –
Turf(340)	33 8 3 6	$285,662 102
Dst⊕(385)	2 0 0 1	$16,500 99

AVEZ J F (72 11 13 7 .15) 2002:(762 148 .19)

Jly02–8Bel fm 1⅜ ⊕ .49 1:13³ 1:37¹ 2:13² 3↑ BowlingGrnH-G2	90 3 52½ 53½ 53½ 72½ 87¼	Gryder A T	L 114	8.90	79–13	Whitmor'sConn112¹¾ StgingPost115hd MoonSolitir116nk	Taken up stretch 9
Jun02–8Bel fm 1¼ ⊕ :50³ 1:14² 1:37⁴ 2:01³ 4↑ Alw 56000C	99 1 41 62¾ 41¾ 3nk 11	Gryder A T	L 120	5.30	84–15	Eltawaasul120¹ Whitmore'sConn113½ Crigsteel116hd	Close up, drew clear 12
May02–7Mth fm 1⅛ ⊕ :51 1:15 1:38² 1:49⁴ 3↑ Alw 45000N$my	97 6 54¼ 41¼ 41¾ 32 21½	Bravo J	L 115	4.70	80–12	Revved Up115¹½ Eltawaasul115nk First Spear115¹¾	Close up,finished well 8
Mar02–8GP fm 1½ ⊕ :46⁴ 1:10¹ 2:00 2:24 3↑ Pan Amrcn H-G2	72 7 24½ 28 54 89½ 919	Aguilar M	L 113	12.50	76–06	Deeliteful Irving113² Cetewayo118½ Mr. Livingston141½	Chased, faded 9
Feb02–8GP yl 1⅜ ⊕ :50² 1:15² 1:40 2:17² 3↑ GP BC H-G1	96 1 1 2½ 21½ 43 46¾	Chavez J F	L 113	9.60	59–34	Cetewayo115³¾ Band IsPassing117¾ ProfitOption115²¾	Stalked, weakened 12
Jan02–10GP fm 1⅜ ⊕ :52¹ 1:17⁴ 1:41¹ 2:16¹ 3↑ MacDiarmdaH-G3	102 2 1½ 11 1hd 1hd 3½	Chavez J F	L 113	9.30	71–25	CrshCourse114½ Unite'sBigRed112no Eltwsul113½	On hedge, held on well 12
Dec01–11Crc fm 1⅜ ⊕ :51³ 1:16² 2:04³ 2:27⁴ 3↑ WLMcKnght H-G2	99 7 11 1½ 1hd 11½ 31¾	Chavez J F	L 114	14.30	90–09	ProfitOption111½ DeelitefullrvIng131½ Eltwsul114½	On hedge, weakened 12
Dec01–11Crc gd 1⅜ ⊕ :47 1:10² 1:35¹ 1:46⁴ 3↑ Trop Turf H-G3	64 11 97 10¹⁰ 74½ 1114 1120¾	Garcia J A	L 114	14.40	74–12	BndlsPssng118³½ CrshCours116² GroomstckStock's114¹	3 wide, faltered 12
Nov01–8Aqu fm 1⅜ ⊕ :50¹ 1:16¹ 1:40³ 2:16⁴ 3↑ Red Smith H-G2	100 1 21 1hd 1hd 11 2¾	Velazquez J R	L 114	*2.50	87–14	Mr.Pleasentfar115¾ Eltawaasul114no ReglDynsty113¹	Vied inside, gamely 9
Oct01–9Bel fm 1⅜ ⊕ :51¹ 1:15⁴ 1:39² 2:02² 3↑ Knickerbckr-G2	102 6 33 43 31½ 32 4¾	Espinoza V	L 113	25.25	78–15	Sumitas115nk Manndar116nk Crash Course115nk	3 wide move, weakened 11
Sep01–5Med fm 1⅜ ⊕ :49² 1:15² 1:40⁴ 2:17⁴ 3↑ Manila75k	99 4 32 32 41½ 31½ 1nk	Velazquez J R	L 114	32.80	71–23	Eltawaasul114nk Spindrift115³ Ready To Roll119½	Boxed 3/16,belatedly 11
Aug01–11Sar fm 1⅜ ⊕ :49 1:12⁴ 1:36³ 1:48³ 4↑ Clm c– (50–40)	86 1 64½ 62½ 62¾ 41 41½	Migliore R	L 121 f	6.20	85–05	Westwood Ho119hd Homeside121¹ Strike Zone121hd	Gamely in traffic late 10
Claimed from Shadwell Stable for $50,000, Peitz Daniel C Trainer 2001(as of 08/25): (76 13 10 5 0.17)							
Aug01–5Sar fm 1¼ ⊕ :49³ 1:13¹ 1:37 1:48⁴ 4↑ Clm 65000 (75–65)	83 5 51¾ 62½ 63 56½ 76½	Migliore R	L 116 f	14.80	86–10	An Oscar For Bert118⁴½ Little Ghazi120no My Request118½	Had no rally 7
Jly01–2Bel fm 1⅛ ⊕ :47⁴ 1:11³ 1:37 1:48⁴ 4↑ Clm 50000 (50–40)	88 3 56 46½ 33 1½ 32	Gryder A T	L 119 f	5.70	87–15	Eltawaasul119½ Ravaro119¾ Spring Street119½	Clear trip inside 9
Jun01–8Bel fm 1⅛ ⊕ :24³ :48² 1:12 1:41² 4↑ Clm 50000	86 4 62½ 61¾ 63½ 43 43	Gryder A T	L 117 f	3.75	86–12	ComOnNowSn119nk Gldsmth117²¾ BlndngSwrds117no	Game finish outside 10
May01–7Aqu fm 1⅛ ⊕ :24¹ :49³ 1:13³ 1:43³ 4↑ Clm 75000 (75–65)	84 6 54½ 63½ 72½ 74 53	Davis R G	L 118 f	7.20	83–14	Ballistic116¾ Little Ghazi118½ Hardy's Halo118¹½	Good finish outside 8
Mar01–9FG fm *1 ⊕ :24² :49 1:14 1:38³ 4↑ OClm 75000	82 5 43½ 31½ 31½ 31½ 2hd	Melancon J	L 119	4.00	83–14	Kris'sSligh117⁵¾ JustLkJmmy117¹ AlcCndns117²	Forward rail, weakened 9
Feb01–9FG fm *1 ⊕ :24⁴ :50¹ 1:14⁴ 1:46² 4↑ Clm 75000	94 6 44 42½ 42½ 31½ 2hd	Melancon J	L 119	4.90	84–18	SoccerGeorge117hd Eltawaasul119½ AlceCndense117¹	Could not get past 9
Feb01–9FG fm *1⅛ ⊕ :24⁴ :50² 1:16² 1:47² 4↑ Alw 35000N3x	89 2 66 54¾ 53 32 1hd	Melancon J	L 117	2.90	79–21	Eltawaasul117hd Just Like Jimmy117½ Blazing Irish117no	Up final stride 7
Jan01–8FG fm *1 ⊕ :23 :47 1:12 1:37 4↑ Clm 65000 (75–65)	89 1 66½ 64½ 53 32½ 1nk	Melancon J	L 114	5.50	100	— Eltawaasul114nk PrivtePower114hd Nt'sBigPrty117¾	Out kicked foe to wire 12

WORKS: Aug7 Sar.tr.⊕ 5f fm 1:03⁴ B 9/11   Jly25 Sar tr.⊕ 5f fm 1:01 H 9/11   Jly11 Bel ⊕ 3f fm :35² B (d)1/2   Jly4 Bel ⊕ 5f fm 1:02 B (d)7/10   Jun12 Bel tr.t 4f fst :48³ B 3/13   Jun6 Bel tr.t 3f fst :36⁴ B 2/10

TRAINER: Turf(88 .11 $1.97)   Routes(166 .11 $1.41)   GrdStk(20 .10 $0.59)

7. **Whitmore's Conn (115)** His victory in the Bowling Green at 14.90-1 was a breakthrough for the 4-year-old New York-bred, his first open stakes victory (see next page). He had raced once at $1\frac{1}{2}$ miles, finishing third by $6\frac{1}{4}$ lengths in the Grade 3 Lawrence Realization Handicap at 16.90-1. Shaun Bridgmohan had ridden Whitmore's Conn in his last two races and maintained the mount.

7 Whitmore's Conn
Own:Shanley Lynn & Michael
Yellow Purple Ball
BRIDGMOHAN S X (45 5 5 5 .11) 2002:(707 109 .15)
Dk. b or br c. 4 FTKJUL99 $150,000
Sire: Kris S. (Roberto) $150,000
Dam: Albonita(Deputed Testamony)
Br: Bud Wolf & Joe D'Agostino (NY)
Tr: Schulhofer Randy(7 3 1 1 .43) 2002:(93 25 .27)
L 115
Life 18 5 3 4 $277,690 103 | D.Fst 5 0 0 2 $23,490 89
2002 5 3 1 0 $151,600 103 | Wet(375) 1 1 0 0 $25,200 78
2001 12 2 2 4 $123,570 93 | Turf(300) 12 4 3 2 $229,000 103
Sar Ⓣ 1 0 1 0 $9,200 84 | DstⓉ(400) 1 0 0 1 $16,500 93

13Jly02–8Bel fm 1⅜ Ⓣ :49 1:133 1:371 2:132 3↑ BowlingGrnH-G2 103 8 62½ 65 63¾ 2hd 11¾ Bridgmohan S X L112 b 14.90 86–13 Whtmor'sConn1121¾ StgngPost115hd MoonSltr116nk 4 wide move, driving 9
21Jun02–8Bel fm 1¼ Ⓣ :503 1:142 1:374 2:013 4↑ Alw 56000C 97 7 73¾ 74½ 63¾ 61½ 21 Bridgmohan S X L113 b 9.30 83–15 **Eltawaasul**1201 *Whitmore'sConn*113½ *Crigsteel*116hd Bumped after start 12
26May02–8Bel fm 1⅛ Ⓣ :474 1:113 1:351 1:47 3↑ Ⓢ Kingston H85k 86 9 41 42½ 42 56 64 Prado E S L121 b 2.60 90–08 CelticSky117¾ RluctntGroom116hd *I'mAllYours*1241¼ Speed 3 wide, empty 10
19Apr02–8Aqu fm 1⅛ Ⓣ :51 1:15 1:39 1:51 4↑ Alw 48000N3X 97 5 32 2½ 2½ 2hd 1½ Prado E S L120 b 3.30 83–19 Whtmr'sCnn120½ WlkngArnd117nk *TpThAdmrl*117nk Stumbled start, drive 9
31Mar02–6GP fm *1$\frac{1}{16}$ Ⓣ :232 :47 1:11 1:424 4↑ Alw 36000N2X 96 8 21 39½ 37 23½ 1½ Prado E S L118 b 5.50 88–15 *Whitmore'sConn*118½ AltrEgo1182 RidoutsPtton1181¼ Late lead, held on 10
Previously trained by Schulhofer Flint S
1Nov01–5Aqu fm 1⅛ Ⓣ :492 1:134 1:382 1:503 3↑ Ⓢ Alw 46000N2X 82 9 916 97 98¾ 95 82¾ Prado E S L116 b *2.20 82–18 Davy Jones1181 *Bicentennial*116nk *Statement*120¾ Had no rally 9
13Oct01–9Bel fm 1½ Ⓣ :494 1:14 2:024 2:27 LRealizatnH-G3 93 2 51¼ 53¾ 42½ 34½ 36¼ Prado E S L114 b 16.90 88–10 ShrpPrformnc1204¼ TgrTrp1162 Whtmr'sCnn1143 3 wide run second turn 6
22Sep01–7Bel fst 1⅛ ⊗ :463 1:102 1:352 1:484 3↑ Ⓢ AshleyTColeH85k 89 4 89½ 810 715 47 32 Prado E S L113 6.60 84–11 Brave One1162 No Bad Habits120no Whitmore'sConn1131¼ Going well late 8
22Aug01–8Sar fst 1⅛ :47 1:113 1:373 1:502 Ⓢ Albany198k 83 5 1221 1212 107 77¼ 58¼ Velazquez J R L117 5.50 81–11 PersonalPro1173¼ SherpGuide1171 *FrmerJke*1172½ 5 wide move, no punch 12
2Aug01–7Sar fm 1$\frac{1}{16}$ Ⓣ :233 :48 1:113 1:413 3↑ Ⓢ Alw 46000N2X 84 10 98¼ 85¼ 88¾ 67¾ 22 Prado E S L116 *1.40 92–10 RlctntGroom1162 Whtmor'sCnn116¾ OnThFn1201¾ Bumped start, 3 wide 10
15Jly01–8Bel fm 1¼ Ⓣ :473 1:111 1:343 1:584 Lexington-G3 89 1 76¼ 69 74¾ 57½ 35¼ Prado E S L114 22.40 92–12 ShrpPerformnc1141 PckgStor1144¼ Whitmor'sConn114½ Inside, no rally 8
16Jun01–7Bel fm 1⅛ Ⓣ :474 1:113 1:354 1:481 Hill Prince-G3 85 1 109 108¼ 108½ 711 65½ Prado E S L114 22.10 83–18 Proud Man122nk Package Store114hd *Navesink*1181¾ Checked far turn 10
17May01–5Bel fm 1¼ Ⓣ :501 1:144 1:384 2:031 3↑ Alw 44000N1X 91 4 32 32½ 21½ 1hd 1hd Prado E S L117 3.90 75–27 Whitmore'sConn117hd Deputy'sLegcy117½ *Yz*1211¼ Bumped deep stretch 8
28Apr01–9Aqu fm 1$\frac{1}{16}$ Ⓣ :224 :472 1:123 1:432 3↑ Ⓢ Alw 44000N1X 75 5 1012 107¾ 106½ 82 2¾ Prado E S L117 *1.45 86–05 Bicentennil115¾ *Whitmore'sConn*117¾ ForvrMn114¾ Fast finish outside 10
30Mar01–6Aqu sly 1⅛ :483 1:151 1:412 1:543 3↑ Ⓢ Md Sp Wt 42k 78 7 54 31½ 2hd 11½ 16¾ Prado E S L115 *.60 63–36 Whitmor'sConn1156¾ MiniMik1156¾ Actury'sSon115¾ With something left 7
17Feb01–1GP fst 1$\frac{1}{16}$:23 :463 1:114 1:452 Md Sp Wt 34k 78 7 610 613 58 36½ 33½ Prado E S 122 15.30 77–14 Equinox1221¾ OffCmpus1221¾ *Whitmor'sConn*122½ Bobbled st, up for 3rd 8
25Jan01–8GP fst 1$\frac{1}{16}$:232 :48 1:124 1:441 Md Sp Wt 31k 67 8 810 89¾ 810 410 411¾ Prado E S 122 12.00 75–23 Date More Minors1224¼ Cielo City1225¼ *Finder*1222¼ 4 wide, passed tired 8
24Nov00–3Aqu fst 1 :231 :471 1:134 1:404 Ⓢ Md Sp Wt 42k 44 7 138½ 1213 107½ 78½ 46¼ Prado E S 119 21.50 58–25 *Bicentnnil*1191 Lstcllforpris1194½ Rndi'sSong114¾ Bumped start, greenly 14
WORKS: Jly22 Sar 4f fst :502 B *26/30* Jly9 Bel 4f fst :494 B *24/37* Jly4 Bel Ⓣ 4f fm :51 B (d) *9/11* Jun29 Bel 4f fst :49 B *38/95* Jun17 Bel 4f fst :50 B *59/79* Jun10 Bel 4f fst :503 B *45/59*
TRAINER: Turf(53 .30 $3.17) Routes(78 .28 $2.52) GrdStk(11 .18 $3.82)

8. Rhythm Band (114) He'd ended a nine-race losing streak by taking a 1⅛-mile nonwinners-of-four allowance race (three other than maiden, claiming, or starter) at Belmont Park in his last start, going off at 6-5. Besides taking a gigantic rise in class, he was stretching out to a distance where he had been seventh by 14½ lengths in his only attempt.

8 Rhythm Band
Own:al Maktoum Mohammed bin
Khaki, Khaki Cap
MIGLIORE R (51 10 6 7 .20) 2002:(588 95 .16)
Gr/ro g. 6
Sire: Cozzene (Caro*Ire) $60,000
Dam: Golden Wave Band(Dixieland Band)
Br: Clifton William L Jr (Ky)
Tr: McLaughlin Kiaran P(10 4 3 1 .40) 2002:(52 16 .31)
L 114
Life 15 4 2 2 $1,319,972 98 | D.Fst 1 0 0 0 $0 –
2002 6 1 1 0 $42,165 98 | Wet(325) 0 0 0 0 $0 –
2001 1 0 0 1 $3,268 – | Turf(335) 14 4 2 2 $1,319,972 98
Sar Ⓣ 0 0 0 0 $0 – | DstⓉ(400) 1 0 0 0 $0 –

17Jly02–5Bel fm 1⅛ Ⓣ :491 1:121 1:36 1:481 4↑ Alw 50000N3X 98 1 52½ 51½ 51¾ 31½ 11¼ Migliore R L119 f *1.30 88–20 RhythmBnd1191¼ SpottdOwl121nk RlctntGroom1161 3 wide move, driving
22Jun02–9Mth fm 1 Ⓣ :231 :464 1:102 1:344 3↑ OClm 50000 (50-45)N 95 2 52¼ 53½ 63¼ 53 2nk Velez J A Jr L118 f *1.50 95–06 *Autonomy*121nk *Rhythm Band*1181¾ Spruce Run1181 Closed gamely
16May02–8Bel fm 1⅜ Ⓣ :474 1:122 1:362 2:131 4↑ Alw 50000N3X 91 4 11½ 16 2hd 21 63½ Migliore R L117 f 4.30 83–19 DeputyStrike1211¼ SovereignKit112½ PerfectStrnger117nk Set pace, tired
Previously trained by Sateesh Seemar
15Mar02 ♦ Jebel Ali(UAE) fst *1 RH 1:373 4↑ Jebel Ali Mile (Listed) 916¼ Durcan T E 123 – Pacino1233½ Zoning123¾ Man Howa1231½
Timeform rating: 77 Stk 95300 *Rated in 6th, weakened 2f out. Jila 4t*
2Mar02 ♦ NadAlSheba(UAE) gd *1⅛ Ⓣ LH 1:52 3↑ Jebel Hatta-G3 41¾ Birrer G 126 – Divine Task1261 Lightning Arrow126½ Superiority126nk
Timeform rating: 111 Stk 95300 *Rated in 5th, 3rd 3f out, one-paced final furlong. Summoner 6t*
24Feb02 ♦ NadAlSheba(UAE) gd *1½ Ⓣ LH 2:323 4↑ Dubai City of Gold-G3 714½ Birrer G 121 – Narrative1193¼ Grandera1193¼ Celtic Silence1191¼
Timeform rating: 95 Stk 95300 *Towards rear throughout. Musha Merr 5th. No bettin*
8Apr01 ♦ Abu Dhabi(UAE) gd *1⅜ Ⓣ RH 2:153 3↑ Abu Dhabi Championship 32 Birrer G 129 – Alva Glen127½ Inchlonaig1261½ Rhythm Band129¾
Timeform rating: 111 Alw 32600 *Rated in 5th, mild bid over 1f out, no late respons*
Previously trained by Suroor Saeed Bin
26Aug00 ♦ Windsor(GB) gd 1¼ Ⓣ RH 2:072 3↑ Winter Hill Stakes-G3 712¾ Dettori L 118 8.00 Adilabad118½ Albarahin1261¼ Forbearing1188
Timeform rating: 97 Stk 57300 *Mid-pack, weakened 3f ou*
21Jun00 ♦ Ascot(GB) gd 1¼ Ⓣ RH 2:072 4↑ Prince of Wales's Stakes-G1 616¾ Durcan T 126 50.00 Dubai Millennium1268 Sumitas126½ Beat All1262½
Timeform rating: 104 Stk 405000 *Steadied start, trailed throughout. Sendawar 4t*
6May00–7CD fm 1⅛ Ⓣ :483 1:122 1:354 1:474 3↑ Woodford-G1 95 8 64 75 73¾ 55½ 43½ Dettori L L123 3.00 93 – *Manndar*1141½ Falcon Flight1181 Yagli1201 Svd grd, mild gain
25Mar00 ♦ NadAlSheba(UAE) gd *1⅛ Ⓣ LH 1:483 4↑ Dubai Duty Free-G3 1¾ Durcan T 126 – Rhythm Band126¾ Easaar1261 Kingsalsa126½
Timeform rating: 119 Stk 2000000 *Trailed, rail bid 3f out, lacked room & bumped, angled out, led lat*
5Mar00 ♦ NadAlSheba(UAE) gd *1$\frac{1}{16}$ Ⓣ LH 1:442 4↑ Jebel Hatta (Prestige) 21¾ Hills R 121 – Siege1221¾ Rhythm Band121½ Spindrift122
Timeform rating: 108 Stk 54400 *Led to over 1f out, second best. No bettir*
3Feb00 ♦ NadAlSheba(UAE) gd *1 Ⓣ LH 1:393 4↑ Al Fahidi Fort Stks (Prestige) 32½ Durcan T 121 – Grazalema124¾ Algunnaas1211¾ Rhythm Band121
Timeform rating: 102 Stk 54400 *Led, quickened 4f out, headed over 1f out, weakened late. No bettir*
14Jly99 ♦ Doncaster(GB) gd 1 Ⓣ Str 1:403 3↑ Arksey Conditions Stakes 11 Supple W J 118 3.50 Rhythm Band1181 Sunstreak1273½ Chief Rebel118no
Timeform rating: 109 Alw 16500 *Tracked leader, led over 2f out, drivir*
Previously trained by Bond Harold James
25Oct98–1Bel fm 1 Ⓣ :23 :46 1:094 1:341 Md Sp Wt 39k 91 4 32½ 32 21 2hd 14 Chavez J F L118 6.60 89–14 Rhythm Band1184 C's Chocolate118¾ *Thanks Franks*1182 Driving
WORKS: Aug5 Sar 4f fst :481 B *4/20* Jly29 Sar 4f fst :51 B *23/29* Jly10 Sar tr.tⓉ 4f fm :50 B (d) *14/19* Jly3 Sar tr.tⓉ 4f fm :49 B (d) *2/10* Jun18 Bel 4f fst :471 H *5/80* Jun11 Bel 4f fst :492 B *13/36*
TRAINER: Turf(61 .23 $1.78) Routes(90 .22 $1.75) GrdStk(1 .00 $0.00)

9. Cetewayo (117) If there was one horse in this field certain to have no trouble with 1½ miles, it was this 8-year-old son of His Majesty who had won 10 of 23 grass starts and more than a million dollars. In 11 starts at the distance, he had five wins, three seconds, and two thirds. He had won the Sword Dancer in 1998 under the same jockey, John Velazquez, at 4.10-1, carrying 115 pounds.

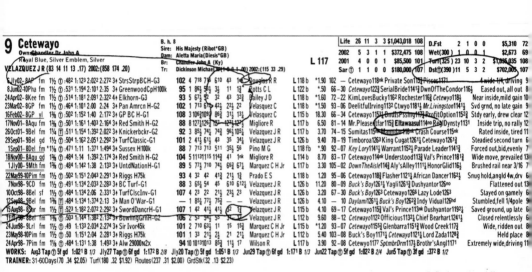

How was his recent form? Under the astute handling of trainer Michael Dickinson, Cetewayo was having a great 2002. He opened his 8-year-old season by winning the Grade 1 Gulfstream Park Breeders' Cup Handicap at 1⅜ miles by 3¼ lengths at 18.30-1. In four consecutive 12-furlong stakes, Cetewayo was second at 3-2 in the Grade 2 Pan American Handicap at Gulfstream, third by 2¾ lengths at 8-5 in the Grade 3 Elkhorn at Keeneland, first by three-quarters of a length at 1-2 in the Greenwood Cup Handicap at Philadelphia Park, and first by a neck at 9-5 in the Grade 3 Stars and Stripes Breeders' Cup Handicap at Arlington Park.

10. With Anticipation (120) How could you not love the 7-year-old gray gelding who reinvented himself when switched back to the grass after a dismal performance—ninth by 55¼ lengths—in the 2001 Grade 1 Gulfstream Park Handicap at 34-1? After winning an allowance race by 8¾ lengths in just his second grass start—he had finished third in the first—With Anticipation won the 1⅜-mile, $109,000 Louisville Handicap at Churchill Downs by six lengths. His gutsy head victory over Senure in the 1⅜-mile United Nations Handicap at Monmouth was taken away when he was disqualified for lightly brushing the second-place finisher, who was placed first.

Regardless, With Anticipation followed with a gritty three-quarter-length win in the 2001 Sword Dancer at 6.30-1, going wire to wire from the 9 post. He added a 2¼-length win in the Grade 1 Man o' War at 1⅜ miles at 2.40-1 before running seventh by 13 lengths in the 1½-mile Breeders' Cup Turf at Belmont and ninth at 22.10-1 in the Group 1 Japan Cup in Tokyo.

When Hall of Fame trainer Jonathan Sheppard unveiled With Anticipation for his 7-year-old debut in 2002, he finished second in a five-furlong allowance race at 6-5. With Anticipation was then second and fourth to Beat Hollow in the $1\frac{1}{8}$-mile, Grade 1 Woodford Reserve Stakes at Churchill Downs and the $1\frac{1}{4}$-mile, Grade 1 Manhattan Handicap at Belmont, at odds of 5.70-1 and 2.80-1, respectively.

But just as people were questioning if his best days were behind him, With Anticipation gamely wore down Denon, taking the $1\frac{3}{8}$-mile, Grade 1 United Nations Handicap by a neck under Pat Day at 2.40-1.

Sheppard returned With Anticipation to Saratoga and gave him a maintenance work for his return in the Sword Dancer, five furlongs in an easy 1:03 breezing.

In three starts at $1\frac{1}{2}$ miles, With Anticipation had hit the board just once, but it was in this stakes at this track.

Could he do it again?

11. Startac (116) Switched back to turf after finishing 10th at 102-1 in the 2001 Kentucky Derby, Startac won the Grade 1, $1\frac{1}{4}$-mile Secretariat Stakes at Arlington Park by a nose at 11.20-1. But he hadn't won since, losing six races heading into the Sword Dancer. He'd been ninth and sixth behind Denon, and, in his last start, was fourth by two lengths behind Whitmore's Conn at 5-1 in the Bowling Green Handicap at $1\frac{3}{8}$ miles. In his lone start at 12 furlongs, Startac was second by three lengths

in the restricted $80,000 Jim Murray Memorial Handicap. On the plus side, Jerry Bailey was replacing Javier Castellano in the saddle.

Analysis: On class and form, Denon, Volponi, Cetewayo, and With Anticipation stood out. Cetewayo had the best record of the quartet at $1\frac{1}{2}$ miles, but had been facing softer. Volponi was unproven at the distance. Denon was an obvious threat, but was getting only one more pound from the horse who had just beaten him, With Anticipation, the previous year's winner. With Anticipation's two possible obstacles were the weight and the post. Carrying 120 pounds would not be a problem, however; he had won carrying 126 in the 2001 Man o' War. The 10 post was a challenge, but there was a long run to the first turn, and the man guiding him, Pat Day, was a Hall of Famer who had won this stakes on him the year before from post 9.

I went for With Anticipation. Denon was the 2.10-1 favorite and With Anticipation was slightly higher at 2.80-1. Denon looked home free at the sixteenth pole, but With Anticipation surged powerfully and got there by a head, an incredible race. Keep in mind that With Anticipation had won this stakes in 2001, wire to wire. This time he rallied from fifth to get the job done. (See *Daily Racing Form* chart, next page.)

NINTH RACE
Saratoga
AUGUST 10, 2002

1½ MILES. (Inner Turf)(2.23¹) 28th Running of THE SWORD DANCER INVITATIONAL HANDICAP. Grade I. Purse $500,000. (Up to $57,000 NYSBFOA). THREE YEAR OLDS AND UPWARD. By invitation only with no subscription, entry or starting fees. The purse to be divided 60% to the owner of the winner, 20% to second, 11% to third, 6% to fourth and 3% to fifth. Trophies will be presented to the winning owner, trainer and jockey. The New York Racing Association reserves the right to transfer this race to the Main Track. In the event that this race it taken off the turf, it may be subject to downgrading upon review by the Graded Stakes Committee.

Value of Race: $500,000 Winner $300,000; second $100,000; third $55,000; fourth $30,000; fifth $15,000. Mutuel Pool $1,373,033.0 Exacta Pool $1,025,378.0 Trifecta Pool $757,027.00 Superfecta Pool $177,186.00

Last Raced	Horse	M/Eqt. A.Wt	PP	¼	½	1	1¼	Str	Fin	Jockey	Odds $1
6Jly02 10Mth¹	With Anticipation	Lb	7 120	10	43½	4½	4½	52½	3hd	1hd	Day P	2.80
6Jly02 10Mth²	Denon	L	4 118	1	3½	3½	3hd	4hd	11	21¾	Prado E S	2.10
26Jly02 8Sar²	Volponi	L	4 115	3	2½	2²	2½	1hd	2hd	3nk	Santos J A	8.70
21Jly02 8Del²	Man From Wicklow	Lb	5 114	2	7²	72½	8½	6hd	6½	41	Castellano J J	47.75
13Jly02 8Bel⁴	Startac	L	4 116	11	6²	6½	6hd	3½	51½	5nk	Bailey J D	8.70
13Jly02 8Bel¹	Whitmore's Conn	Lb	4 115	7	10²	11	11	8hd	85	61¾	Bridgmohan S X	14.70
6Jly02 8AP¹	Cetewayo	Lb	8 117	9	81½	101½	9½	72½	71	7nk	Velazquez J R	7.30
21Jly02 6Hol¹	Grammarian	L	4 115	5	11	11½	1½	2hd	41½	84¾	Blanc B	23.20
5Jly02 San²	Hawkeye-IR	b	4 118	4	5hd	5¹	5hd	10½	1010	9²	Samyn J L	11.40
13Jly02 8Bel⁸	Eltawaasul	L	6 114	6	11	8hd	103½	94½	9²	1012¼	Chavez J F	45.75
17Jly02 5Bel¹	Rhythm Band	L	6 114	8	92½	92½	7½	11	11	11	Migliore R	36.75

OFF AT 5:35 Start Good. Won driving. Course firm.
TIME :23¹, :47¹, 1:11³, 1:36², 2:00², 2:24 (:23.34, :47.23, 1:11.74, 1:36.54, 2:00.59, 2:24.06)

$2 Mutuel Prices:
10-WITH ANTICIPATION	7.60	3.80	3.00
1-DENON		3.50	3.00
3-VOLPONI			5.50

$2 EXACTA 10-1 PAID $21.60 $2 TRIFECTA 10-1-3 PAID $120.50 $2
SUPERFECTA 10-1-3-2 PAID $2,483.00

Gr/ro g, by Relaunch–Fran's Valentine, by Saros*GB. Trainer Sheppard Jonathan E. Bred by George Strawbridge, Jr. (Pa).

WITH ANTICIPATION raced in hand while outside, advanced three wide on the final turn, dug in resolutely in the stretch and was up in time, driving. DENON was urged up inside after the start, saved ground while close up early, came through inside, drew clear leaving the eighth pole and dug in determinedly but could not resist the winner. VOLPONI raced with the pace from the outside and stayed on gamely through the stretch. MAN FROM WICKLOW clipped heels entering the first turn, stumbled, dropped back early, rallied wide on the final turn and finished gamely outside. STARTAC raced close up early, rallied wide nearing the stretch and lacked a solid finishing kick. WHITMORE'S CONN was steadied in tight quarters early on, dropped back, rallied wide approaching the stretch and finished well outside. CETEWAYO was taken back early, raced inside and lacked a rally. GRAMMARIAN quickly showed in front, set the pace and tired in the final furlong. HAWKEYE (IRE) bobbled at the start, was in tight quarters early on, raced inside and tired in the stretch. ELTAWAASUL was steadied after the start, raced wide and tired. RHYTHM BAND was steadied in tight quarters after the start, dropped back, put in a run along the inside nearing the final turn and tired.

Owners— 1, Augustin Stable; 2, Gann Edmund A & Flaxman Stable; 3, Amherst Stable & Spruce Pond Stable; 4, Violette Richard A et al Jr; 5, Allen E Paulson Living Trust; 6, Shanley Michael & Lynn; 7, Chandler Dr John A; 8, Pacific Heritage Farm; 9, Tanaka Gary A; 10, Connors Christopher G; 11, al Maktoum Mohammed b

Trainers— 1, Sheppard Jonathan E; 2, Frankel Robert; 3, Johnson Philip G; 4, Violette Richard A Jr; 5, Mott William I; 6, Schulhofer Randy; 7, Dickinson Michael W; 8, Gorder Kellyn; 9, Jarvis Michael A; 10, Reynolds Patrick L; 11, McLaughlin Kiaran P

3

IT'S ALL ABOUT THE DAM

A THOROUGHBRED STALLION WILL father dozens of horses every year. A dam has only one shot at producing a foal each year, and she might not be able to deliver one every time. Because she has fewer chances to succeed, a mare that does produce winners is a precious commodity, and her influence is crucial.

Think about the buzz that surrounded Juddmonte Farms' Empire Maker in 2002. Of course he drew attention because he was trained by Hall of Famer Bobby Frankel and because he was working sensationally for his 2-year-old debut and because his sire, Unbridled, was a Kentucky Derby and Breeders' Cup Classic winner who ranked as one of the top stallions in the world.

But the exciting part of Empire Maker's pedigree was the "bottom" side—his dam, Toussaud. Named 2002 Kentucky Broodmare of the Year, she earned more than half a million dollars herself, then produced Grade 1 stakes winners Chester House, who took the 2000 Arlington Million on turf and won nearly $2 million; Honest

Lady, who won the 2000 Santa Monica Handicap, and earned just under $900,000; and Chiseling, who won the 2002 Secretariat Stakes on grass. Another of Toussaud's foals, Decarchy, won the Grade 2 Frank E. Kilroe Mile Handicap and almost $600,000. Decarchy's pedigree was not a secret when he made his debut September 15, 1999, at Yarmouth in Great Britain. Sent off at 6-5, he aired by seven lengths.

Empire Maker's victory in the 2003 Florida Derby gave Toussaud her fourth Grade 1 stakes winner and fifth graded stakes winner from just six foals. His subsequent victory in the Belmont Stakes just added to her legacy.

While broodmares as successful as Toussaud are rare, there are hundreds of very good grass mares who, as she did, follow their own success on the racetrack by producing multiple turf winners, and a few who produce multiple turf-stakes winners.

Being aware of a horse's royal connections when he or she debuts on grass or steps up to stakes company can lead to many winning wagers.

Here's my personal favorite: North of Eden, a daughter of Northfields (a son of Northern Dancer), out of Tree of Knowledge, by Sassafrass.

North of Eden's third dam was Pange, who produced 1964 Prix de l'Arc de Triomphe winner and Italian champion Prince Royal II.

North of Eden's second dam, Sensibility, won just one of seven starts in Europe but produced stakes winners Beyond the Lake and Lake Champlain.

North of Eden's dam, Tree of Knowledge, also won just one of seven starts, but produced grass champion Theatrical, who won nearly $3 million, and Taiki Blizzard, a multiple stakes winner in Japan. According to the March 30, 2003, edition of *DRF Simulcast Weekly*, Theatrical's 18 percent turf winners ranked No. 1 among the 100 top turf sires from March 20, 2000, through March 19, 2003.

Like her dam and granddam, North of Eden raced seven times. Although she did not win a race, that did not prevent her from becoming one of the greatest grass broodmares in racing history.

Her first foal, Elliot Bay, by Seattle Song, won 8 of 50 starts and $54,951.

North of Eden's second foal, Paradise Creek, by Irish River, won 14 of 25 starts, more than $3.4 million, and was voted champion turf male. His Grade 1 stakes victories were the Arlington Million; Washington, D.C., International; Hollywood Derby; and Early Times Manhattan Stakes, when he set a Belmont Park course record by getting $1\frac{1}{4}$ miles in 1:57.79.

North of Eden's third foal, Celestial Bliss, by Relaunch, was winless in two starts, but her fourth, I'm Very Irish, by Pleasant Colony, won 5 of 17 starts, including the ungraded Smoke Screen Stakes, and bankrolled just under $200,000.

Bred to Seattle Slew, North of Eden produced Cayell, who won 2 of 11 starts and $63,319.

Then North of Eden was bred to Wild Again, and she produced Wild Event, who was bred and owned by Arthur I. Appleton and trained by Lou Goldfine. He won 1 of 2 dirt starts as a 3-year-old.

It's hard to believe, with his outstanding turf pedigree, but Wild Event was not favored in his grass debut as a 4-year-old, an allowance race at Arlington Park, June 12, 1997 (see next page). Sent off at 2.90-1 under Mark Guidry, Wild Event won by a neck. That didn't impress too many people, because he was only bet down to 2.30-1 in his next start, also in allowance company. He won by five lengths. Wild Event kept his turf record unblemished by winning the Grade 2 Arlington Park Handicap by a head at 8.50-1.

Now bettors were impressed. They sent off Wild Event at 1-2 in his next start, another allowance race, and he won by $2\frac{1}{2}$ lengths.

Wild Event took his 4-for-4 turf record on the road for the Grade 3 Keeneland Breeders' Cup Mile. Sent off at 9-1, Wild Event won by half a length.

His win streak was snapped in the 1997 Breeders' Cup Mile at Hollywood Park when he finished ninth in the field of 12, beaten 8¾ lengths by Spinning World, who ran the mile in 1:32.77. That was hardly a disgrace. Wild Event, who went off 21-1, was, according to the chart, steadied on the first turn, steadied in the upper stretch, and brushed the inside rail. Yet he'd only missed fifth by two lengths.

Wild Event then raced twice in dirt stakes in Florida before returning to grass. Racing six-wide from the 10 post, he finished a tiring ninth by 7¾ lengths in the 1⅜-mile, Grade 2 Gulfstream Park Handicap, February 14, 1998.

Wild Event was finally given some time off by his connections and returned on July 25, in the Grade 3 Robert F. Carey Memorial Handicap at Hawthorne, finishing third by two lengths at 9-2 to Soviet Line, who got the mile in 1:33²/₅. Given that it was Wild Event's first start in more than five months, his comeback was solid and there was no reason that he wouldn't move forward in his next start, which—luckily for me—came in the 1¹/₁₆-mile, Grade 3 Fourstardave Handicap at Saratoga, August 29, 1998, on the Travers Stakes undercard.

The 2-1 favorite in the field of 11 was none other than Soviet Line, who had won that Hawthorne stakes by three-quarters of a length at 7-5.

The 7-2 second choice in the Fourstardave was Garbu, who had won all four of his grass starts for trainer Bill Mott. Garbu, however, would be making his stakes debut in a Grade 3 event off a life-and-death allowance win earlier in the meet at Saratoga.

Given the class he had shown earlier in his career, I believed that if Wild Event moved forward, as he should in his second start back, he was the horse to beat. He went off the third choice, but that was a generous 6.70-1. With a flawless ride by Mark Guidry, Wild Event edged front-running 11-1 Bomfim by a head to pay $15.40. The exacta came back $237. (See chart, next page.)

I couldn't imagine ever getting such a generous price on Wild Event again, but I nearly did the next year. I was at Aqueduct for the Carter Handicap on May 2, 1999, and was able to bet Wild Event on the simulcast from Churchill Downs, where he was sent off at 5.60-1 in the Early Times Classic. He won again.

He would finish his career with 10 victories from 22 starts and earnings of $937,274.

North of Eden's next foal, Paradise River, by Irish River, was winless in seven starts.

Bred to Pleasant Colony again, North of Eden foaled a handsome dark bay colt named Forbidden Apple, who showed up at Saratoga to make his grass debut on August 22, 1998, a week before his older half-brother would win the Fourstardave.

In his dirt debut, July 24, 1998, for owner-breeder Appleton and trainer Christophe Clement, Forbidden Apple was last in a field of seven at 5-1, beaten 28¾ lengths, with Jerry Bailey riding.

But that would be irrelevant with respect to his ability on turf, right? That's what I thought when I picked Forbidden Apple, again ridden by Bailey, in the ninth-race finale at Saratoga, August 22, despite his drawing the outside 10 post in a $1\frac{1}{16}$-mile maiden grass race. With Bailey aboard, his great grass pedigree, and the way he had been bet in his dirt debut, I expected Forbidden Apple to be a short price. Instead, he went off at 6.40-1.

He didn't win, but he did finish a distant second, tipping off his

1 1/16 MILES. (Turf)(1.38⁴) 14th Running of THE FOURSTARDAVE HANDICAP. Grade III. Purse $100,000 Added (plus up to $19,400 NYSBFOA.) 3–year–olds and upward. By subscription of $100 each, which should accompany the nomination, $500 to enter and $500 to start, with $100,000 added. The added money and all fees to be divided 60% to the owner of the winner, 20% to second, 11% to third, 6% to fourth and 3% to fifth. Weights: Sunday, August 23. Starters to be named at the closing time of entries. In the event the Fourstardave overfills, preference will be given to highweights (age and sex allowance considered.) Ties broken by gross lifetime earnings. Trophies will be presented to the winning owner, trainer and jockey. The New York Racing Association reserves the right to transfer this race to the main track. Closed Saturday, August 15.

Value of Race: $114,900 Winner $68,940; second $22,980; third $12,639; fourth $6,894; fifth $3,447. Mutuel Pool $1,097,383.0 Exacta Pool $996,895.00 Trifecta Pool $713,616.00

Last Raced	Horse	M/Eqt.	A.Wt	PP	St	1/4	1/2	3/4	Str	Fin	Jockey	Odds $1
25Jly98 9Haw3	Wild Event	L	5 116	4	2	3¹	3¹½	3½	2¹½	1hd	Guidry M	6.70
8Aug98 7Sar1	Bomfim	L	5 114	5	3	1½	1¹	1½	1¹½	2⁵	Davis R G	11.90
9Aug98 6Pen1	Rob 'n Gin	L	4 119	11	9	2½	2½	2¹	3²	3¹¼	Bravo J	12.50
9Aug98 6Pen2	Boyce	L	7 115	3	1	5hd	5hd	5¹½	5½	4⁴¾	Krone J A	10.80
29Jly98 8Sar1	Garbu		4 114	8	8	4²	4⁴	4³	4¹½	5¹	Bailey J D	3.50
25Jly98 9Haw4	Honor Glide	L	4 115	1	6	10²	10²½	8½	7½	6¹	Perret C	12.90
26Jly98 8WO5	Long War	L	4 113	7	10	8hd	8hd	6hd	6²½	7³	Santos J A	33.00
20Jun98 10Rkm7	Thesaurus		4 113	6	4	7¹	7¹	9¹	8²	8hd	Gryder A T	22.70
31Jly98 8Sar2	Tahmid	L	5 114	9	11	11	11	11	9hd	9¹	Migliore R	14.80
31Jly98 8Sar3	Jambalaya Jazz	L	6 114	10	5	6¹½	9¹	10hd	10½	10⁵½	Sellers S J	18.30
25Jly98 9Haw1	Soviet Line-IR	L	8 118	2	7	9²	6hd	7¹	11	11	Velazquez J R	2.00

OFF AT 4:28 Start Good. Won handily. Time, :23, :46, 1:09², 1:33¹, 1:39¹ Course firm.

$2 Mutuel Prices:

5–WILD EVENT	15.40	9.70	6.80
6–BOMFIM		11.80	9.30
11–ROB 'N GIN			6.30

$2 EXACTA 5–6 PAID $237.00 $2 TRIFECTA 5–6–11 PAID $2,149.00

B. h, by Wild Again–North Of Eden*Ire, by Northfields. Trainer Goldfine Lou M. Bred by Appleton Arthur I (Fla).

WILD EVENT, close up inside while in hand, saved ground into the stretch, angled out for running room in upper stretch, dug in resolutely from the outside and caught pacesetter BOMFIM in the final strides. BOMFIM flashed good speed, set the pace while in hand, drew clear in upper stretch then dug in determinedly but could not hold off the winner. ROB 'N GIN, with the pace from the outside under wraps, put in a wide run on the second turn but faded in the stretch. BOYCE, rated outside, raced wide and had no solid closing kick. GARBU chased the pace for three quarters and tired in the stretch. HONOR GLIDE, outrun early, came wide for the drive but had little to offer when roused. LONG WAR had no response after a wide trip. THESAURUS raced inside and had no response when roused. TAHMID, taken back in the early going, raced wide on the second turn and had no response. JAMBALAYA JAZZ tired badly. SOVIET LINE was steadied on the first turn and outrun thereafter.

Owners— 1, Appleton Arthur I; 2, Live Oak Plantation; 3, Sabine Stable; 4, Marsh Hazel B; 5, Paulson Allen E; 6, Robert G Schaedle; 7, Diane Perkins; 8, Cella Charles J; 9, Shadwell Stable; 10, Oxley John C; 11, al Maktoum Sheikh Maktoum

Trainers—1, Goldfine Lou M; 2, Kelly Patrick J; 3, Barbara Robert; 4, Forbes John H; 5, Mott William I; 6, Vestal Peter M; 7, Attfield Roger L; 8, Vestal Peter M; 9, McLaughlin Kiaran P; 10, Ward John T Jr; 11, McLaughlin Kiaran P

Scratched— Concerto (7Aug98 6SAR4)

$2 Pick Three (2–65) Paid $273.00; Pick Three Pool $296,679.
$2 Pick Six (11–6–1–2–6–5) 6 Correct Paid $28,283.00; Pick Six
Pool $201,124. $2 Pick Six (11–6–1–2–6–5) 5 Correct Paid $438.00

immense turf talent. He complemented that with a great heart, consistency, and versatility, posting eight wins, six seconds, eight thirds, and five fourths in 30 grass starts while working his way up to the highest level of competition in races from one mile to $1\frac{1}{4}$ miles.

Yet he never really got enough respect, especially at Belmont Park, where he was nearly unbeatable. Forbidden Apple won the 2000 running of the Grade 2, $1\frac{1}{8}$-mile Belmont Breeders' Cup Handicap by $1\frac{1}{4}$ lengths at 21-1, and, in his next start, the one-mile, Grade 2 Kelso Handicap at Belmont by a neck at 8-1. In 2001, Forbidden Apple won the $1\frac{1}{4}$-mile, Grade 1 Manhattan Handicap at Belmont by three-quarters of a length at 7-1 and the Kelso Handicap again by half a length as the 2-1 favorite.

Off that race, Forbidden Apple took his second shot at the Breeders' Cup Mile at Belmont Park. The year before at Churchill Downs, he was sent off at 29-1 in the field of 14 out of the nearly impossible 13 post and was beaten all of $2\frac{1}{2}$ lengths while finishing seventh to War Chant.

I knew he would run his heart out in the 2001 Breeders' Cup Mile and was thankful for the 8.20-1 odds under Corey Nakatani. Forbidden Apple fought his way to the lead, opened a $1\frac{1}{2}$-length advantage at the top of the stretch, and battled to the wire, losing by $1\frac{3}{4}$ lengths to Val Royal in an amazing 1:32.05 for the mile. Forbidden Apple held off Bach by three-quarters of a length for second and paid $8.60 to place.

As a 7-year-old in 2002, Forbidden Apple ran second in the Grade 1 Manhattan, third by a neck in both the Grade 2 Bernard Baruch Handicap and the Grade 1 Arlington Million, and second by half a length in the Kelso to Green Fee, who denied Forbidden Apple a three-peat.

North of Eden was bred to Jolie's Halo in 1996 and foaled Far East of Eden, who won 1 of 3 starts. Her next two foals died, but in 2000, she foaled a colt by Unbridled.

When foals out of North of Eden turn up in turf races, pay attention.

But you don't have to dive into years of charts to find female families such as North of Eden's. We've done it for you. The following list of more than 800 dams of graded stakes winners, as well as a few influential dams of ungraded stakes winners, will be producing grass winners for years. Especially important dams are indicated with an asterisk before their names. With this list, you're going to find first-time turf winners that others will miss.

DAMS OF GRADED STAKES WINNERS, 1996—APRIL 2003

Abigailthewife	Antoinetta	Battle Drum
Acharmer	Appealing Look	Beautiful Bedouin
Admiration	Appealing Story	Beautiful Bid
Adorable Micol	Arbela	Becky Be Good
Adored	Arborea	* Becky Branch
Affection Affirmed	Ardmelody	Been Dazzled
Ahead	Ardy Arnie	Belle Nuit
Albonita	Ascend	Bermuda Classic
Alberta Johnson	Athyka	Bert's Valentine
* Aletta Maria	Auspiciante	Betrayer
Alexandria	Aviance	Bid Dancer
Allage	Awaasif	Bidding Bold
All My Memories	* Awesome Account	Bird House
* Al Sylah	Azzurina	Blazing Kadie
Alywow	Ba Bish	Blue Begum
Amazing Love	* Ballerina Princess	Bluemont
Amelia Bearhart	Balletomane	Blue Wedding
Ameriflora	Banchory Faye	Bold Senorita
Amour Celtique	Bangkok	Bonnie's Axe
Anastastia Honey	Bank Privee	Bonny Guest
Angela Serra	Bannockburn	Boom Bird
Angelic Song	Barari	* Buckeye Gal
Angle Puss	Barely Rarely	Buck The Odds
Annie Edge	Barnard Gal	* Burst Of Sound
Anthis	* Battle Creek Girl	Buttercup

Buzzovertomyhouse

Cadeaux d'Amie

Cagey Exuberance

Call Box

Calling Guest

Cal Norma's Lady

Candid Moments

Captive Queen

Carats Please

Carmanetta

Caro Keri

Caromist

Caro Queen

Caro's Beauty

Carrolton Zip

Carry

Carson City Gal

Cellar's Best

Central City

Chain Fern

Champagne Cocktail

Charlotte Amalie

Charlotte Augusta

Charm a Gendarme

Charming Bride

Charming Kain

Chase the Dream

* Chateaubaby

Chaudennat

Cheap Appeal

Chelsey Dancer

Cherlindrea

Chimes of Freedom

Christmas Bonus

* Circus Act

City Ex

* City Fortress

Claire Stevens

Clashfern

Classic Value

Classy 'n Smart

* Claxton's Slew

Coastal Connection

Colonial Witch

Colony Bay

Come on Texas

Comical Cat

* Committed

Confident Writer

* Continental Girl

Cope's Light

Corvettin

Costly Doll

Countess Olivia

Courtesane

* Cozumel Kitty

Cozzena

Crazy Fitz

Crazy for You

Creaking Board

Cryptoqueen

Cup Of Honey

Current Guest

Cute Move

Cut the Twinkle

Cymbaline

Czar Gal

Dabaweyaa

* Daltawa

Damask Sky

Dame Avie

Dancer's Candy

Dancer's Gate

Dance Song

Dancing Affair

Dancing Devlette

Dancing Monarch

Dancing Road

Dangerous Native

Danka

Dart Star

Dawn's Flame

Dear Colleen

Debbie's Next

Debutante Dance

Declamation

Deep Discount

Deputy Clerk

Desert Run

Desirable

De Stael

Dhaka

Dicken's Miss

Diese

Diferente

Distaff Magic

Distant Doll

Doblique

Donnegalle

Don't Be Foolish

Doradoradora

Do's Gent

Douce Annie

Downtown Blues

Dramatical

Duchess Zia

Duty Free

Easter Heroine

Easter Queen

Ebony Dancer

* Echoes of Eternity

Edge Of Morning

Ela's Gold

Elegance in Design

Elegant Glance

Emeraude

Empress Tigere

Endearingly

English Trifle

Enola

Epicure's Garden

Epitome

Erstwhile

Escape Reality

* Esprit d'Escalier

Eurolink Mischief

Eversince

Evil's Sister

Exangular Lady

Exciting Fandance

* Exing

Fab's Melody

* Fabuleux Jane

Fair Advantage

Fairforband

* Fair Picture

Falcon Dancer

Fama

Fanning The Flame

Fantastic Look

Fantastic Ways

Farewell Partner

Fast Flow

Femme De Fer

Femme Fatale

Finally Found

Finlaggan

Firey Affair

First Approach

Fitnah

Flamenco Wave

Flaming Gold

Flashing Eyes

Fleet Secretariat

Fleetside Review

Florentink

Florie

* Flying Circus

Fly It Betsy

Forest Key

Forever Lady

Forli's Song

Francfurter

Fran's Valentine

Free At Last

Frigid Zone

From Sea To Sea

Frosty Straw

Full Board

Fun Forever

Funistrada

* Gaijin

Garimpeiro

Gay Fantastic

Ghariba

Ginger Candy

Gioconda

Gleaming Glory

* Glitzi Bj

Glorious Calling

* Glowing With Pride

Go Bananas

Go For Bold

Golden Bloom

Golden Galaxy

Golden Goldie

Golden Seal

Golden Thatch

Golden Wolfen

Gold 'n Desire

Gold Nickle

* Goodbye Heart

Good Faith Woman

Green Boundary

Grisonnante

Guardian Spirit

Guiza

* Halloween Joy

Halo At Dawn

Halory

Handsewn

Harmless Albatross

Harouniya

Hasili

Hasty Appeal

Hattab Voladora

Heartland

* Heavenly Music

Heavenly Ray

Herbs And Spices

Here's Look Adder

Highbrow

Highest Score

His Ginger

Hofuf

Hold to Fashion

Hollywood Wildcat

Hooray Lady

Horphaly

Hot Option

Housatonic

Ideal Home

Idle Affair

I Dream

If Liloy

Ile Mamou

Image Of Super

I'm an Issue

I'm Harriet

Impulsive Lady

I'm Select

Incha

Infamy

In Neon

* Inreality Star

Insipid

In Unison

Ioya

Irish Brick

Irish Order

Irving's Girl

* Island Jamboree

Island Spirit

Isle Of View

Itquan

Ivorine

Ivor's Love

* Jacky Max

Jammu

Jangada

Jinger Feathers

Joan L.

Jolly Saint

Jood

Jour du Soleil

Julie La Rousse

June's Weapon

Kacella

Kalamba

Kamkova

Kasora

Katerina Key

Kazaviyna

* Key Buy

Key Mist

Key Special

* Key To Khartoum

Key to My Heart

Khoruna

Kiss the Wind

Kisumu

Kool Arrival

Kshesinskaya

La Affirmed

* Ladies Double

* Lady Blackfoot

Lady Di

* Lady Duvach

Lady Fandet

Lady Longmead

Lady Lush

* Lady Of Glamour

Ladyshill

* Lady Vixen

Lady Winborne

Lady Winner

La Favorita

* La Gueriere

Lailati

La Perruca

Laquifan

Lara's Star

Last Glance

Latin Puzzle

Laughing Keys

Laughing Look

* Lazy Fables

Leandra

Leaping Water

Legit

Lemons to Lemonade

Lettre de Cachet

Liberia

Licena

Lightning Fire

Light Run n Lady

Like A Train

Likely Split

Lilaya's For Real

Linkage Love

* Lisa Leigh

Lismore Lady

Listen Here

Listen Well

Lit'l Rose

Little Miss Miller

Little Niece

Little Worker

Lizzie Rolfe

Loa

Logical

Logical Lady

Loon

Lovelier Laura

Love Lost

Love Potion

Love's Reward

Louisiana Flash

Loving Cup

* Lucky Sally

Luminosity

Lunaire

Luth de Crystal

Luxurious

Lyphard Gal

Mackie

Madame Gold

Madame Norclifffe

Madame Nureyev

Madam Guillotine

Madam Sandie

Madam Schu

Madeleine's Joy

Madiriya

Madura

Magic Par

Mahasin

Mahonie

Mahrah

Majuba

Mamara Reef

* Mandera

Mangala

Manureva

Marie De Chantilly

Marina Dugg

Marked Well

Mark's Magic

Mazarine Blue

Meadow Spirit

Metair

Meteor Stage

Michelle's Monarch

Midnight Air

Milaoshu

Millie Do

Millie's Choice

Ming China

Miracles Happen

Mira Monte

Miss Angel T

Miss Buck Trout

Miss Cross

Miss D'Ouilly

Miss Enjoleur

Miss High Blade

Miss Jove

Miss Lenora

Miss Rudy T

Miss Swiss

Miss Toot

Miss Turlington

Miss Verbatim

Misty Gleam

Misty Moon

* Molly's Colleen

Money Player

Moondust Mink

More Than Willing

Mosaique Bleue

Mostly Misty

* Most Precious

Moucha

Ms. Arrowsmith

Mstoyou

Muffies Muffin

Music Bell

Music Zone

My Dearest Love

My Jessica Ann

* My Sharp Lady

Mystery Tune

Mystic Moves

Mythomania

Naboa

Nakterjal

Nancy's Place

Napoli

Nasty Affair

Nataka

Native Fancy

Navarchus

Navarra

Naziriya

Neat Dish

Nemea

Never Tarnished

Nifty

Night Girl

Nightlong

Night Tan

* Nijinsky's Best

* Nijinsky's Lover

No Class

* Nomo Robbery

Norland

North East Dancer

Northern Dynasty

Northern Goddess

Northern Pageant

Northern Sting

* North Of Eden

Not So Careless

Now That's Funny

Nunatak

Obeah

Oh My Jessica Pie

Oh Silly Me

Oh So Well

Olden Roberta

One More Breeze

Only Above

Oops I Am

Orange Motiff

Oriental Answer

Or Vision

Oscura

Our Friend Terry

Our Locket

Our Tina Marie

Our Wildirish Rose

Outlasting

Out Ruled

Packer Legend

Palm Dove

Paloma Blanca

* Papsie's Pet

* Parade Of Roses

Park Walk

Passionate Pursuit

Pat Wolsh

Pearl Bracelet

Pearl of Dawn

Pedicure

Penny's Chelly

Penny's Valentine

Petal Girl

Petite Diable

Piazza's Pride

Pick Up Your Cards

Pillow Dancer

Pinaflore

P J Floral

Plains Indian

Platinum Queen

Platinum Ring

Pleasantly Free

Pleasant Tale

Plumeria Lei

Poco Lolo

Poligala

Political Intrigue

Possibly Perfect

Powder Doll

Prankstress

Prayer Wheel

Preciseness

Precious Jet

Pretty Flame

Pretty Tricky

Princess of Note

Principle

Prodigious

Proflare

Prom Knight

Proskona

Prospect Digger

Proud Entrance

Proud Lou

Proud Nova

Proud Puppy

Purer Than Pure

Pure Speed

Pushoff

Puzzle Book

Queena

Queen Marrea

Queen of Women

Question D'Argent

Quick Strike

Quiet Cleo	Rose De Crystal	Serena
Quite Honestly	Rosy Sunset	Serena's Song
Rabadella	Rowdy Bird	Sewing Lady
Rainbow's End	Royal Angellique	Shannkara
Raise A Reason	Royal Honoree	Sharata
Raised Clean	Royalivor	Shared Reflections
Rajas Secret	Royal Run	Shareefa
Ramanouche	Royal Setting	* Sharp Briar
Rare Sound	Ruby Ransom	* Sharp Call
* Rascal Rascal	Runaway Marcie	Sharp Looking Lady
Raska	Runaway Royalty	Sherkiya
Ratings	Run Spot	She's A Talent
Rays Joy	Sabria	* Shore Line
Reach For It	Sagar Island	Shy Pirate
* Reactress	Sailing Minstrel	Side View
Reckless Rose	Salluca	Silabteni
Regal Sherry	Salsabil	Silk Dancer
Regal Wonder	Samalex	Silken Ripples
* Reina Terra	Sand Dancer	Silver Echo
Relax And Enjoy	San Empery	Silvery Swan
* Rensaler	Santa Linda	* Sioux Narrows
Respectfully	Saraa Ree	Siren Song
Richard's Choice	Saratoga Fleet	Sistabelle
Right Connection	Savannah Slew	Skisette
Right Word	Sayyara	Sky Love
Rising Spirits	Screening Room	Slew Boyera
* River Jig	Sea Regent	Slew n Easy
River Ried	Seattle Kaper	* Slightly Dangerous
River Sans Retour	Secret Threat	Slipscreen Queen
Road To Heaven	Seductive Smile	Smart Queen
Rollicking Road	Sennon Cove	Snowbowl
Romanche	Senora Tippy	Snow Colony
Romantic Fibs	Sentimental Gift	Snow House
Romantic Story	Serape	Soaring Jewel

Social Lesson	Suntrap	Tintaburra
So Cozy	Sunyata	Tochar Ban
Sofala	Super Chef	Topacio
Soft Dawn	Super Me	Totham
Sol de Terre	Supreme Angel	To the Rainbow
Sounding Off	Supreme Excellence	* Touch of Greatness
* Source d'Orezza	Sweet Reality	Toussaud
South Cove	Sweet Silver Star	Towering Success
South Sea Dancer	Syria	Track Gossip
* Spanish Parade	Syrian Summer	Tricky Game
Spe	Table Frolic	Trinity Place
Special Idea	* Takarouna	* Tropical Royalty
Special Quest	Tappity Tap	True Charmer
Spectacular Joke	Tarabilla	Truly Do
Spectacular Motion	Tarte Aux Pommes	Trusted Partner
Spectacular Native	Taruma	Truth Above All
Splash Em Baby	Tash	Trying for Gold
Stage Queen	Tasseled	Tudor Loom
Stalique	Tea And Roses	* Tuesday Evening
Star Deputy	Tea House	Tuk'n Run
Star Gem	Tenga	* Turkeina
Star of Wicklow	Thakhayr	Turk O Witz
Stella Madrid	That's My Hon	Turn Native
St. Lucinda	Theatre Flight	Tuscoga
Stormette	The Bink	Twine
Storm The Bank	* The Lip	Twitchet
Stormy Spell	* Ticked	Twixt
Strawberry Night	Tidal Reach	Ulanowa
Stronghold	Tiffany's Gem	Vadlava
* Stylish Sister	Tijara	* Valdemosa
Subia	Time Deposit	Valid Victress
Sultry Sun	Timely Reserve	Vana Turns
Summer Fashion	Timely Times	Vands
Sunset Queen	Tinaca	Verbal Intrigue

Very Special Lady

Very Special Lite

Victorian Village

Vienna Knickers

* Virginia Reef

Viviana

Waders

Wancha

Wander Storm

Wanton

* Watch the Time

Wavering Girl

Waviness

Wavy Reef

Wedding Picture

Wemyss Bight

Wendy's Ten

Wewarrenju

What a Future

Whiffling

Whimsical Wolf

Whisper Who Dares

Wicklow Royalty

Wide River

Wild and Bold

Wild Planet

Willie's Cobra

Willow Runner

Win Approval

Wind in Her Hair

Windsharp

* Windy Mindy

Win For Me

Winglet

Wings Of Grace

Winters' Love

Wising Up

Wooden Crown

Wood o Binn

Words of War

Worldly Bold

Worldly Possession

Wortheroatsingold

Written Word

Yafill

Yes She's Sharp

York Woods

Young Flyer

Yukon Connie

Zurl

*Worth special consideration

4

STALLIONS AND TOMLINSONS

*T*HE *DAILY RACING FORM* offers Tomlinson Ratings for turf, wet tracks, and distance. Tomlinson Ratings are an evaluation of the male influence of a horse's pedigree. Stallions are rated on the basis of their offspring's success in turf, wet track, or distance racing. The Tomlinson Rating is calculated by adding the full score of a horse's sire's rating to half the rating of the broodmare sire (dam's sire).

Tomlinson Ratings were devised by Art Kaufman, a former vice president of a Wall Street brokerage firm who was born in the Bronx and weaned on Thoroughbred racing at Jamaica and Aqueduct.

"I started going to the races when I was 15 with my dad," Kaufman said. "I handicapped. In the mid-80's, I was getting clobbered on sloppy tracks. The *Racing Form* used to have mud marks, but they were only given to horses who had performed well on an off track. I said, 'There has to be a better way.'"

On Thanksgiving weekend in 1986, Kaufman took stacks of *Daily Racing Form*s into his bedroom and closed the door. "I told my wife, Jackie, not to bother me," he said. "I had about 500 or 600 *Racing Forms*. Maybe 700. And I went to work. I looked at every chart I could find."

Kaufman simply noted the sires of horses who did well on wet tracks and slowly compiled a list, which he and his friend, Lee Tonelson, began using with success. "Lee and I starting using this and we were cashing tickets," Kaufman said. "Lee said, 'You can sell this.' I said, 'I can't use my name because of Wall Street.' He said, 'Use mine.'"

Kaufman, though, had been calling Tonelson "Tomlinson" since they were kids. So Kaufman used that name. He eventually added a list of grass sires, and, in the summer of 2000, sold his business to the *Form*.

Here's what a near month-long sample of grass races in March 2003 revealed. Examining grass races at Fair Grounds, Golden Gate Fields, Gulfstream Park, and Santa Anita, 19 of 99 top-figure Tomlinson-rated horses won. Four were in maiden races, five in claimers, one in a stakes, and nine in allowance company.

The odds of those 19 winners? One was 4-5, two were even money, two were 6-5, one was 3-2, one was 8-5, one was 2-1, two were 5-2, one was 7-2, three were 4-1, one was 5-1, three were 7-1, and one was 13-1. The 13-1 winner was Bourbon County, who won an allowance race at Santa Anita on March 8, with a 335 rating. The 7-1 winners were Jilo (355) in a $62,500 claimer at Santa Anita on March 7, Champion Lodge (400), a six-length winner of the Grade 2 San Luis Rey Handicap at Santa Anita on March 15, and Rhythm of Life (334), who took an allowance race at Santa Anita on March 20.

One of the best ways to use Tomlinson turf ratings is as a barometer in maiden races for horses who have not previously started on grass. A maiden grass race at Aqueduct, April 25, 2003, featured four first-time turfers. With their Tomlinson Ratings in parentheses, they were Minstrel's Melody (285), Hard Dance (300), I'ma A Fax (180), and Logger (278). None of their ratings came close to that of Supreme Regime (395), who had started once on grass for trainer Jimmy Toner and finished fifth at 8.60-1 off a 4½-month layoff. Sent off at 4.30-1, Supreme Regime won by a head and paid $10.60. None of the four first-time turfers finished in the money.

Tomlinson turf ratings should be used as a tool to help you determine the strength of a horse's grass pedigree. Knowing the best turf sires will help you more.

In progeny earnings for 2002, the top 75 turf sires were:

Sadler's Wells	Lost Soldier	Judge T C
Dynaformer	Gone West	Barathea
Lear Fan	Caerleon	A.P. Indy
Theatrical	Broad Brush	Danzig
Sky Classic	Lord At War	El Gran Senor
Pleasant Colony	Alphabet Soup	Mister Baileys
Nureyev	Thunder Gulch	Private Terms
Pivotal	Lord Avie	Ghazi
Woodman	Unbridled	Kissin Kris
Affirmed	Mt. Livermore	Distant View
Royal Academy	Belong to Me	Quiet American
Danehill	Hennessy	Tabasco Cat
Relaunch	Indian Ridge	Wild Again
With Approval	Glitterman	River Special
Rahy	Night Shift	Bertrando
Green Dancer	Mendocino	Honor Grades
Kris S.	Persian Bold	Irish River
Smart Strike	Storm Cat	Runaway Groom
Cozzene	Mr. Prospector	Mr. Greeley
Red Ransom	General Meeting	Forest Wildcat
Kingmambo	Skywalker	Unbridled's Song
Prized	Flying Continental	Miesque's Son
Polish Numbers	Candy Stripes	Gulch
El Prado	Harlan	
Storm Creek	Sword Dance	

But that's by earnings. By percentage, the following stallions were exceptional. Sadler's Wells, Theatrical, Royal Academy, Danehill, Green Dancer, Nureyev, Rahy, Alphabet Soup, Night Shift, Danzig, Storm Creek, Sword Dance, El Gran Senor, and Irish River.

These sires are also worth paying attention to: Sky Classic, Lear Fan, Kris S., Red Ransom, Belong to Me, With Approval, Prized,

Lord Avie, Dynaformer, Polish Numbers, Woodman, Relaunch, Cozzene, Marquetry, Flying Continental, Candy Stripes, and Honor Grades.

But if you pick up any issue of *DRF Simulcast Weekly*, you get three-year winning percentages of leading grass sires.

Here are 16 sires whose progeny won at least 15 percent of their grass starts the past three years (March 27, 2000, through March 26, 2003).

STALLION	RECORD (WINS-STARTERS)	PERCENTAGE
Lord At War	126-566	22.26
Theatrical	126-686	18.36
In Excess	33-182	18.13
Danzig	40-224	17.85
Nureyev	51-288	17.70
Glitterman	47-278	16.90
Affirmed	84-498	16.86
Smokester	16-96	16.66
Storm Cat	62-381	16.27
Hennessy	19-125	15.97
El Gran Senor	44-276	15.94
Polish Numbers	115-724	15.883
Bertrando	54-340	15.882
Go for Gin	49-318	15.40
Dynaformer	202-1323	15.26
Honour and Glory	19-125	15.20

Any of the above stallions demand your attention, but which sires have undesirable percentages on grass? These sires checked in at five percent or less for the past three years: Carson City, Claramount, Cryptoclearance, Deputy Minister, Distinctive Pro, Meadowlake, and Memo.

What about value? *Simulcast Weekly* also divulges the average win price for each stallion's progeny. At the time of this writing, the lowest were Cherokee Run ($7.80), Claramount ($8.80), Danzig ($8.20), General Meeting ($9.24), Hadif ($9.54), Kingmambo ($7.78), Lost Code ($9.66), Maria's Mon ($8.94), Memo ($4.30), Montbrook ($8.92), Red Ransom ($9.66), Seeking the Gold ($9.48), and Theatrical ($7.12).

The highest were Cee's Tizzy ($19.54), Cryptoclearance ($17.54), Distinctive Pro ($32.98), Fly So Free ($21.72), Hennessy ($17.18), Honour and Glory ($22.26), Jeblar ($16.04), Meadowlake ($29.82), Mountain Cat ($22.46), Mr. Greeley ($16.98), Notebook ($22.54), Phone Trick ($19.38), Seattle Slew ($16.04), Smokester ($18.22), and Tactical Advantage ($17.20).

Use common sense. If you are compelled to play one of the extremely low-percentage stallions, make sure it's not Claramount, Memo, or Montbrook, who combine limited success with low payoffs.

There is one more crucial list of sires, and that is broodmare sires. This is especially important, and frequently profitable, for turf racing. Pay special attention to these broodmare sires if one of their descendants is racing on grass: Hoist the Flag, Lord At War, Nijinsky II, Seattle Slew, Sea-Bird, Prince John, Roberto, In Reality, Pleasant Colony, Stage Door Johnny, Tom Rolfe, Lyphard, Secretariat, Affirmed, and Riverman.

Farther back in pedigrees, any horse with His Majesty in his bloodlines deserves extra attention.

This list is based on progeny earnings:

Buckpasser	Vice Regent	High Line
Hoist the Flag	Blushing Groom	Java Gold
Pieces of Eight II	Nureyev	Top Ville
Rahy	Sea-Bird	Snow Sporting
Lord At War	Prince John	King's Bishop
Darshaan	Mari's Book	Boldnesian
Seeking the Gold	Alydar	Prominer
Graustark	Lashkari	Pleasant Colony
Dr. Fager	Alysheba	Stage Door Johnny
Gulch	Never Bend	Smarten
El Gran Senor	Miswaki	Le Fabuleux
Seattle Song	Strawberry Road	Ribot
Northern Dancer	Tunerup	Ruritania
Round Table	Danzig	Fappiano
Hail to Reason	Desert Wine	Viceregal
Nijinsky II	Roberto	Tom Rolfe
Turkoman	Fast Play	Val de Loir
Troy	Assert	Lyphard
Northfields	In Reality	Dahar
Mr. Prospector	Wavering Monarch	Secretariat
Key to the Mint	Deputy Minister	Affirmed
Seattle Slew	Storm Cat	Riverman
Dancing Brave	Tentam	First Landing

Northern Dancer's influence is incredible. He not only tied with Seattle Song on this list 13 years after his death, but sired nine other sires on this list: El Gran Senor, Nijinsky II, Northfields, Vice Regent, Nureyev, Mari's Book, Danzig, Viceregal, and Lyphard.

5

THAT FIRST TIME

*I*T IS DIFFICULT ENOUGH for any Thoroughbred to win the first start of his career, particularly if he is racing against experienced competition. The longer the distance, the harder that debut victory becomes. Winning a debut in a grass route requires an exceptionally precocious individual and great preparation work by his trainer.

Yet every summer, handicappers and bettors are confronted with maiden grass races for 2-year-olds, frequently at route distances, that are composed of most, if not all, first-time starters. And many 3-year-old maiden grass races are chock full of inexperienced turfers.

Tread lightly here. Never has Harvey Pack's adage—don't take a short price asking a horse to do something for the first time—rung truer.

There is, however, nothing wrong with taking a stand against an overbet first-time starter going long on grass or taking shots when there is no clear-cut favorite.

Here's how. The table on page 71 is a sample of winners at racetracks all over the world that you would have had simply by betting first-time starters whose dams appear in Chapter 3's list of dams of graded stakes winners. That list gives you an edge for years to come, because time after time the mares on that list will produce another winner or another stakes winner.

The fifth race at Gulfstream Park, April 17th, 2003, was for 3-year-old fillies going about $1\frac{1}{8}$ miles on grass. It attracted a field of 10, just one of whom had ever raced on grass. That was Significant Risk, who had the worst possible post, the 10.

The horse with the best post, the rail, was Honor Bestowed, trained by Jimmy Toner. One of the best grass trainers in the country, Toner has cranked out several top grass fillies, including Memories of Silver, Soaring Softly, and Wonder Again, and is featured in a later chapter. From January 1, 2002, through April 30, 2003, Toner had won with 4 of 16 first-time turf starters, an excellent 25 percent.

Honor Bestowed's lone start as a 2-year-old was on dirt in a sprint at Belmont Park, September 6, 2002, when she was a distant sixth at 29-1. It was irrelevant. Honor Bestowed was not only turning to the surface she had been bred to run best on, but also was adding Lasix. And Toner had won with two of his last 14 horses starting off more than a 180-day layoff.

1	Honor Bestowed	B. f. 3 (Feb)		Life	1 M 0 0	$0 40	D.Fst	1 0 0 0	$0 40
Rel	Own: John W Phillips & Hank Snowden	Sire: Honor Grades (Danzig) $15,000		2002	1 M 0 0	$0 40	Wet(365)	0 0 0 0	$0 —
	White, Beige Sash, White Cap	Dam: Wings of Grace (Key to the Mint)		2001	0 M 0 0	$0 —	Turf(285)	0 0 0 0	$0 —
		Br: Hank Snowden Lynn Snowden & John Phillips (Ky)	121	2001	0 M 0 0				
	TURNER T G (53 0 5 5 .00) 2003:(55 0 .00)	Tr: Toner James J(6 0 2 0 .00) 2003:(18 2 .11)		GP ①	0 0 0 0	$0 —	Dst①(315)	0 0 0 0	$0 —

6Sep02–6Bel fst 6f :22² :46 :58 1:10³ ⑰Md Sp Wt 45k 40 7 7 7¹³ 8⁸¼ 6¹⁸ 6¹⁷¼ Prado E S 119 29.50 67–12 FastCookie1195½ StormClipper1191¼ OurNncyLee119⁶ Greenly, inside trip 8

WORKS: Apr11 Pay5f fst 1:03² B 1/1 ●Apr3 Pay5f fst 1:03¹ B 1/5 Mar27 Pay4f fst :51⁴ B 22/34 ●Mar21 Pay ① 4f fm :50 B 1/5 Mar15 Pay3f fst :37⁴ B 3/24 ●Mar8 Pay3f fst :37⁴ B 1/20

TRAINER: +180Days(14 .14 $5.16) 2ndStart(12 .08 $5.25) 1stTurf(14 .21 $8.47) 1stLasix(16 .06 $1.09) Sprint/Route(11 .09 $5.73) Turf(81 .17 $2.67)

In Tomlinson turf ratings of the nine first-time grass horses, Honor Bestowed's 285 was tied for sixth. But Honor Bestowed was the only firster whose dam, Wings of Grace, had won a graded stakes since 1996 to make the list in Chapter 3. When a good first-out turf trainer shows up with a horse whose dam is on the list, go for it. Sent off at 7.70-1 in the field of 10, Honor Bestowed won by 1¼ lengths to pay $17.40. If you used a $2 exacta wheel with her on top, you were lucky because Aud finished second at 21-1 and the $2 exacta paid $271.20.

Bet the first-timers whose dams pop up on this list. They may not all pay boxcar numbers like Miss Marcia, a daughter of Mr. Greeley out of Runaway Marcie, who won her grass maiden at Gulfstream Park, January 10th, 2002, and paid $110.20, but the list will consistently produce good-paying winners.

Stay Forever, out of Forever Lady, won her career debut, November 6, 2000, at Calder at odds of 10.70-1 (see next page). After running second at 2-1 in her next start, she won four straight at odds of 4-1, 7-5, 2-1, and 2-1. The last two were in stakes. After finishing a close third, she won her 2003 debut in the Sunshine Millions Turf at 3.60-1. That gave her six wins, a second, and a third in her first eight starts.

Go Helen Go, out of Snow Colony, made her career debut at Calder, June 4, 2002, winning by five lengths and paying $24.80.

11 Stay Forever
Gray
Own:Santa Cruz Ranch Inc
Black, Red Cross Sashes, Red Bars
CASTANON J L (—) 2003:(445 86 .19)

Ch. m. 6
Sire: Stack (Nijinsky II)
Dam:Forever Lady(Forever Sparkle)
Br: Santa Cruz Ranch Inc (Fla)
Tr: Wolfson Martin D (—) 2003:(38 4 .11)

L 117

Life	9	6	1	1	$328,453	96	D.Fst	0	0	0	0	$0 –
2003	2	1	0	0	$198,500	96	Wet(255*)	0	0	0	0	$0 –
2002	5	4	0	1	$113,123	94	Turf(295)	9	6	1	1	$328,453 96
Crc Ⓣ	7	5	1	1	$129,953	94	DstⓉ(295)	5	5	0	0	$110,123 9

2Mar03-10GP fm 1⅛ Ⓣ :493 1:131 1:362 1:474+ 3↑ ⒻSuwanneeRvrHG3 91 9 75 77 77 64¼ 42¾ Santos J A L 117 b 2.70 93–02 Amonita1172½ What A Price114no Calista118nk Mild response
25Jan03-9GP fm 1⅛ Ⓣ :474 1:114 1:354 1:474+ 4↑ Ⓕ[R]SnshnMilTurf350k 96 5 109¾109¼ 105½ 63¾ 11¼ Santos J A L 120 b 3.60 96–19 StayForever1201¼ *CellarsShiraz*118nk Maliziosa118½ Bumped start, up late 1
16Nov02-9Crc gd 1⅛ Ⓣ :492 1:122 1:362 1:481 3↑ [S]B HeathTurfH150k 94 2 53½ 65 64½ 54 31 Cruz M R L 114 b 5.60 88–14 Msq'sApprvl116hd SrBrn'sSwrd1161 *StyFrvr*1141½ Steadied leaving bkstr
2Nov02-8Crc gd 1 1/16 Ⓣ :231 :472 1:111 1:412 3↑ ⒻSolo Haina45k 91 8 64½ 73¾ 52¾ 31½ 1½ Cruz M R L 119 b *2.20 89–11 Stay Forever119½ Pembroke Palace117nk Banderia1171¾ 4 wide, up late 1
28Sep02-4Crc gd 1 1/16 Ⓣ :242 :494 1:134 1:443 3↑ ⒻNobleRoyltyH50k 89 1 56½ 66¾ 65 4¾ 13 Cruz M R L 116 b 2.00 73–29 *StyForever*1163 PembrokPlc114nk AbulEsthr114no Angled in, going away 8
25Aug02-5Crc fm 1 1/16 Ⓣ :24 :49 1:13 1:422 3↑ ⒻOClm 25000(25-22.5)N 90 1 74¼ 65 52½ 3nk 1¾ Cruz M R L 122 b *1.40 84–18 *StyForever*122¾ CeeKnowsEvil119¾ *WhtAPrice*1194¾ Rail rally, prevailed 10
22Jly02-2Crc fm 1 1/16 Ⓣ :242 :50 1:15 1:463 3↑ ⒻAlw 26000N1X 81 8 710 76¾ 74 2hd 14 Cruz M R L 119 b 4.00 63–37 *StayForever*1194 Icnseeclerly1191½ *Jeblette*1191 Angled out, going away 8
29Nov00-5Crc gd 1⅛ Ⓣ :472 1:114 1:37 1:494 3↑ ⒻAlw 18500N1X 75 1 88 814 74 43½ 23½ Douglas R R L 118 bn 2.20 76–20 RaceyLady1153½ *StyForever*1181½ Singsingsong1151¾ Svd grnd, up for 2nd 10
6Nov00-2Crc fm 1 1/16 Ⓣ :23 :463 1:104 1:424 3↑ ⒻMd Sp Wt 20k 74 5 1012 1019 98½ 67 11¼ Douglas R R L 118 bn 10.70 82–18 StyForvr1181¼ Syndiction1181½ *Ohbygoshbyglly*1181 Hesitated st, up late 10

WORKS: Apr21 Crc 5f fst 1:03 B *3/13* Apr15 Crc 4f fst :522 B *18/19* Apr8 Crc 4f fst :502 B *9/14* Mar27 Crc 4f fst :503 B *18/23* Mar18 Crc 4f fst :512 B *14/20* Mar13 Crc 4f fst :502 B *14/16*
TRAINER: 31-60Days(47 .28 $2.28) Turf(86 .17 $1.57) Routes(166 .22 $1.59) Stakes(49 .27 $2.75)

6 Go Helen Go
Black
Own:Albatroz Bloodstock
Green/black Stripes White Sleeves
JARAMILLO E (30 2 2 1 .07) 2002:(16 1 .06)

B. f. 4 (Feb) OBSOCT99 $12,000
Sire: Island Whirl (Pago Pago) $1,000
Dam:Snow Colony(Pleasant Colony)
Br: David G Lozensky (Fla)
Tr: Ziadie Kirk(5 1 2 0 .20) 2002:(66 4 .06)

L 119

Life	8	2	0	2	$37,610	77	D.Fst	1	0	0	1	$3,240 59
2003	1	0	0	0	$360	77	Wet(330)	1	0	0	0	$230 60
2002	7	2	0	2	$37,250	77	Turf(255)	6	2	0	1	$34,140 77
GP Ⓣ	1	0	0	0	$360	77	DstⓉ(200)	0	0	0	0	$0 –

20Jan03-8GP fm *1⅛ Ⓣ :501 1:15 1:404 1:524+ 4↑ ⒻAlw 36000N2X 77 8 109¾ 1011 107½ 75 85¼ Velasquez C L 121 38.70 72–22 SomethingVnturd117½ Bijou1191¼ FlotAndSting117½ No speed,6wd,tired 10
Previously trained by Ziadie Ralph
29Nov02-4Crc fm 1 1/16 Ⓣ :23 :472 1:112 1:424 3↑ ⒻAlw 24000N2L 77 6 88¾ 86¼ 73½ 41½ 1nk Velasquez C L 119 4.60 82–14 GoHlnGo119nk StrshipWondr1161½ VctorousVck1221 Steadied str, just up 8
Previously trained by Ziadie Kirk
28Oct02-5Crc fm 1 Ⓣ :231 :472 1:11 1:36 ⒻAlw 21000N1X 65 7 87½ 76 85½ 85¾ 83½ Coa E M L 118 2.60 84–12 Ziada121no Marlenica118nk Takealetter121hd Failed to menace 10
12Oct02-9Crc fm 1⅛ Ⓣ :491 1:131 1:37 1:484 ⒻCalder Oaks200k 75 4 78¾ 76½ 85½ 76¾ 88½ Nunez E O L 112 49.10 77–11 CellrsShirz1182½ Mlizios118nk SomthingVnturd1151½ Saved grnd, no factor 9
29Sep02-8Crc fst 1 ⊗ :25 :492 1:143 1:412 3↑ ⒻAlw 30000N2L 59 5 65 43 43 33 38¼ Beasley J A L 118 *1.70 66–24 Dough Girl1101¾ Coco Bay1226½ Go Helen Go118nk Rail, flattened out 9
18Aug02-9Crc fm 1 1/16 Ⓣ :231 :483 1:132 1:44 ⒻAlw 30000N1X 73 4 75 74½ 83½ 41 33¼ Beasley J A L 117 *1.70 73–24 ChitChtter1173 *FbulousHwii*117nk GoHelenGo117½ Lacked room stretch 10
5Aug02-8Crc sly 1 1/16 ⊗ :233 :474 1:122 1:463 ⒻAlw 23000N1X 60 8 52¾ 32½ 44½ 57½ 613¾ Beasley J A L 120 4.20 65–21 JadeButterfly1179¾ *ChitChtter*117¾ She'sfullofhope117¾ Inside, faltered 8
4Jun02-8Crc fm 1 Ⓣ :231 :47 1:12 1:372 3↑ ⒻMd Sp Wt 23k 74 5 710 67 61¾ 13½ 15 Beasley J A 117 11.40 81–15 GoHelenGo1175 AngelBeGreat1121 Takeletter117¾ Hit rail, checked late 10

WORKS: Jan15 Crc 5f fst 1:032 B *8/18* Jan6 Crc 5f fst 1:033 B *10/22* Dec28 Crc 1 fst 1:483 B *2/5* Dec18 Crc 3f fst :393 B *14/15* Nov24 Crc 5f fst 1:041 B *17/24*
TRAINER: Turf(25 .04 $0.99) Routes(40 .08 $1.25) Alw(13 .15 $4.72)

Despite a paucity of turf racing in the winter and spring, through the end of April 2003, the dam's list had already produced Frisco Johnny (Side View), who won at Golden Gate Fields on January 9 and paid $13, and three winners at Gulfstream Park: Remind (Watch the Time), who paid $12.60 on January 22 despite the consistently overbet Bill Mott-Jerry Bailey connection; Silver Tree (Blue Begum), who paid $11.80 on March 27, and Honor Bestowed.

Here's a sample of horses whose dams were on the list in Chapter 3 and who won their turf debuts during a 2½-year period from October 2000 through April 2003.

HORSES FROM DAM'S LIST WHO WON FIRST GRASS START

Date	Horse (Dam)	Odds and Track
Oct. 28, 2000	Aldebaran (Chimes of Freedom)	5-2 at Doncaster
Nov. 6, 2000	Stay Forever (Forever Lady)	10.70-1 at Calder
Feb. 2, 2001	Party Queen (Miss Lenora)	2.80-1 at Calder
Mar. 22, 2001	Beefeater Baby (Tiffany's Gem)	5.80-1 at Santa Anita
May 13, 2001	High Society (Ela's Gold)	7-1 at Leopardstown
May 28, 2001	Quite Careless (Not So Careless)	6-1 at Hollywood
July 25, 2001	War Zone (Proflare)	1-2 at Maison-Lafitte (France)
Sept. 8, 2001	Della Francesca (La Affirmed)	2-5 at Leopardstown
Oct. 19, 2001	Studio Time (Ratings)	2-5 at Newmarket
Nov. 11, 2001	Sun Seasons (Epicure's Garden)	2-1 at Leopardstown
Jan. 10, 2002	Miss Marcia (Runaway Marcie)	54.10-1 at Gulfstream
Jan. 29, 2002	Charm a Song (Charm a Gendarme)	6.10-1 at Hollywood
Feb. 6, 2002	Royal Gem (Tiffany's Gem)	5.80-1 at Santa Anita
April 12, 2002	Heat Haze (Hasili)	1-1 at Chantilly
June 4, 2002	Go Helen Go (Snow Colony)	11.40-1 at Calder
June 22, 2002	French Charmer (Queen of Women)	4-5 at Delaware
July 14, 2002	Van Nistelrooy (Halory)	1-2 at The Curragh
Aug. 17, 2002	Winaprize (Distaff Magic)	4-5 at Ellis Park
Aug. 26, 2002	Man Among Men (La Favorita)	8.20-1 at Del Mar
Sept. 16, 2002	Fiscally Speaking (Tuesday Evening)	2.60-1 at Kentucky Downs
Jan. 3, 2003	Gentlemen JJ (Confident Writer)	1-1 at Fair Grounds
Jan. 9, 2003	Frisco Johnny (Side View)	5.50-1 at Golden Gate
Jan. 22, 2003	Remind (Watch the Time)	5.30-1 at Gulfstream
March 27, 2003	Silver Tree (Blue Begum)	4.90-1 at Gulfstream
April 17, 2003	Honor Bestowed (Wings of Grace)	7.70-1 at Gulfstream

But just because a first-time turfer's dam isn't on our list doesn't mean you can't find a well-bred first-time turfer at an inviting price. Strizzi, a son of Lit de Justice out of Mysteriously, by Afleet, made his grass debut at Gulfstream Park in a $1^1/_{16}$-mile allowance race, January 8, 2003, after winning 1 of 3 dirt starts. Paul Malecki did the *Form*'s horse-by-horse analysis, "A Closer Look," and he pointed out that Lit de Justice has a turf pedigree and that Mysteriously had won a turf stakes. Strizzi's trainer, Malcolm Pierce, had an excellent record with first-time turf starters, 6 for 15. Yet Strizzi went off at 8.30-to-1 under Mark Guidry, winning by $4\frac{1}{2}$ lengths.

4 Strizzi **Own:Stronach Stable** Black, Black A & Red Arrow On Gold Ball, **GUIDRY M** (22 3 0 2 .14) 2002:(1030 156 .15)	Gr/ro c. 3 (Feb) Sire: Lit de Justice (El Gran Senor) $7,500 Dam:Mysteriously(Afleet) Br: Adena Springs (Ont–C) Tr: Pierce Malcolm(2 0 0 0 .00) 2002:(150 32 .21)	**Life** 3 1 0 0 $42,117 62 **D.Fst** 3 1 0 0 $42,117 62 2001 3 1 0 0 $42,117 62 Wet(275*) 0 0 0 0 $0 – **L 120** 2001 0 M 0 0 $0 – Turf(280*) 0 0 0 0 $0 – **GP** ① 0 0 0 0 $0 – Dst①(320) 0 0 0 0 $0 –

1Dec02–7WO fst 1¼ :232 :48 1:133 1:494   Alw 69900N1x   61 7 107¾ 96¼ 72¾ 5² 5²   Ramsammy E   L 117   .95e 55 – 28 Aba Daba Doo122no Symmetron117¾ Strikingly120¾   Late rally 4 wide 12
3Nov02–5WO fst 1⅟₁₆ :23 :48 1:141 1:481   Md Sp Wt 66k   62 8 43½ 51½ 42½ 1hd 1nk   Ramsammy E   L 114   7.95 65 – 26 Strizzi114nk Solihull1152½ Raw Power1141¾   Split horses, driving 12
12Oct02–4WO fst 5f :221 :46 :59   Md Sp Wt 60k   43 8 6 67½ 6⁹ 715 712½   Ramsammy E   114 b   1.35e 72 – 19 Lucky Tom115nk Quiet Dare114⁴ Aba Daba Doo119²   No factor 8
WORKS: Dec31 GP 4f fst :48² B 10/71 Dec24 GP 4f fst :49 B 24/86 Dec16 GP 4f fst :48² B 4/26 Nov25 WO 5f fst 1:03² H 7/7 Nov19 WO 4f fst :48 H 6/20 Oct30 WO 3f fst :37² Hg5/7
TRAINER: 1stTurf(15 .40 $5.22) 31-60Days(34 .24 $1.78) Turf(85 .26 $2.49) Routes(71 .24 $2.33) Alw(74 .19 $1.61)

The following table of more than 275 trainers' records with first-time turf starters can only help your handicapping. Why settle for a short price on a first-time turfer if his trainer didn't win with a first-time grass horse from January 1, 2002, through the end of April 2003?

There were a large number of trainers who failed to win with a first-time turfer during that time period, including such notables as Pat Kelly (0 for 22) and Joe Orseno (0 for 19). Other trainers who had oh-fers with at least 10 starters were: William Morey (0 for 19), Beau Greely (0 for 18), R. B. Hess Jr. (0 for 14), John Terranova (0 for 14), Juan Garcia (0 for 13), Alan Seewald (0 for 13), Michael Tammaro (0 for 12), Rafael Becerra (0 for 11), Manuel Estevez (0 for 11), Ross Wolfendale (0 for 11), Jennifer Pedersen (0 for 11), A. C. Avila (0 for 10), and John Servis (0 for 10).

This does not mean those trainers will never have a first-time turf winner. What it does mean is that if you risk betting one of those trainers, demand value and be sure there are not other negatives. If you bet a short-priced first-time turfer trained by Joe Orseno breaking from the 12 post at Aqueduct, good luck.

Also take a deep breath if the first-time turfer you've fallen in love with is trained by Barry Abrams (1 for 23), George "Rusty" Arnold

(1 for 26), Clifford Sise (1 for 26), or Ralph Ziadie (1 for 27). Even Shug McGaughey, a tremendous trainer, has had little recent success with first-time turfers (1 for 20), reflecting his patience in bringing young horses along.

Conversely, it is always a plus to bet trainers who consistently do well with first-time grass horses. Some successful first-turf trainers have high national profiles: Christophe Clement (22.43 percent), Michael Dickinson (22.86), Richard Dutrow Jr. (21.05), Bobby Frankel (25.84), Ron McAnally (22.44), Bill Mott (19.20), and Todd Pletcher (17.38). Other trainers are not as well known nationally and are worth your attention, especially if you bet simulcast races from their home bases. Don't hesitate betting these trainers who have high percentages with at least 20 starters: Jim Bond (19.04), Simon Bray (23.08), Dale Capuano (28.85), Gary Capuano (38.09), Mark Hennig (17.50), Jeff Mullins (18.18), Doug O'Neill (17.65), and Gary Sciacca (16.66).

TRAINERS WITH FIRST-TIME TURF STARTERS

FROM JANUARY 1, 2002, THROUGH APRIL 30, 2003

Trainer	Record	Percentage
Barry Abrams	1-23	0.43
*Anthony Aguirre	0-5	0.00
*Paul Aguiree	5-26	19.23
*Edward Allard	4-26	15.38
Enrique Alonson	0-13	0.00
Rene Amescua	1-8	12.50
*Tom Amoss	8-36	22.22
Pablo Andrad	0-4	0.00
Joe Aquilino	3-10	30.00
*Rene Araya	1-7	4.28
*George Arnold	1-26	0.39
Paul Assinesi	2-10	20.00
*A.C. Avila	0-10	0.00
Michael Azpurua	0-8	0.00

*Bob Baffert	6-48	12.50
*Robert Bailes	2-22	9.09
*Kelly Bailey	0-2	0.00
Bobby Barbara	0-4	0.00
Rafael Becerra	0-11	0.00
*Charles Bell	0-4	0.00
*Tom Bell	0-9	0.00
Tim Bellasis	1-12	8.33
Patrick Biancone	2-14	14.28
Vincent Blengs	3-18	16.66
*Jim Bond	4-22	18.18
Jeff Bonde	3-18	16.66
David Braddy	1-13	7.69
*William Bradley	1-12	8.33
*Simon Bray	6-26	23.08
Michael Brice	0-2	0.00
*Steve Brown	0-2	0.00
*John Buc	0-4	0.00
Susan Bump	0-3	0.00
*Barbara Burdick	0-4	0.00
Pat Byrne	2-18	11.11
Joe Calascibetta	0-14	0.00
*William Campbell	0-3	0.00
*Francis Campitelli	1-11	9.09
*John Candlin	1-12	8.50
Julian Canet	1-4	25.00
*Dale Capuano	15-55	27.27
Gary Capuano	8-21	38.09
Eduardo Caramori	0-3	0.00
Ruben Cardenas	2-11	18.18
Jeffrey Carle	0-2	0.00
*Del Carroll	0-10	0.00
*Julio Cartagena	1-8	12.50
Ronald Cartwright	0-4	0.00
James Cassidy	4-34	11.76

B.D.A. Cecil	2-13	15.38
Jesus Chavez	0-6	0.00
William Christmas	0-5	0.00
*Christophe Clement	23-107	22.43
John Connor	3-9	33.33
*Gary Contessa	4-49	8.16
*Javier Contreras	0-15	0.00
Michael D'Angelo	0-3	0.00
Jose De Lima	1-3	33.33
*Buddy Delp	2-12	16.66
Richard Demola	0-3	0.00
*Suzanne Dempsey	0-5	0.00
Laura De Seroux	4-24	16.66
*John Destefano	0-5	0.00
*Michael Dickinson	8-35	22.86
*Jacob Dillon	0-3	0.00
Damon Dilodovico	0-7	0.00
Steve DiMauro	1-28	3.57
*Craig Dollase	4-17	23.53
Carl Domino	0-6	0.00
David Donk	2-33	6.06
Anthony Dutrow	0-3	0.00
Richard Dutrow Jr.	4-19	21.05
Jerry Dutton	0-6	0.00
Oliver Edwards	1-5	20.00
*Hassan Elamri	0-6	0.00
*Ron Ellis	1-20	5.00
*Manuel Estevez	0-11	0.00
Scott Everett	0-6	0.00
David Fawkes	2-17	11.76
*Ben Feliciano	2-10	20.00
Jim Ferraro	0-5	0.00
*Allen Ferris	2-30	6.66
William Fires	1-8	12.50
*John Fisher	3-6	50.00

Bernie Flint	3-22	13.63
Greg Foley	0-3	0.00
John Forbes	0-6	0.00
Bobby Frankel	23-89	25.84
Edward Frederick	0-5	0.00
John Friedman	0-2	0.00
*Mitch Friedman	0-2	0.00
*Ron Gaffney	0-2	0.00
Dominic Galluscio	1-8	12.50
*Carlos Garcia	4-12	33.00
Juan Garcia	0-13	0.00
Rodolfo Garcia	1-12	8.33
*Edmond Gaudet	0-10	0.00
*Greg Gilchrist	1-9	11.11
*Mark Glatt	1-17	5.88
Frank Gomez	1-18	5.55
Paco Gonzalez	4-12	33.33
*Michael Gorham	0-9	0.00
*Beau Greely	0-18	0.00
Christopher Grove	3-29	10.34
*Bessie Gruwell	0-6	0.00
Leah Gyarmati	0-10	0.00
David Habeeb	1-4	25.00
Robert Hale	3-12	25.00
Daniel Hartak	0-8	0.00
*Gary Hartiage	1-6	16.66
Charles Harwatt	0-8	0.00
Phil Hauswald	1-14	7.14
*Bev Heckrotte	0-2	0.00
Nancy Heil	0-6	0.00
Dan Hendricks	2-11	18.18
*Mark Hennig	7-40	17.50
*Ramon Hernandez	0-7	0.00
John Hertler	0-8	0.00
*R. B. Hess Jr.	0-14	0.00

Denette Hicks	0-3	0.00
Timothy Hills	3-28	10.71
N. J. Hines	1-4	25.00
David Hoffmans	2-22	9.09
Jerry Hollendorfer	9-73	12.32
*Stanley Hough	3-17	17.53
*Neil Howard	4-17	23.53
*William Huffman	0-6	0.00
Bernard Hughes	0-4	0.00
Byron Hughes	0-2	0.00
*Mike Hushion	1-11	9.00
*Joe Imperio	1-6	16.66
Bruce Jackson	2-11	18.18
*Ellen Jackson	0-4	0.00
*Rodney Jenkins	2-15	13.33
*Kent Jensen	0-4	0.00
*Jimmy Jerkens	1-7	14.28
*Allen Jerkens	2-23	9.09
Murray Johnson	1-8	12.50
*Phil Johnson	5-22	22.73
LeRoy Jolley	0-6	0.00
Harold Jordan	1-2	50.00
Ian Jory	3-21	14.28
*Pat Kelly	0-22	0.00
Martin Kenney	0-6	0.00
*John Kimmel	3-13	23.07
Wendy Kinnamon	1-7	14.28
*Steve Klesaris	3-7	42.86
Steve Knapp	0-2	0.00
Brian Koriner	2-10	20.00
*Terry Knight	2-9	22.22
*David La Croix	0-4	0.00
Armando Lage	5-49	10.20
*Gail Lattimer	1-3	33.33
*James Lawrence	1-14	7.14

Craig Lewis	2-17	11.76
Lisa Lewis	1-10	10.00
Joshua Lilt	2-2	100.00
Charles Lopresti	0-5	0.00
Joseph Lostrito	0-6	0.00
*D. Wayne Lukas	4-29	13.79
Brian Lynch	0-4	0.00
*Michael Machowsky	3-22	13.64
Stephen Margolis	2-6	33.33
Phil Marino	0-2	0.00
Alfredo Marquez	4-11	36.36
*Greg Martin	0-5	0.00
Michael Matz	3-21	14.28
Ron McAnally	11-49	22.44
*Gregg McCarron	0-3	0.00
Dan McFarlane	3-22	13.63
*Shug McGaughey	1-20	5.00
*Paul McGee	1-14	7.14
Bill McLean	1-5	20.00
Kenny McPeek	4-47	8.51
*Mike Miceli	2-12	16.66
*Darvin Miller	0-4	0.00
F. Bruce Miller	1-3	33.33
Wayne Mogge	0-7	0.00
Kathy Mongeon	1-5	20.00
William Morey	0-19	0.00
*Graham Motion	6-31	19.35
*Bill Mott	19-99	19.20
Jeff Mullins	4-22	18.18
*James Murphy	2-14	14.28
*Lawrence Murray	3-12	25.00
*Carl Nafzger	3-12	25.00
*Harry Nelson	0-3	0.00
Michael Nevin	0-8	0.00
*Morris Nicks	1-7	14.28

Donna Nolan	0-3	0.00
Colum O'Brien	0-3	0.00
*Gerald O'Brien	0-5	0.00
Keith O'Brien	1-4	25.00
Niall O'Callaghan	1-10	10.00
Kathleen O'Connell	2-27	7.40
*Jeff Odintz	0-6	0.00
Victoria Oliver	1-6	16.66
*Doug O'Neill	6-35	17.09
*Joe Orseno	0-19	0.00
*Juan Ortiz	1-3	33.33
Patrick Quick	0-3	0.00
*David Pate	0-3	0.00
Anthony Pecoraro	3-11	27.27
*Jennifer Pedersen	0-11	0.00
Dean Pederson	2-6	33.33
*Chuck Peery	0-20	0.00
Danny Peitz	0-3	0.00
Mag Perez	0-2	0.00
*Maria Pinzon	0-4	0.00
Ed Plesa Jr.	4-24	16.66
*Todd Pletcher	16-92	17.38
Terri Pompay	1-18	5.55
*Laura Posada	0-11	0.00
Doug Potter	0-7	0.00
Gerald Procino	0-5	0.00
Faustino Ramos	0-3	0.00
Anthony Reinstedler	3-13	23.07
Pat Reynolds	2-7	28.57
Karel Ridder	0-3	0.00
Timothy Ritvo	2-28	7.15
*John Robb	1-10	10.00
Craig Robertson	1-9	11.11
*Dale Romans	4-40	10.00
Harold Root	0-3	0.00

Richard Root	0-7	0.00
*Sal Russo	1-3	33.33
Steve Rydowski	0-2	0.00
*John Sadler	3-20	15.00
*John Salzman	4-17	23.53
Sally Schu	1-4	25.00
*Randy Schulhofer	2-18	11.11
Gary Sciacca	5-30	16.66
Roy Sedlacek	0-3	0.00
Alan Seewald	0-13	0.00
Phil Serpe	0-7	0.00
*John Servis	0-10	0.00
Jonathan Sheppard	5-58	8.62
Art Sherman	3-19	15.78
Sanford Shulman	2-11	18.18
Mark Shuman	3-39	7.69
Juan Pablo Silva	0-8	0.00
Keith Sirota	0-2	0.00
Clifford Sise Jr.	1-26	3.84
*Hamilton Smith	9-51	17.65
Gary Socco	0-5	0.00
Antonio Soto	0-2	0.00
Bill Spawr	1-24	4.16
*Albert Stall	2-23	8.69
Steve Standridge	0-6	0.00
*Dallas Stewart	4-29	13.79
*Ken Streicher	0-3	0.00
Mel Stute	0-8	0.00
*Taryn Tagg	0-3	0.00
*Michael Tammaro	0-12	0.00
John Terranova	0-14	0.00
Howie Tesher	0-7	0.00
*Gary Thomas	0-4	0.00
Ray Thomas	1-2	50.00
*Michael Thompson	0-4	0.00

Jim Toner	4-16	25.00
Michael Trivigno	0-3	0.00
*Charles Treece	0-2	0.00
Michael Trombetta	1-6	16.66
*Timothy Tulluck	0-4	0.00
Billy Turner	1-10	10.00
David Vance	0-9	0.00
*Gamallel Vasquez	1-8	12.50
Rick Violette	2-15	13.33
David Vivian	0-5	0.00
Elliott Walden	7-39	17.95
Wesley Ward	2-32	6.25
*Donald Warren	1-12	0.85
Fred Warren	1-12	0.85
Joseph Waunch	1-5	20.00
*Lucy Webb	0-3	0.00
*Ted West	2-11	18.18
William White	2-39	5.12
*Jesse Wigginton	1-6	16.66
Ross Wolfendale	0-11	0.00
*Marty Wolfson	3-17	17.65
Milton Wolfson	0-5	0.00
Steve Young	2-7	28.57
Ricardo Zamora	1-3	33.33
Dante Zanelli	0-9	0.00
Ralph Ziadie	1-27	3.70
*Howard Zucker	3-8	37.50

Source: *Daily Racing Form*
*As of May 11, 2003

6

RIDING HIGH

LET'S FACE IT. SOME jockeys are just better on grass. Nobody is better than Jerry Bailey. His 20.05 turf win percentage from January 1, 1976, through January 14, 2003, is well clear of his contemporaries' numbers. This does not imply that Bailey is a bum on dirt. Heck, he's winning 18.28 percent of his dirt starts. The important point here is that he's better on turf than on dirt.

Who else is? And who's better on dirt than on turf?

The table on pages 91-92 examines 35 top jockeys' winning percentages on dirt versus turf. Collectively, the sample size is about 600,000 races, which guarantees that those percentages are meaningful.

Which jockeys' win percentages are better on turf than dirt? Robby Albarado, Bailey, Julie Krone, Corey Nakatani, and Jean-Luc Samyn.

And that's it.

But there are a lot of jockeys in this table whose win percentage is significantly higher on dirt than on grass. They are Manny Aguilar,

Norberto Arroyo, Russell Baze, Gary Boulanger, Shaun Bridgmohan, Victor Carrero, Javier Castellano, Heberto Castillo, Jorge Chavez, Eibar Coa, Pat Day, Kent Desormeaux, Victor Espinoza, David Flores, Aaron Gryder, Mark Guidry, Charles Lopez, Frank Lovato Jr., Mike Luzzi, Donnie Meche, Richard Migliore, Edgar Prado, Mike Smith, Pat Valenzuela, and John Velazquez.

This doesn't mean that it's a bad decision to bet one of those riders on turf. Some of them have extremely high grass win percentages, as the table indicates.

What's important is to realize when there is a significant jockey change on a grass horse you are considering to either bet or eliminate.

A jockey switch from Bailey to Prado or vice versa isn't significant, but a switch from either Bailey or Prado to, let's say, Norberto Arroyo or Jose Espinoza or Mike Luzzi is. Obviously, the converse is also true. A switch from Arroyo to either Bailey or Prado is a huge plus, one that should be factored into your decision as you handicap a grass race.

Celtic Sky was a telling example when he stepped into the starting gate May 26, 2002, in the Kingston Handicap. Trained by Christophe Clement, Celtic Sky had not raced since December 1, 2001, a substantial layoff of nearly six months. But by starting at the bottom of his past performances and moving up, you discover that Celtic Sky had won off a similar layoff—from December 17, 2000, to June 7, 2001—by $3\tfrac{3}{4}$ lengths at 6-5.

In his race on December 1, 2001, Celtic Sky had finished third by 4¼ lengths as part of a 1-2 entry in a 1⅛-mile open-company allowance for nonwinners of two. Norberto Arroyo rode.

Celtic Sky was returning to the races in the Kingston, for New York-breds at 1⅛ miles, with Jose Santos up. Santos had previously finished third on Celtic Sky at 7-5 in another New York-bred grass stakes at the same distance, the Mohawk. In that race, I'm All Yours had gone off at 2.35-1, winning by half a length.

The switch to Santos was huge, yet with I'm All Yours being bet down to 1.70-1, Celtic Sky went off at 4.80-1, winning by three-quarters of a length.

They met again in the West Point Handicap for New York-breds at Saratoga at the same 1⅛-mile distance. I'm All Yours went off at 6-5 and Celtic Sky 3.20-1. Celtic Sky won by a nose and I'm All Yours finished fourth.

In general, young riders struggle on grass. The table shows that Arroyo, who was the runner-up for an Eclipse Award as top apprentice jockey in 2000, is winning at a 14.61 percent clip on dirt, but 10.68 percent on turf. Victor Carrero wins with 12.6 percent of his dirt mounts, but just 6.76 percent on grass. Even the highly accomplished 23-year-old New York rider Shaun Bridgmohan still needs to improve on grass, where he has won just 9.36 percent of his races compared to 13.46 percent on dirt.

The New York jockeys I'm most comfortable betting on turf are Jerry Bailey, Javier Castellano, Jorge Chavez, Mark Guidry, Richard Migliore, Edgar Prado, Jean-Luc Samyn, Jose Santos, and John Velazquez. One jockey who rides at Saratoga every year, Pat Day, is frequently overbet, and his horses rarely offer value.

The jockey of greatest interest is Bailey. Though it's hard to believe, there are, occasionally, situations where you can get a fair price on him in a grass race. But there are a lot more situations where he is overbet. I thought one of them was the fifth race at Saratoga on August 21, 2000. Bailey was riding Great Will in a New York-bred allowance race at 1¹⁄₁₆ miles on Saratoga's inner turf course. Great Will was trained by Michael Dickinson, who almost always gets overbet in New York turf races. He had post 7. The horse I liked was a closer, Imperial Roger, who would be ridden from post 2 by Julio Pezua.

Pezua's winning rides at Saratoga are rare, but Imperial Roger seemed capable of winning a race that seemed to have quite a bit of early speed, including the favorite, Great Will. In the morning line, Great Will was 6-5, but went off at a surprising 2.05-1, suggesting that he might have a chink in his Dickinson-Bailey armor. Imperial Roger was 12-1 on the morning line, but went off at 9.50-1, the fifth choice in the field of 10. My picks in the paper from the previous day had been Imperial Roger, Great Will, and Platinum Setting.

FIFTH RACE
Saratoga
AUGUST 21, 2000

1¹⁄₁₆ MILES. (Inner Turf)(1.39⁴) ALLOWANCE. Purse $46,000. For Three Year Olds And Upward, foaled in New York State and approved by the New York State-Bred Registry Which Have Never Won Two Races Other Than Maiden, Claiming, Or Starter Or Which Have Never Won Three Races. Three Year Olds 118 lbs.; Older 123 lbs. Non-winners of $25,000 at a mile or over on the turf since June 1 allowed, 2 lbs. (Races where entered for $35,000 or less not considered in allowances). (Preference by condition eligibility).

Value of Race: $46,000 Winner $27,600; second $9,200; third $5,060; fourth $2,760; fifth $1,380.   Mutuel Pool $448,228.00 Exacta Pool $451,183.00   Trifecta Pool $324,113.00

Last Raced	Horse	M/Eqt. A.Wt	PP	St	¼	½	¾	Str	Fin	Jockey	Odds $1
6Aug00 2Sar⁴	Imperial Roger	Lb	5 121	2	1	6hd	7hd	92½	87	1hd	Pezua J M	9.50
1Dec99 5Lrl¹	Great Will	L	5 121	7	7	3½	3½	3²	2hd	2½	Bailey J D	2.05
8Jly00 7Bel¹	Platinum Setting	f	4 123	3	8	92½	9²	6½	5½	3nk	Chavez J F	3.75
6Aug00 2Sar⁵	Rate Base	L	4 121	8	5	4hd	5hd	5¹	4¹½	4no	Espinoza J L	29.25
6Aug00 2Sar³	Galactic		4 121	5	9	7¹½	8²½	7¹½	6hd	5¹	Ebina M	6.80
6Aug00 2Sar⁸	College Point	Lb	7 121	10	6	2½	2²	2½	3hd	6nk	St Julien M	42.25
6Aug00 2Sar²	York Harbor	L	5 121	4	3	8²½	6¹	4hd	7hd	7nk	Samyn J L	4.30
28Sep98 9Bel²	Go Mikey Go	Lf	5 121	6	4	1¹	1½	1hd	1hd	87¾	Vergara O	11.20
5Aug00 5Sar⁹	Jimeric	Lb	4 121	1	2	5²	4hd	8½	9¹	9½	Prado E S	16.60
14Aug00 5Sar⁶	Indian Style	Lb	5 121	9	10	10	10	10	10	10	Davis R G	25.75

OFF AT 3:24 Start Good. Won driving. Course firm.
TIME :24¹, :48⁴, 1:13³, 1:37², 1:43³ (:24.30, :48.93, 1:13.75, 1:37.58, 1:43.63)

$2 Mutuel Prices:

3-IMPERIAL ROGER	21.00	8.00	4.70
7-GREAT WILL		3.80	3.30
4-PLATINUM SETTING			3.20

$2 EXACTA 3-7 PAID $83.50 $2 TRIFECTA 3-7-4 PAID $322.50

B. g, by Belong to Me-Roberta Babe, by Roberto. Trainer Tesher Howard M. Bred by Regent Farms (NY).

IMPERIAL ROGER broke awkwardly, bobbled after the start, was steadied along the inside on the second turn, swung wide, finished fast and was up in the final stride. GREAT WILL raced close up while in hand, rallied three wide on the second turn and stayed on gamely to the finish. PLATINUM SETTING rallied three wide on the second turn and finished gamely outside. RATE BASE raced close up while in hand and stayed on gamely along the inside. GALACTIC finished gamely in traffic. COLLEGE POINT prompted the pace from the outside and weakened in the final furlong. YORK HARBOR raced along outside and had no impact on the outcome. GO MIKEY GO set the pace along the inside and tired in the stretch. JIMERIC raced inside and tired. INDIAN STYLE had no rally.

Owners— 1, Regent Farms; 2, Seven Furlong Farm; 3, Our Seven Stable; 4, C'est Tout Stable; 5, Aragon Zacarias; 6, Flying Zee Stable; 7, Gerrity Joseph W Jr; 8, Cholakis John; 9, Olson James F; 10, Goodman Gerald

Trainers—1, Tesher Howard M; 2, Dickinson Michael W; 3, Lostritto Joseph A; 4, Daggett Michael H; 5, Martin Carlos F; 6, Serpe Philip M; 7, Hertler John O; 8, Contessa Gary C; 9, Brida Dennis J; 10, Pregman John S Jr

Scratched— Blazing Saddle (28Jly00 9SAR⁴)

$2 Pick Three (2-6-3) Paid $671.00; Pick Three Pool $68,503.

Publicly picking Pezua over Bailey in a turf race at Saratoga is an invitation to feel mighty dumb afterward. But not this day. Imperial Roger broke poorly, bobbled early, and was steadied on the second turn before rallying extremely wide and nipping Great Will by a head. Platinum Setting finished third as the 3.75-1 second choice. Imperial Roger paid $21 to win; the exacta returned $83.50 and the triple $322.50.

Now, how about catching a fair price on a Bailey grass race? Young Star seemed to fit the bill when she showed up in the eighth at Gulfstream Park on Janurary 11, 2003, a 1 1/16-mile allowance for nonwinners of three races for fillies and mares.

Young Star had not raced since September 27, 2002, when she won a race taken off the turf at The Meadowlands. Over a sloppy track, she'd won by seven lengths as the 4-5 favorite under Jorge Chavez.

4 Young Star
Own:Live Oak Plantation
Yellow White, Red Dots, Black Sleeves, Red Cap
AILEY J D (9 1 2 3 .11) 2002:(832 213 .26)

Dk. b or br f. 4 (May)
Sire: Capote (Seattle Slew) $30,000
Dam: Agotaras(Saratoga Six)
Br: Live Oak Stud (Ky)
Tr: Mott William I(6 0 2 1 .00) 2002:(710 149 .21)

L 117

Life	11	2	3	3	$71,360	87	D.Fst	8	1	1	3	$35,760	87
2002	4	1	2	1	$40,110	84	Wet(390)	2	1	1	0	$27,200	84
2001	7	1	1	2	$31,250	87	Turf(260)	1	0	1	0	$8,400	78
GP Ⓣ	0	0	0	0	$0	–	DstⓉ(295)	1	0	1	0	$8,400	78

Sep02-8Med sly	1	⊗	:23 $:46^{4}$ 1:12 $1:37^{3}$	3↑ ⒻAlw 30000N1X	84	6	2^{2}	2^{2}	$1^{1½}$	$1^{3½}$	1^{7}	Chavez J F	L114	*.80	84-18	$YoungStar114^{7}$ SpiceIsland114¾ *KissMeTwice*$116^{1¼}$	Mostly own courage	6
Aug02-4Sar my	1⅛	⊗	$:47^{1}$ $1:12^{2}$ $1:39^{1}$ $1:53^{1}$	ⒻClm 75000 (75-65)	79	2	1½	1½	1½	1½	2¾	Day P	L119	3.20	72-26	Cut AWager119¾ *YoungStar*$119^{2½}$ *JesterRahab*119^{6}	Set pace, outfinished	6
Jly02-9Sar gd	$1\frac{1}{16}$	Ⓣ	$:24^{2}$ $:49^{2}$ $1:14^{3}$ $1:43^{2}$	ⒻClm 60000 (60-50)	78	6	1^{1}	1½	1^{hd}	2^{hd}	2^{3}	Bailey J D	L119	8.50	76-18	Minni $Sangue122^{3}$ $YoungStar119^{1}$ EarthShaker121½	Stayed on for place	12
Jan02-7Aqu fst	6f	⊡	$:23^{2}$ $:47^{1}$ $1:00^{1}$ $1:13^{2}$	ⒻClm 60000 (60-50)	49	6	1	3½	3^{1}	$5^{2¼}$	$3^{5¾}$	Bridgmohan S X	L121	*1.55	71-18	*Jester Rahab*$115^{1¼}$ $Fruits121^{4½}$ Young Star121½	3 wide, no rally	6
Dec01-8Aqu fst	6f	⊡	$:23^{3}$ $:47^{3}$ $:59^{4}$ $1:12^{4}$	ⒻAlw 43000N1X	48	5	1	1^{hd}	2^{hd}	4^{7}	6^{14}	Pimentel J	L119	2.85	67-25	$Vesta117^{5¼}$ Salem $Willow117^{1}$ Lost $Expectations117^{6½}$	Bobbled,pace,tired	6
9Nov01-5Aqu fst	6f		$:22^{3}$ $:46^{1}$:58 1:10	ⒻMd 60000 (60-50)	87	9	4	1^{hd}	1½	$1^{4½}$	$1^{4¼}$	Pimentel J^{5}	L114	*1.10	87-17	Young $Star114^{4¼}$ Gem's $Wager114^{no}$ $CoolChicken119^{7}$	Pace, clear, driving	10
5Oct01-2Bel fst	6f		$:22^{2}$ $:46^{1}$ $:58^{3}$ 1:12	ⒻMd 75000	64	2	1	$1^{1½}$	1^{hd}	2^{2}	$3^{6¾}$	Bailey J D	118	*1.35	71-24	$Vesta118^{6¼}$ Spectacular Place118½ *Young Star*$118^{1¾}$	Set pace, tired	7
3Sep01-3Bel fst	5½f		$:22^{2}$ $:45^{4}$:58 $1:04^{2}$	ⒻMd 75000 (75-65)	74	7	4	2^{hd}	2^{hd}	2½	2^{5}	Bailey J D	119	*2.60	85-17	*Wopping*119^{5} $YoungStr119^{4¼}$ *Bringhomthloot*119^{2}	Vied outside, 2nd best	10
8Aug01-6Sar fst	5½f		$:21^{4}$ $:45^{2}$ $:58^{4}$ 1:06	ⒻMd Sp Wt 41k	34	2	2	1½	1^{hd}	$3^{2½}$	$5^{7½}$	Prado E S	118	3.55e	79-12	Win's $FairLady118^{2}$ $SwingAgain118^{hd}$ $SuperPunch118^{1½}$	Vied inside, tired	10
3Jly01-6Sar fst	6f		$:22^{3}$ $:46^{2}$ $:59^{1}$ 1:12	ⒻMd Sp Wt 41k	46	5	5	3½	1^{hd}	3^{nk}	$3^{8½}$	Prado E S	118	10.70e	75-14	$MagicStorm118^{4¼}$ $Maria'sOnlyOne118^{4¼}$ YoungStr118½	Vied outside, tired	8
9Jun01-3Bel fst	5½f		$:22^{2}$ $:46^{3}$ $:58^{4}$ $1:05^{2}$	ⒻMd Sp Wt 41k	42	9	9	5^{3}	$5^{1¾}$	$4^{5½}$	$6^{8½}$	Bailey J D	117	10.70	76-17	$SavannhByou117^{1¾}$ Arriviste117½ $NotAProblem117^{2¼}$	Chased 3 wide, tired	9

WORKS: Jan5 Pay 4f fst $:52^{1}$ B *25/26* Dec30 Pay 5f fst $1:03^{2}$ B *2/3* ●Dec23 Pay 4f fst $:49^{2}$ B *1/27* ●Dec8 Pay 3f fst :37 B *1/6* Dec2 Pay 3f fst :37 B *1/3*
TRAINER: 61-180Days(71 .13 $0.79) Dirt/Turf(62 .26 $2.62) Turf(338 .22 $1.56) Routes(494 .22 $1.55) Alw(263 .24 $1.67)

I had seen Young Star make the lone turf start of her career the previous summer at Saratoga. Racing off a six-month layoff for trainer Bill Mott and Bailey, Young Star went off at 8.50-1 in a $60,000 claimer. Mott doesn't normally saddle claimers, but he is among the best in the world with layoff horses. Young Star's grass breeding was okay. A daughter of Capote, she was out of the Saratoga Six mare Agotaras. The 8-1 odds meant she had no chance, right? Wrong. She raced very well, dueling on the lead and weakening late to finish second by three lengths to Minni Sangue.

At Gulfstream, she was reacquiring Bailey off a 3½-month layoff. The *Daily Racing Form* trainer stats showed Mott had won with 13 percent of his layoffs from 61-180 days since January 1, 2002. The 2-1 favorite in the race, When I Grow Up, had not raced since October 25 for trainer Dale Romans, who wins at a 10 percent rate with layoffs that long. Young Star could have been 2-1 or 5-2. Instead, she went off at 5-1, paying $12.80 after winning by a length.

When I'm handicapping a grass race in New York, I expect any top trainer with a horse in that race will be using his regular jockey.

EIGHTH RACE
Gulfstream
JANUARY 11, 2003

ABOUT 1$\frac{1}{16}$ MILES. (Turf)(1.40^{2}) ALLOWANCE. Purse $36,000 For Fillies and Mares Four Years Old And Upward Which Have Never Won Two Races Other Than Maiden, Claiming, Or Starter Or Which Have Never Won Three Races. (Condition Eligibility) Weight 121 lbs. Non-winners of a race other than maiden, claiming, or starter at a mile or over since November 15 allowed, 2 lbs. Such a race since October 15, 4 lbs. (Rail at 20 feet).

Value of Race: $36,000 Winner $21,600; second $6,480; third $3,960; fourth $1,800; fifth $360; sixth $360; seventh $360; eighth $360; ninth $360; tenth $360. Mutuel Pool $416,090.00 Exacta Pool $356,382.00 Trifecta Pool $257,493.00 Superfecta Pool $71,851.00

Last Raced	Horse	M/Eqt.	A.Wt	PP	St	¼	½	¾	Str	Fin	Jockey	Odds $1
27Sep02 ^{8}Med^{1}	Young Star	L	4 117	4	2	$2^{\frac{1}{2}}$	2^{1}	2^{1}	1^{hd}	1^{1}	Bailey J D	5.40
7Jly02 ^{7}Del^{3}	Beyond The Waves	L	6 117	5	3	8^{hd}	8^{hd}	$8^{1\frac{1}{2}}$	4^{1}	$2^{\frac{1}{2}}$	Decarlo C P	5.80
22Dec02 ^{7}Crc^{4}	Devon Rose	L	4 117	1	1	1^{hd}	1^{1}	$1^{\frac{1}{2}}$	$2^{2\frac{1}{2}}$	$3^{1\frac{3}{4}}$	Velazquez J R	6.30
25Oct02 ^{6}Kee^{1}	When I Grow Up	Lb	4 119	2	4	$4^{\frac{1}{2}}$	4^{hd}	5^{1}	$3^{\frac{1}{2}}$	$4^{1\frac{1}{4}}$	Day P	2.40
22Dec02 ^{7}Crc^{3}	Roses For Ruby	L	4 117	7	7	$3^{\frac{1}{2}}$	3^{hd}	3^{hd}	$5^{1\frac{1}{2}}$	5^{hd}	Guidry M	8.70
12Dec02 ^{5}Crc^{1}	Lisa's Deelites	L	4 116	6	6	5^{hd}	5^{1}	$6^{\frac{1}{2}}$	$6^{1\frac{1}{2}}$	$6^{\frac{3}{4}}$	Castillo L A^{5}	39.10
6Aug02 Dea^{3}	Negueva-FR		4 117	8	10	10	10	9^{hd}	$7^{1\frac{1}{2}}$	$7^{2\frac{1}{2}}$	Prado E S	5.30
8Dec02 ^{4}Crc^{6}	Michael's Queen	Lb	5 117	3	5	9^{1}	$9^{1\frac{1}{2}}$	10	$8^{\frac{1}{2}}$	8^{nk}	Toribio Aurelio Jr	44.20
8Dec02 ^{4}Crc^{5}	Tasso Run	L	4 117	9	8	6^{1}	7^{hd}	7^{hd}	$9^{\frac{1}{2}}$	$9^{1\frac{3}{4}}$	Chavez J F	9.80
21Oct02 ^{7}Del^{3}	Sass N' Class	Lb	6 117	10	9	7^{hd}	$6^{\frac{1}{2}}$	$4^{\frac{1}{2}}$	10	10	Coa E M	17.80

OFF AT 4:09 Start Good. Won driving. Course firm.
TIME :25^{1}, :53^{1}, 1:18^{1}, 1:43, 1:48^{2} (:25.29, :53.36, 1:18.37, 1:43.00, 1:48.50)

$2 Mutuel Prices:			
4–YOUNG STAR	12.80	7.00	4.40
5–BEYOND THE WAVES		6.40	5.40
1–DEVON ROSE			5.80

$2 EXACTA 4–5 PAID $76.40 $2 TRIFECTA 4–5–1 PAID $334.00 $2 SUPERFECTA 4–5–1–2 PAID $780.80

Dk. b. or br. f, by Capote–Agotaras, by Saratoga Six. Trainer Mott William I. Bred by Live Oak Stud (Ky).

YOUNG STAR stalked the pace outside DEVON ROSE, moved to gain the lead at the eighth pole and was under steady pressure to prevail. BEYOND THE WAVES unhurried after being steadied in the early going, saved ground into the stretch, angled out and closed to be up for the place. DEVON ROSE set the pace along the rail to inside the eighth pole and weakened. WHEN I GROW UP steadied in behind DEVON ROSE on the first turn and again on the backstretch, tracked the pace into the stretch and had no late response. ROSES FOR RUBY chased the pace three wide into the stretch and tired. LISA'S DEELITES raced in striking position into the stretch and failed to rally. NEGUEVA (FR) was no factor after being outrun early. MICHAEL'S QUEEN showed little. TASSO RUN raced three wide and faltered. SASS N' CLASS rated off the pace, made a run four wide to reach contention on the far turn, then faded.

Owners— 1, Live Oak Plantation; 2, Augustin Stable; 3, Englander Richard A; 4, Ramsey Kenneth L & Sarah K; 5, Schwartz Martin S & Santangelo B; 6, Rea Joe & Kathy; 7, Puglisi Stables; 8, Pincus Anna B; 9, Robinson Jesse M; 10, P T K Racing Ltd

Trainers—1, Mott William I; 2, Sheppard Jonathan E; 3, Iwinski Allen; 4, Romans Dale; 5, Matz Michael R; 6, McCarthy Michael J; 7, Dutrow Richard E Jr; 8, Dwoskin Steven; 9, Gomez Frank; 10, Allen A Ferris III

Scratched— Affirmed Future (30Dec02 ^{8}CRC^{9}), Kiss Me Twice (19Oct02 ^{7}MED^{3}), Sonatina (16Dec02 ^{9}CRC^{6}), Flying Marlin (8Nov02 ^{10}CD^{1})

$2 Pick Three (5–6–4) Paid $7,951.20; Pick Three Pool $79,512.

I want to see Bailey, or more recently, Mike Luzzi, show up for Mott, John Velazquez for Todd Pletcher, Richard Migliore for John Kimmel, etc. There is one important exception. When a top jockey shows up riding a horse for a top trainer he usually does not ride for, pay attention.

On January 29th, 2003, Bailey rode Statement, a horse trained by John Kimmel, in Gulfstream Park's ninth race, a $46,000 allowance. Kimmel, one of the nation's best trainers, rarely uses Bailey.

Statement, a New York-bred, had won his previous start, an open allowance at Gulfstream Park, on January 19 of the year 2002. He was literally off a bit more than a year, and he was moving up in class. Statement showed six unspectacular works at the Payson Park training center, yet there was Bailey riding for Kimmel, who had won with 20 percent of his horses laid off more than 180 days, according to his stats in the *Form*.

It was easy to dismiss Statement off the layoff or the class rise, but a review of his past-performance lines showed just one poor race in seven turf starts, and that was on a yielding course. He had only been beaten half a length by I'm All Yours, a multiple stakes winner, from the 10 post in a New York-bred stakes.

Statement would have offered little value had he been bet down to 4-1 or 5-1 because of Bailey. But Statement went off 11-1, got through on the inside thanks to another flawless ride by Bailey, and won.

In his next start, a $100,000 claimer with Eibar Coa replacing Bailey, Statement won again at 9.90-1, paying $21.80.

Winning-percentage breakdowns of trainer-jockey combos are sometimes indicated in the *Daily Racing Form* and should be treated like trainer stats, pedigree stats, and other useful tools that have been added to the *Form* in the past five years.

If a trainer routinely uses three or more different jockeys, and none of them is riding his horse in a grass race, interpret it as a decided negative.

If a trainer who doesn't routinely use a specific top jockey has one on board his horse in an upcoming race, interpret that as a definite plus. Though it was not on grass, there was a great example last year. Hall of Fame trainer Allen Jerkens usually rides Jean-Luc Samyn or one of a cadre of seldom-used jockeys who also exercise his horses in the morning, such as Ray Ganpath or Raul Rojas. I couldn't ever remember Jerkens using Jorge Chavez, but Chavez showed up on a live Jerkens contender, Missing Miss, in the sixth race at Saratoga on August, 14, 2002. Missing Miss won easily and paid $8.50.

If you are going to be an apprentice jockey on grass, be sure you're getting value. Ten-pound apprentice Shannon Uske had made a favorable first impression in New York in 2003, winning on four of her first 45 mounts.

On May 7, 2003, at Belmont Park, she was up on Keith O'Brien's 7-year-old claiming mare Rose Esther. Rose Esther had made more than $125,000 in her career, but had been 0 for 7 in 2002. In her first start in 2003 off a seven month layoff, Rose Esther took some action, going off at 7-1 in a $35,000 claimer at $1\frac{1}{16}$ miles. She broke in the air, then settled down and rallied strongly to finish second by $3\frac{1}{4}$ lengths in the field of 10.

Her second 2003 start would be at the same claiming level and at the same distance. If she improved any off her impressive return, she was a major player here. With a more experienced jockey, Rose Esther could have been 3-1 or lower. Instead, she went off at exactly the same odds as in her return, 7-1 in the field of 10. Still, she was the third choice. Both Longingtobeme and La Croisette, who like Rose Esther hadn't won a race in 2002 or 2003, went off at 2-1. I picked Rose Esther that morning in the *Daily Gazette* and made her my best longshot. She won by four lengths, paying $16.20.

JOCKEYS' RECORDS FROM JANUARY 1, 1976, THROUGH JANUARY 14, 2003

	Dirt			Grass		
	Starts	**Wins**	**%**	**Starts**	**Wins**	**%**
Manny Aguilar	2,966	413	**13.83**	659	63	**9.56**
Robbie Albarado	14,119	2,204	**15.61**	2,525	424	**16.79**
Norberto Arroyo	2,984	436	**14.61**	571	61	**10.68**
Jerry Bailey	20,442	3,736	**18.28**	7,647	1,533	**20.05**
Russell Baze	33,359	7,317	**21.93**	3,636	690	**18.98**
Gary Boulanger	15,945	2,320	**14.55**	2,385	275	**11.53**
Shaun Bridgmohan	5,202	700	**13.46**	1,132	106	**9.36**
Victor Carrero	1,436	181	**12.60**	370	25	**6.76**
Javier Castellano	5,960	1,009	**16.93**	1,495	184	**12.31**
Heberto Castillo	13,225	1,731	**13.09**	2,471	258	**10.44**
Jorge Chavez	17,530	3,206	**18.29**	3,909	519	**13.28**
Eibar Coa	8,834	1,811	**20.50**	2,671	458	**17.15**
Pat Day	30,088	6,940	**23.07**	5,434	1,012	**18.62**
Kent Desormeaux	17,210	3,533	**20.53**	4,159	762	**18.32**
Jose Espinoza	3,362	317	**9.43**	930	83	**8.92**
Victor Espinoza	7,263	1,082	**14.90**	1,865	239	**12.82**
David Flores	14,382	2,181	**15.16**	2,644	290	**10.97**
Aaron Gryder	16,380	2,217	**13.53**	3,238	337	**10.41**
Mark Guidry	24,502	4,054	**16.55**	2,318	302	**13.03**
Julie Krone	16,825	2,069	**12.30**	3,837	701	**18.27**
Charles Lopez	22,432	3,235	**14.42**	2,689	340	**12.64**

JOCKEYS' RECORDS FROM JANUARY 1, 1976, THROUGH JANUARY 14, 2003

	Dirt			Grass		
	Starts	Wins	%	Starts	Wins	%
Frank Lovato Jr.	12,168	1,350	**11.09**	2,320	217	**9.35**
Mike Luzzi	14,762	2,052	**13.90**	2,229	192	**8.61**
Donnie Meche	6,837	977	**14.29**	1,102	114	**10.34**
Lonnie Meche	7,966	928	**11.65**	1,233	133	**10.79**
Richard Migliore	20,687	3,145	**15.20**	4,278	511	**11.94**
Corey Nakatani	10,959	1,807	**16.49**	3,643	654	**17.95**
Edgar Prado	21,520	4,145	**19.26**	3,320	581	**17.50**
Jean-Luc Samyn	14,650	1,660	**11.33**	6,491	754	**11.62**
Jose Santos	15,948	2,594	**16.27**	6,321	975	**15.42**
Mike Smith	20,613	3,603	**17.48**	4,444	670	**15.08**
Alex Solis	21,262	3,103	**14.59**	5,462	792	**14.50**
Pat Valenzuela	15,227	2,796	**18.36**	3,844	472	**12.28**
John Velazquez	11,956	2,062	**17.25**	3,768	456	**12.10**

Source: Equibase

7

TURF TRAINERS

THE 20 PERCENT CLUB for turf success over the past three years is exclusive. Only Bobby Frankel (24.71), Bill Mott (22.05), Christophe Clement (21.78), Jeff Mullins (21.73), Tom Amoss (21.24), Neil Drysdale (21.11), Gary Capuano (20.93), Neil Howard (20.32), Ron Ellis (20.30), and Julio Canani (20.00) of the 66 trainers in the table on pages 107-109 have been able to win with at least one of every five grass starters.

It's highly difficult to get value playing any of those top three—Frankel, Mott, and Clement—but it does happen.

What's easier to do is avoid or limit wagers on a low-percentage grass trainer, particularly if there is any other nagging doubt about his horse, be it the post position, a poor grass rider, or suspect form. If you are going to play a Nick Zito horse on grass, be sure you're getting value for using a trainer who only wins 5.61 percent of his turf starts.

The more familiar you become with the trainers at the track you're playing, the better you will do. Some are more adept with layoff horses. "Mott, McGaughey, and Frankel," jockey Jerry Bailey said. "There's only a handful."

Mott, actually, is the most adept trainer in New York, if not the entire country, with extremely long layoffs. Which is why I selected Delta Princess to win an allowance race at Saratoga on September 1, 2002. She had raced just once in her life, but it was quite a performance, an eight-length maiden win at Belmont Park at odds of 3.10-1 under Jerry Bailey. She showed just three works for her second start, but the *Daily Racing Form* trainer stats showed Mott won with 17 percent of his horses off longer than 180 days. Bailey's presence was even more meaningful. Despite her connections, she was let go at 3.30-1 and got the job done, paying $8.30.

8	Delta Princess	Dk. b or br f. 3 (Feb)		Life	1	1	0	0	$25,200	82	D.Fst	0	0	0	0	$0
	Own:Khaled Saud bin	Sire: A.P. Indy (Seattle Slew) $300,000		2001	1	1	0	0	$25,200	82	Wet(420)	0	0	0	0	$0
	White/emerald Green Diagonal	Dam: Lyphard's Delta(Lyphard)	117	2000	0	M	0	0	$0	–	Turf(330)	1	1	0	0	$25,200
	BAILEY J D (162 41 20 19 .25) 2002:(623 164 .26)	Br: Palides Investments N V Inc (Ky) Tr: Mott William I (76 17 12 7 .22) 2002:(463 108 .23)		Sar ⑦	0	0	0	0	$0	–	Dst⑦(380)	1	1	0	0	$25,200

6Nov01–3Aqu fm 1½ ⑦ :224 :474 1:13⁴ 1:44⁴ ⑥Md Sp Wt 42k   82 7 4² 32½ 2ʰᵈ 1⁷ 1⁸   Bailey J D   118   3.10   80–14 Delta Princess118⁸ Marfin Dancer118ʰᵈ Betty B118ʰᵈ   When asked, drivin
WORKS: Aug29 Sar 3f fst :37² B 6/11   Jly26 CD 4f fst :49⁴ B 10/27   Jly19 CD 4f fst :48¹ B 3/22
TRAINER: +180Days(64 .17 $1.06)   2ndStart(113 .22 $1.89)   Turf(600 .23 $1.70)   Routes(844 .23 $1.64)   Alw(464 .24 $1.73)

Some trainers do better with fillies than colts. And one underrated New York trainer, Jimmy Toner, is as good as anyone at developing grass fillies. He won a bundle of stakes with Memories of Silver and developed champion grass filly Soaring Softly. Yet the filly he entered on opening day at Saratoga in 2002, Wonder Again, did not get much attention at the betting windows, producing one of the biggest turf overlays of the six-week season.

Scratches left a field of 12 fillies in a $48,000, 1³/₁₆-mile allowance for nonwinners of two (one other than maiden, claiming, or starter) on the Mellon (main) turf course. Let's take a detailed look in post-position order by program number (the scratch of half an entry meant they did not correspond):

2. **Dynamic Lady** She was 1 for 12 on turf, though at one point she did have a string of five consecutive finishes in the money. She sure had a better position, the rail, than in her previous start, when she finished seventh from the 12 post at Belmont

Dynamic Lady
Own:C K Woods Stable
Black/blue Blocks Blue Sleeves
GMOHAN S X (—) 2002:(661 104 .16)

Dk. b or br f. 3 (Jan) KEENOV99 $80,000
Sire: Dynaformer (Roberto) $50,000
Dam: Quick Courtship(Fast Play)
Br: Centaur Farms Inc (Ky)
Tr: Badgett William Jr (—) 2002:(77 13 .17)

L 116

Life	12	1	2	2	$49,940	88	D.Fst	0	0	0	0	$0	–
2002	7	1	2	1	$42,860	88	Wet(320)	0	0	0	0	$0	–
2001	5	M	0	1	$7,080	75	Turf(330)	12	1	2	2	$49,940	88
Sar Ⓣ	1	0	0	0	$0	54	DstⓉ(340)	0	0	0	0	$0	–

02-7Bel fm 1 1/16 Ⓣ :23⁴ :47¹ 1:10⁴ 1:40¹ ⒻAlw 46000N2L 78 12 12⁶¾ 12⁷½ 10⁷¾ 9⁸¼ 7⁸ Gryder A T L 119 b 29.25 89-11 Nunatall117³¾ Hottentot119ʰᵈ *Sugar Dipped*119³ Had no rally 12
02-6Bel fm 1⅛ 🅃 :49¹ 1:14 1:38¹ 1:49³ 3↑ ⒻAlw 46000N1X 82 7 6⁶ 7⁵ 7⁴ 4⁵½ 4⁴¾ Gryder A T L 115 b 8.30 76-22 Sonata Cosmos121³ Miss Playbill117½ Sky Cover121¼ Inside, no rally 9
02-7Bel fm 1 Ⓣ :23² :46⁴ 1:10³ 1:34² ⒻAlw 46000N2L 78 5 12⁴¼ 11⁴½ 11⁵½ 8⁵ 6⁵½ Luzzi M J L 122 b 5.80 82-14 She's Vested117¹½ *High Maintenance*122¹ Attico117¾ Mild rally outside 12
02-6Aqu fm 1⅛ Ⓣ :47³ 1:13 1:38³ 1:51¹ 3↑ ⒻMd Sp Wt 42k 88 7 8¹³ 8¹⁶ 8⁸ 2⁵ 1⁵ Santos J A L 114 b *1.35 82-18 DynmicLdy114⁵ Rivr'sSolution111³ Gbb'sDix111²½ Going away, hand ride 12
02-2FG fm *1 Ⓣ :25 :50³ 1:16⁴ 1:42¹ ⒻMd Sp Wt 28k 84 6 7⁷ 7⁷ 7⁴¾ 3² 2ⁿᵒ Albarado R J L 119 b *2.10 74-27 Cabri119ⁿᵒ *Dynamic Lady*119¹½ Port A119½ Determined, missed 8
02-10FG fm *1 Ⓣ :24² :49 1:15 1:40¹ ⒻMd Sp Wt 30k 65 8 5⁴½ 5⁵ 4²½ 3² 3¹½ Albarado R J L 119 b 2.80 82-11 Hottentot119¹ *Trixie Wac*119½ Dynamic Lady119² Green in drive 11
02-6FG fm *1 Ⓣ :24¹ :49² 1:14³ 1:39¹ ⒻMd Sp Wt 30k 67 7 7⁵½ 7⁶½ 7⁶½ 5⁴ 2ⁿᵏ Albarado R J L 119 b 6.60 89-10 DynaPenny119ⁿᵏ DynamicLady119¹ LindEder119½ Rallied midtrack, late 12
01-6FG fm *1 Ⓣ :25 :50⁴ 1:16³ 1:40² ⒻMd Sp Wt 30k 65 8 7⁴¾ 7⁴½ 7⁴½ 4⁵ 3¹½ Martin E M Jr L 119 b 6.80 81-17 *Ntombi*119½ Woodsia119¹ Dynamic Lady119ⁿᵏ Unhurried, game rally 12
01-3Aqu fm 1 1/16 Ⓣ :22⁴ :47⁴ 1:13⁴ 1:44⁴ ⒻMd Sp Wt 42k 63 9 7⁶¼ 5⁴½ 3½ 3⁸ 5⁸¾ Castillo H Jr L 118 b 4.70 71-14 Delta Princess118⁸ Marfin Dancer118ʰᵈ Betty B118ʰᵈ 3 wide move, faded 11
01-6Bel gd 1 Ⓣ :23⁴ :48⁴ 1:14² 1:38⁴ ⒻMd Sp Wt 42k 75 7 6⁸¼ 7³½ 5¹¾ 3¹ 4¹¾ Castillo H Jr L 118 17.90 62-33 Attico118¹½ Warm Weather118ⁿᵏ Betty B118ⁿᵒ Bumped start, rallied 10
01-6Sar fm 1 1/16 Ⓣ :23¹ :47⁴ 1:13 1:44¹ ⒻMd Sp Wt 42k 54 10 8⁷ 7³¼ 4¹¼ 9⁷½ 9⁹¼ Castillo H Jr L 118 6.80e 66-18 **Another Storm**118³¼ Consort Music118¾ Woodsia118ⁿᵏ Wide trip, tired 11
01-6Bel fm 6f Ⓣ :21⁴ :44⁴ :56⁴ 1:09 ⒻMd Sp Wt 41k 41 6 5 6³½ 7⁵¾ 6¹² 6¹⁵ Castillo H Jr 118 23.10 83-02 *Cyclorama*118³½ Consort Music118² Party Finale118¹¾ 3 wide trip, tired 8
KS: Jly16 Bel 5f fst 1:02⁴ B *10/11* Jly11 Bel 5f fst 1:03 B *17/22* ●Jun6 Bel 5f fst 1:00³ B *1/5* May27 Bel 5f fst 1:01² B *5/17* May11 Bel 5f fst 1:02³ B *24/45* May5 Bel 4f fst :48¹ H *9/67*
NER: 31-60Days(47 .11 $0.83) Turf(82 .07 $0.62) Routes(129 .08 $0.71) Alw(59 .12 $2.04)

Park at 29-1 in a shorter grass route. Regardless, she was tough to endorse.

3. **Another Storm** This filly had shown considerable potential, winning her career debut, a 1¹/16-mile grass race, in 2001 at Saratoga by 3¹/4 lengths as the 8-5 favorite. She was freshened and next appeared in the Grade 3 Herecomesthebride Stakes at Gulfstream Park, February 3. Sent off at 4-1 in the 1¹/16-mile stakes, she was "bounced around early," according to the *Form*, and finished ninth of 10. She again received time off before finishing fourth by seven lengths in a grass allowance race at Belmont Park at 9-2, also at 1¹/16 miles. Edgar Prado had ridden Another Storm in all three starts, but this time he was

Another Storm
Own:Alnoff Stable
Royal Blue And Silver Diamonds, Blue Cap
RRERO V (—) 2002:(368 48 .13)

B. f. 3 (Jan) KEESEP00 $1,000,000
Sire: Gone West (Mr. Prospector) $125,000
Dam: Storm Song(Summer Squall)
Br: Equiné Stable Ltd (Ky)
Tr: Bond Harold James (—) 2002:(127 24 .19)

L 111⁵

Life	3	1	0	0	$27,960	81	D.Fst	0	0	0	0	$0	–
2002	2	0	0	0	$2,760	81	Wet(355)	0	0	0	0	$0	–
2001	1	1	0	0	$25,200	74	Turf(285)	3	1	0	0	$27,960	81
Sar Ⓣ	1	1	0	0	$25,200	74	DstⓉ(315)	0	0	0	0	$0	–

un02-7Bel fm 1 1/16 Ⓣ :23⁴ :47¹ 1:10⁴ 1:40¹ ⒻAlw 46000N2L 81 7 11⁵¼ 8⁴¼ 8⁵¼ 5⁶ 4⁷ Prado E S L 117 4.90 90-11 Nunatall117³¾ Hottentot119ʰᵈ *Sugar Dipped*119³ Inside, no punch 12
eb02-9GP gd 1 1/16 Ⓣ :24³ :50 1:14 1:43¹+ ⒻHrcomsthbrd-G3 72 9 4¹½ 4²½ 4³½ 7⁷½ 9⁸¾ Prado E S L 117 b 4.80 70-17 *CellrsShirz*117¹¼ AugustStorm121² She'sVstd115¹ Bounced around early 10
ug01-6Sar fm 1 1/16 Ⓣ :23¹ :47⁴ 1:13 1:44¹ ⒻMd Sp Wt 42k 74 6 6⁵ 4¹½ 3ⁿᵏ 1¹½ 1³¼ Prado E S L 118 b *1.65 75-18 Another Storm118³¼ Consort Music118¾ Woodsia118ⁿᵏ 3 wide, driving 11
RKS: Jly17 Sar tr.tⓉ 5f hd 1:00 B *3/22* Jly10 Sar tr.tⓉ 5f fm 1:02 B (d)*6/15* Jly3 Sar tr.tⓉ 5f fm 1:01² B (d)*2/18* Jun11 Sar tr.t 3f fst :37⁴ B *6/54* ●Jun5 Sar tr.tⓉ 5f fm 1:01³ B (d)*1/18* ●May28 Sar tr.t 4f fst :50³ B *1/6*
AINER: 31-60Days(81 .16 $1.42) Turf(93 .23 $2.42) Routes(262 .21 $2.06) Alw(140 .20 $1.41)

aboard Wonder Again. The jockey switch to Victor Carrero was not enticing.

4. **Bluebird Day** The Irish import had one win in five starts, scoring by 1½ lengths at Gulfstream Park at 9-10. She was fifth, fourth, and seventh in three subsequent starts. The rider in her

4 Bluebird Day (Ire) Gr/ro f. 3 (Apr) TATHOU00 $373,269
Own:Humphrey G W Jr — Sire: Sadler's Wells (Northern Dancer)
Green And White Diamonds, Green Sleeves, — Dam: Desert Bluebell(Kalaglow*GB)
Br: Tullamaine Castle Stud and Partners (Ire)
SAMYN J L (—) 2002:(279 37 .13) — Tr: Arnold George R II (—) 2002:(132 23 .17) — L 116

Life	5	1	0	0	$23,708	83	D.Fst 0 0 0 0 $0
2002	5	1	0	0	$23,708	83	Wet(330) 0 0 0 0 $0
2001	0	M	0	0	$0	–	Turf(355*) 5 1 0 0 $23,708
Sar Ⓣ	0	0	0	0	$0	–	DstⓉ(365) 1 0 0 0 $2,760

12Jun02-6Bel fm 1⅛ Ⓣ :491 1:14 1:381 1:493 3↑ ⒻAlw 46000N1X 77 9 21 21 2½ 66 76½ Prado E S L115 5.80 74-22 SonataCosmos1213 MissPlybill117½ SkyCover1211¼ Speed outside, tir
27May02-4Bel fm 1¼ Ⓣ :494 1:132 1:372 2:014 3↑ ⒻAlw 46000N1X 83 6 33½ 33 21½ 23 42½ Prado E S L115 4.20 80-17 Duchcov121hd **Cozie Advantage**1151½ Sunstone1211 3 wide move, fad
19Apr02-5Kee fm 1⅛ Ⓣ :474 1:134 1:382 1:501 ⒻAlw 55580N1X 75 6 31 33½ 3½ 52½ 54½ Day P L120 3.40 81-14 AffirmedDncer1201½ Disygo123nk *TrnishdLdy*1202¼ Tracked,4w,flatten c
22Mar02-10GP fm *1⅛ Ⓣ :511 1:154 1:42 1:541+ ⒻMd Sp Wt 32k 71 8 32½ 31 1½ 11½ 11½ Prado E S L121 *.90 67-30 Bluebird Day1211½ Glowing Halo1212½ *Dizzy*121no 3 wide, prevail
10Jan02-7GP fm *1 1/16 Ⓣ :23 :481 1:141 1:474 ⒻMd Sp Wt 32k 70 8 96½ 912 106½ 83¼ 54 Day P 121 *1.90 59-40 *MnhttnSkylin*121nk TrnishdLdy1212½ Dvid'sDoll1211 Blocked, taken up
WORKS: Jly14 Bel 5f fst 1:04 B *24/27* ● Jly7 Bel 5f fst 1:00 H *1/31* Jun30 Bel 4f fst :513 B *39/49* Jun8 Bel 3f fst :36 B *2/12* May21 Bel 5f fst 1:034 B *24/26* May15 Bel 4f fst :502 B *42/53*
TRAINER: 31-60Days(122 .18 $1.61) Turf(138 .14 $1.48) Routes(281 .17 $1.77) Alw(164 .18 $1.72)

last two starts was none other than Prado. Jean-Luc Samyn was aboard this time.

5. **Supposedly** After losing her only start at 2 on the dirt at Aqueduct, she had raced three times on turf at Tampa Bay, following a pair of seconds with an 8¾-length win at 9-10 with the addition of blinkers. Shipped to New York, she finished fifth by seven lengths off a two-month layoff and then a game second by half a length, a head in front of one of today's opponents, Cozie Advantage, at 8-1 with Javier Castellano

5 Supposedly Dk. b or br f. 3 (Mar) EASOCT00 $70,000
Own:Lerman Roy S — Sire: Polish Numbers (Danzig) $20,000
Yellow, Brown Triangular Panel, Brown — Dam: Allegedly(Sir Ivor)
Br: Dr & Mrs T Bowman & M P Higgins III & H T McKnight (Md)
CASTELLANO J J (—) 2002:(633 103 .16) — Tr: Lerman Roy S (—) 2002:(27 5 .19) — 116

Life	6	1	3	0	$22,880	85	D.Fst 1 0 0 0 $2,520
2002	5	1	3	0	$20,360	85	Wet(410) 0 0 0 0 $0
2001	1	M	0	0	$2,520	–	Turf(340) 5 1 3 0 $20,360
Sar Ⓣ	0	0	0	0	$0	–	DstⓉ(320) 1 0 1 0 $9,200

7Jly02-4Bel fm 1¼ Ⓣ :492 1:132 1:373 2:01 3↑ ⒻAlw 46000N1X 85 2 44½ 35 31½ 32 2½ Castellano J J 117 b 8.20 86-15 Terri'sToy122½ Supposedly117hd **CoziAdvntg**117hd Gamely between riv
20Jun02-7Bel fm 1 1/16 Ⓣ :234 :471 1:104 1:401 ⒻAlw 46000N2L 80 8 105 115 95¾ 86¾ 57 Davis R G 119 b 36.75 90-11 Nunatall1173¾ Hottentot119hd *Sugar Dipped*1193 Wide trip, no ra
22Apr02-10Tam fm *1 Ⓣ :243 :50 1:161 1:412 ⒻMd Sp Wt 10k 72 5 33 51¾ 41¼ 12 18¾ Bell D C 120 b *.90 77-23 Supposedly1208¾ Six Zeroes1202¼ Gotta Go Now1202 Much the be
19Mar02-4Tam fm 1 1/16 Ⓣ :231 :474 1:124 1:432 ⒻMd Sp Wt 9k 59 5 63 75¼ 57 38 23¼ Umana J L 120 *.90 78-18 Hydrtion1203¼ *Supposedly*1201½ *SomethingVenturd*1202½ Outfinished r
19Feb02-4Tam fm 1 1/16 Ⓣ :23 :48 1:133 1:444 ⒻMd Sp Wt 9k 59 2 75¼ 64¾ 63¼ 2½ 21¼ Umana J L 120 4.60 73-20 MercyMission1201¼ Supposedly1205½ LadyLenore1203 Mid m 4w,bid,2n
2Nov01-6Aqu fst 1 :231 :471 1:121 1:374 ⒻMd Sp Wt 40k -0 4 21½ 45 412 427 448½ Smith A E 118 12.90 -29-15 Indyfault118½ *Clear Destiny*11810 Hold The Lime11837 Brief speed, ti
WORKS: Jun18 Sar tr.t 4f fst :522 B *37/42*
TRAINER: Turf(40 .10 $0.68) Routes(54 .09 $0.63) Alw(23 .00 $0.00)

replacing Robbie Davis. Castellano was on today, but the filly did not show a single work since her last race on July 7.

6. Wonder Again The 3-year-old daughter of Silver Hawk, out of the Danzig mare Ameriflora, began her career on dirt, finishing eighth at 78-1, then a distant third at 16-1 with Lasix added. She made her grass debut under Castellano in a 1$\frac{1}{8}$-mile maiden race at Belmont Park on May 31, and fought bravely the entire way, finishing second by half a length at 7-2. Prado replaced Castellano for her last start, a 1$\frac{1}{16}$-mile maiden race at Belmont Park. She had drawn the 10 post in the field of 10, yet was sent off at 7-5. She didn't disappoint. Despite

6 **Wonder Again**	B. f. 3 (Feb)		Life	4 1 1 1	$40,040 88	D.Fst	1 0 0 0	$0 47
Own:Phillips Joan G & John W	Sire: Silver Hawk (Roberto) $75,000					Wet(295)	1 0 0 1	$4,840 49
White, Kelly Green Diamond Hoop, Green	Dam: Ameriflora(Danzig)		2002	4 1 1 1	$40,040 88			
	Br: Phillips Racing Partnership & John Phillips (Ky)	L 118	2001	0 M 0 0	$0 –	Turf(325)	2 1 1 0	$35,200 88
PRADO E S (—) 2002:(860 161 .19)	Tr: Toner James J (—)2002:(73 9 .12)		Sar ⊕	0 0 0 0	$0 –	Dst⊕(330)	0 0 0 0	$0 –

26Jun02-4Bel fm 1$\frac{1}{8}$ ⊕ :241 :482 1:123 1:424 3↑ⓕMd Sp Wt 44k   83 10 31 41 3$\frac{1}{2}$ 1hd 13$\frac{1}{2}$ Prado E S   L 118   *1.45   84–15 WondrAgin118$\frac{3}{4}$ Allison'sEys118no ClirsyWrsy118$\frac{1}{2}$ Speed 3 wide, driving 10
31May02-1Bel fm 1$\frac{1}{8}$ ⊕ :491 1:133 1:374 1:492 3↑ⓕMd Sp Wt 44k   88 1 32 2$\frac{1}{2}$ 2hd 1hd 2$\frac{1}{2}$ Castellano J J   L 117   3.85   81–13 MadeirMist117$\frac{3}{4}$ WonderAgin118$\frac{3}{4}$ SobrinDelRey123no   With pace, gamely 9
18May02-3Bel my 1$\frac{1}{8}$ ⊗ :234 :474 1:132 1:442 3↑ⓕMd Sp Wt 44k   49 6 1$\frac{1}{2}$ 1$\frac{1}{2}$ 3$\frac{1}{2}$ 311 316$\frac{1}{2}$ Castellano J J   L 115   16.20   61–29 Dubai Fall115$\frac{1}{4}$ Title Nine115$\frac{2}{1}$ Wonder Again115nk   Set pace, tired 8
14Apr02-3Aqu fst 7f   :22 :444 1:102 1:233   ⓕMd Sp Wt 41k   47 1 8 610 813 815 816$\frac{3}{4}$ Castellano J J   120   ,78.50   65–23 Strike The Sky120$\frac{3}{4}$ Zawzooth120$\frac{1}{2}$ My Golden Girl120$\frac{2}{1}$ Inside trip, tired 10
WORKS: Jly18 Bel⊕5f fm 1:03$\frac{1}{3}$ B (d)6/10 Jly10 Bel4f gd :483 B 5/13 Jun19 Bel4f fst :49 B 25/49 May11 Bel4f fst :483 B 19/76 Apr25 Bel5f fst 1:01 H 7/29
TRAINER: Turf(139 .13 $2.33) Routes(190 .12 $1.93) Alw(59 .15 $1.55)

racing three wide early, she drew off to a 3$\frac{1}{4}$-length win. She had two maintenance works since for the step up today.

1. Showlady The 3-year-old filly was the half of the Kiaran McLaughlin entry that did not scratch. In her debut at Belmont Park, she was sent off at odds of 7-1 against Wonder Again despite the presence of Bailey in the saddle. The *Form* said she had an awkward start and raced between horses to finish fourth, 2$\frac{3}{4}$ lengths behind Wonder Again, who had gone off at 7-2. Showlady then won a maiden race from the 10 post in a field of 12, scoring by 3$\frac{1}{4}$ lengths at 1$\frac{1}{4}$ miles and going off at .95-to-1 under Bailey, who was back on board today. She, too, had two maintenance works since her last start.

Showlady	B. f. 3 (Mar) KEESEP00 $4,000,000		Life	2 1 0 0	$29,040 85	D.Fst	0 0 0 0	$0 –
Own:al Maktoum Mohammed bin	Sire: Theatrical*Ire (Nureyev)					Wet(320)	0 0 0 0	$0 –
Maroon, White Sleeves, Maroon Cap, White	Dam: Claxton's Slew(Seattle Slew)		2002	2 1 0 0	$29,040 85			
	Br: Allen E. Paulson (Ky)	L 118	2001	0 M 0 0	$0 –	Turf(365)	2 1 0 0	$29,040 85
KLEY J D (—) 2002:(454 122 .27)	Tr: McLaughlin Kiaran P (—)2002:(42 12 .29)		Sar ⊕	0 0 0 0	$0 –	Dst⊕(375)	1 1 0 0	$26,400 85

un02-5Bel gd 1$\frac{1}{4}$ ⊕ :49 1:141 1:383 2:022 3↑ⓕMd Sp Wt 44k   85 10 43$\frac{1}{2}$ 31$\frac{1}{2}$ 2hd 1$\frac{1}{2}$ 13$\frac{1}{4}$ Bailey J D   L 118   *.95   80–21 Showlady118$\frac{3}{4}$ Atherbest124$\frac{1}{2}$ Missy Kiri118no   Close up, driving 12
ay02-1Bel fm 1$\frac{1}{8}$ ⊕ :491 1:133 1:374 1:492 3↑ⓕMd Sp Wt 44k   82 5 96 93$\frac{3}{4}$ 62$\frac{1}{2}$ 44 43$\frac{1}{2}$ Bailey J D   L 117   7.00   79–13 MdirMist117$\frac{1}{2}$ WondrAgin117$\frac{3}{4}$ SobrinDlRy123no   Awkward start, between 9
RKS: Jly20 Sar3f fst :364 B 5/10 Jly12 Bel4f fst :502 B 37/45 Jun25 Bel4f fst :512 B 30/35 Jun18 Bel4f fst :502 B 69/80 May24 Bel4f fst :483 B 6/32 May18 Bel4f fst :493 B 1/1
AINER: Turf(52 .19 $1.58) Routes(80 .20 $1.64) Alw(47 .21 $2.34)

7. Boana The German filly was one of the three 4-year-olds in this race. Following nine starts in Germany, she had raced twice in the U.S. On December 29, 2001, she had been ambitiously placed in the Grade 2 La Prevoyante Handicap at Calder. Sent off at 33-1, she rallied to finish fifth in the 10-horse field, an impressive American debut. Boana was given time off as she switched trainers from Peter Rau to Steve Asmussen. She returned to the track at Churchill Downs, June 9, in a 1 1/16-mile allowance. Adding Lasix, she was sent off at 1-2 from the rail, broke slowly, and rallied to finish second by 1 1/4 lengths under Donnie Meche, who was back on today.

7 Boana (Ger)
Own:Tanaka Gary A
Emerald Green, White Sash, Gold Blocks
MECHE D J (—) 2002:(420 70 .17)

Dk. b or br f. 4
Sire: Goofalik (Lyphard)
Dam: Borama*Ger(Meinberg*Ger)
Br: Rahlfes K (Ger)
Tr: Asmussen Steven M (—) 2002:(1001 228 .23)

L 121

Life	11	1	5	0	$59,665	91	D.Fst		0	0	0	0	$0
2002	1	0	1	0	$7,100	86	Wet(280)		0	0	0	0	$0
2001	7	0	3	0	$38,060	91	Turf(278)		11	1	5	0	$59,665
Sar (T)	0	0	0	0	$0	–	Dst(T)(298)		1	0	0	0	$0

9Jun02-7CD fm 1 1/16 (T) :24 :483 1:124 1:432 3↑ (F)Alw 43660N1X 86 1 106 1/2 104 3/4 95 1/4 43 1/2 21 1/4 Meche D J L116 *.50 86-10 As Told112 1 1/4 Boana116hd Maltese Indy118 1 1/2 Broke slow,8w lane
Previously trained by Rau Peter
29Dec01-8Crc fm 1 1/2 (T) :491 1:14 2:024 2:263 3↑ (F)LaPrevoyntH-G2 91 8 1011 108 3/4 87 1/4 78 1/2 52 1/2 Chavez J F 114 33.30 96-09 Krisada115nk Sweetest Thing115hd Great Fever113 3/4 3 wide, passed tired
4Nov01♦ Frankfurt(Ger) sf *1 5/16 (T) RH 2:23 3↑ (F)Frankfurter Stutenpreis (Lstd) 21 1/2 Mundry T 123 8.50 Nouvelle Fortune124 1 1/2 Boana123nk Nicara131nk
Timeform rating: 103 Stk 46100 *Rated in 6th,late gain into*
30Sep01♦ Dortmund(Ger) sf *1 3/4 (T) LH 3:072 Deutsche St Leger(Ger StLeger)-G2 528 Mundry T 123 5.00 Fair Question12810 Stingray128 2 1/2 Saldenschwinge12413
Timeform rating: 70 Stk 95000 *Rated in 6th,never a fac*
9Sep01♦ Hannover(Ger) sf *1 1/2 (T) LH 2:343 3↑ (F)Deutscher Stutenpreis-G3 21 Mundry T 121 7.50 Saldenschwinge1211 Boana1211 Abitara13211
Timeform rating: 106 Stk 57900 *Rated in mid-pack,3rd 3f out,bumped and angled left,2nd 100y*
4Aug01♦ Bremen(Ger) gd *1 3/8 (T) RH 2:221 3↑ (F)Gr Stutenpreis von Bremen(Rst) 2nk Mundry T 120 4.30 Nicara130hd Boana120nk Pearlmix128nk
Timeform rating: 106 Stk 45200 *Tracked in 3rd,dueled between horses,gamely.Well Minded*
27May01♦ Baden-Baden(Ger) gd *1 1/8 (T) LH 1:531 (F)Idee-Festa-Rennen (Listed) 42 Helfenbein A 128 17.00 Dakhla Oasis128 1 1/2 Dunnella124 1/2 Kimbajar128hd
Timeform rating: 102 Stk 31500 *Rated in 7th,mild late g*
7Apr01♦ Dresden(Ger) sf *1 3/16 (T) RH 2:101 Preis von Dahlwitz (Listed) 53 3/4 Koplik R 123 3.50 Peu a Peu123 Street Poker123 Foreman123
Timeform rating: 96 Stk 15700 *Towards rear,never threate*
29Oct00♦ Hannover(Ger) sf *1 (T) LH 1:463 (F)Quebrada-Rennen (German-breds) 2 3/4 Mundry T 121 3.30 Schlenderaca121 3/4 Boana1212 Sang Sun121 3/4
Timeform rating: 85 Stk 43800 *Tracked in 4th,late bid into*
1Oct00♦ Hannover(Ger) gd *6 1/2 f (T) LH 1:204 GP Landesjagerschaft(Ger-bred) 52 1/4 Koplik R 120 8.70 Diamond Moon128hd Asta Luego119nk Andrelhina1191
Timeform rating: 85 Stk 46000 *Chased in 6th,evenly late.Rosenstern*
6Aug00♦ Hannover(Ger) gd *1 (T) LH 1:453 Preis der Hannover Region-EBF 1 1/2 Mundry T 120 1.30 Boana120 1/2 Rosenstern1262 Basento128
Maiden 5200 *Led throughout,held v*
WORKS: Jly9 CD 5f fst 1:051 B *12/12* Jly2 CD (T) 4f fm :531 B (d) *6/7* Jun25 CD (T) 6f sf 1:181 B (d) *4/5* Jun18 CD (T) 4f fm :52 B *10/10* Jun4 CD (T) 4f fm :502 B (d) *10/11* ●May28 CD (T) 6f fm 1:182 B (d) *1/5*
TRAINER: 31-60Days(665 .20 $1.30) Turf(484 .14 $1.09) Routes(861 .19 $1.50) Alw(708 .19 $1.34)

8. Risotto She began her career in Great Britain, finishing second, 13th, and first in three starts. Sent to trainer Jonathan Sheppard, she finished eighth in a nonwinners-of-two allowance at Gulfstream at 12-1, and dead-heated for fourth in the same class at Pimlico while adding Lasix. She had never raced farther than 1 1/16 miles. Pat Day, who had ridden her in Florida, was up.

8 Risotto
Own: Augustin Stable
White/green Halves White Sleeves
DAY P (—) 2002:(653 149 .23)

Dk. b or br f. 3 (Feb)
Sire: Kris S. (Roberto) $150,000
Dam: Routilante*Ire(Rousillon)
Br: George Strawbridge Jr. (Pa)
Tr: Sheppard Jonathan E (—) 2002:(230 30 .13)

L 116

Life	5	1	1	0	$9,937	78	D.Fst	0	0	0	0	$0	–
2002	2	0	0	0	$1,510	78	Wet(340*)	0	0	0	0	$0	–
2001	3	1	1	0	$8,427	–	Turf(315)	5	1	1	0	$9,937	78
Sar Ⓣ	0	0	0	0	$0	–	DstⓉ(370)	0	0	0	0	$0	–

9May02-5Pim fm 1 1/16 Ⓣ :24 :492 1:133 1:451 3↑ ⒻAlw 26000N1X 78 6 42½ 32½ 31½ 51¾ 41½♦ Bartram B E L 114 3.60 75-25 Bowkeen117¾ Leebearski117¾ NoBettorLove112no Flipped prerace,faded 8
1Feb02-7GP fm *1 1/16 Ⓣ :243 :502 1:14 1:451 ⒻAlw 34000N1X 73 9 85½ 85¾ 85¾ 54½ 84½ Day P 117 12.80 71-18 Manhattan Skyline121¾ Always Country119nk Katie Kreitz1171½ Outrun 10
Previously trained by Ian Balding
4Sep01♦ Epsom(GB) gd 7f Ⓣ LH 1:254 ⒻEBF Brian Angove Maiden Stakes 1nk Duffield G 123 2.75 Risotto123nk Atarama123½ Westmead Empress1231¼ 5
Timeform rating: 70 Maiden 9400 *Pressed pace,dueled 2f out,hard ridden to lead 150y out,just held*
7Aug01♦ Newbury(GB) gd 6f Ⓣ Str 1:132 ⒻPub-Enterprises.co.uk Mdn Stks 137¼ Fallon K 123 5.50 Misterah1231¼ Pretty Clear1232½ Homespun123½ 21
Timeform rating: 64 Maiden 12500 *Tracked leaders,weakened final furlong*
24Jun01♦ Pontefract(GB) gd 6f Ⓣ LH 1:182 ⒻEBF Maiden Stakes 2½ Fallon K 123 6.00 Hufflepuff123½ Risotto123nk Sophorofic123nk 13
Timeform rating: 66+ Maiden 11500 *Tracked in 5th,led briefly 150y out,gamely*
WORKS: ●Jly21 Del 5f fst 1:01 B *1/14* Jun1 Del 5f fst 1:023 B *14/39*

9. Hangingbyamoment As bad as her last race was, 10th by 14 lengths at 61-1 at Belmont Park, she had won a maiden race at Saratoga by 1¼ lengths in her grass debut the year before. Jorge Chavez replaced Dennis Carr.

9 Hangingbyamoment
Own: Flying Zee Stable
Light Blue, White Yoke/zz, White
CHAVEZ J F (—) 2002:(690 137 .20)

Ch. f. 3 (Apr) KEESEP00 $45,000
Sire: Thunder Gulch (Gulch) $14,036
Dam: Kermis(Graustark)
Br: D J Stable (Ky)
Tr: Serpe Philip M (—) 2002:(100 9 .09)

L 116

Life	7	1	0	1	$33,871	77	D.Fst	2	0	0	0	$1,230	27
2002	2	0	0	0	$0	73	Wet(305*)	0	0	0	0	$0	–
2001	5	1	0	1	$33,871	77	Turf(305)	5	1	0	1	$32,641	77
Sar Ⓣ	1	1	0	0	$25,200	64	DstⓉ(330)	0	0	0	0	$0	–

0Jun02-7Bel fm 1 1/16 Ⓣ :234 :471 1:104 1:401 ⒻAlw 46000N2L 65 11 63 63½ 74¼ 1113 1014 Carr D L 117 61.25 83-11 Nunatall1173¾ Hottentot119hd *Sugar Dipped*1193 Wide trip, tired 12
7May02-7Bel fm 1 Ⓣ :232 :464 1:103 1:342 ⒻAlw 46000N2L 73 1 2hd 2hd 3½ 73½ 87¾ Carrero V5 L 112 19.20 80-14 She's Vested1171½ *High Maintenance*1221 Attico117¾ Vied inside, tired 12
4Nov01-6Aqu fst 1⅛ :483 1:132 1:374 1:502 ⒻDemoiselle-G2 27 1 31 31 76 730 741 Castellano J J L 115 f 38.50 43-16 Smok'nFrolic1214½ LdyShr121nk *ProxySttmnt*1174¼ Stumbled start, inside 7
4Nov01-9Aqu fm 1⅛ Ⓣ :48 1:132 1:39 1:513 ⒻMiss Grillo86k 77 12 97¼ 86¾ 53 54½ 53¼ Castellano J J L 116 36.50 77-18 Riskaverse1181¼ Lujien Lujien118¾ Kathy K D118½ Wide throughout 12
20Oct01-4Bel fm 1 Ⓣ :222 :454 1:102 1:344 ⒻAlw 44000N1X 67 5 76 88¼ 63¾ 44½ 39¼ Velazquez J R 120 9.00 75-15 LujinLujin1205¼ GloblVson1184 Hngngbymomnt1205½ Inside trip, mild bid 8
3Aug01-5Sar fm 1 1/16 Ⓣ :24 :484 1:133 1:442 ⒻMd Sp Wt 42k 64 2 21½ 2½ 2hd 2hd 11¼ Castillo H Jr 118 40.25 74-16 Hangingbymoment1181¼ Allison'sEyes118nk ElNor118nk With pace, driving 10
5Aug01-5Sar fst 5f :214 :45 :574 ⒻMd Sp Wt 41k 13 1 1 613 69 515 520¾ Guidry M 118 19.30 78-05 Goodness1184½ Ballagren118½ As Told11811 Inside trip, tired 6
WORKS: Jly18 Bel Ⓣ 5f fm 1:02 B (d)*4/10* Jly7 Bel 4f fst :493 B *14/30* Jun16 Bel tr.t 4f gd :501 B *10/15* Jun9 Bel Ⓣ 5f gd 1:032 B (d)*2/3* May9 Bel Ⓣ 5f fm 1:024 B (d)*6/9* Apr30 Bel tr.t 5f fst 1:04 B *13/16*
TRAINER: 31-60Days(61 .18 $1.58) Turf(106 .09 $1.57) Routes(165 .09 $1.27) Alw(108 .09 $0.90)

10. Polyandry An Irish-bred 4-year-old filly now in Christophe Clement's barn, Polyandry had two impressive U.S. races in as many starts, finishing second by a head in a 1 1/16-mile allowance race as the 2-1 favorite and then second by a nose in the same company at 4-5. That made her 1 for 13 on grass with four seconds and one third. In her lone start longer than 1 1/16 miles, she had finished a tiring fourth in a 1¼-mile race in France the year before. Clement's main man, Jose Santos, maintained the mount.

10 Polyandry (Ire)
Own:de Rothschild Edouard
Yellow, Royal Blue Hoop On Sleeves, Blue
SANTOS J A (—) 2002:(602 85 .14)

B. f. 4
Sire: Pennekamp (Bering*GB) $8,482
Dam: Dashing Colours*Ire(Be My Native)
Br: McGregor Duncan A (Ire)
Tr: Clement Christophe (—) 2002:(190 44 .23)

L 121

Life	13	1	4	1	$53,967	90	
2002	2	0	2	0	$18,400	90	
2001	6	0	1	1	$16,673	–	
Sar Ⓣ	0	0	0	0	$0	–	
D.Fst	0	0	0	0	$0		
Wet(204*)	0	0	0	0	$0		
Turf(204*)	13	1	4	1	$53,967		
DstⓉ(244)	1	0	0	0	$2,996		

21Jun02-6Bel fm 1 Ⓣ :23 :454 1:093 1:341 3↑ ⒻAlw 46000N1X 90 3 76 76¼ 64½ 54¾ 2no Santos J A L121 *.80 89-15 Sandr'sSong121no Polyndry121½ *PrimeQueen*121hd Dug in gamely, missed

15May02-7Bel gd 1 1/16 Ⓣ :243 :491 1:133 1:432 3↑ ⒻAlw 46000N1X 90 5 103½ 84 62 2hd 2hd Santos J A L122 *2.00 81-22 Tarnished Lady115hd Polyandry122¾ **Miss Halory**1151 Came wide, gamely

Previously trained by Henri-Alex Pantall

21Aug01♦ Deauville(Fr) yl *1 Ⓣ Str 1:423 ⒻPrix de Lieurey (Listed) Stk 36300 12 Junk A 123 27.00 Shawara1233 Les Yeux Mauves123½ Five Fishes123nk
Timeform rating: 91 *Trailed,tracking leaders halfway,weakened 2f out.Love Roi*

4Aug01♦ Deauville(Fr) sf *1 Ⓣ RH 1:481 ⒻPrix de la Calonne (Listed) Stk 34900 73¾ Soumillon C 123 2.50 Canasita128nk Linea d'Ombra1231½ First1231½
Timeform rating: 97 *Towards rear,some late progress.Spaulwaki*

5Jly01♦ La Teste(Fr) yl *1 Ⓣ RH 1:392 ⒻPrix La Sorellina (Listed) Stk 30600 2nk Soumillon C 123 5.00 Ing Ing123nk Polyandry1232½ Spaulwaki123¾
Timeform rating: 99 *Tracked leader,led 1f out,headed near li*

8Jun01♦ M-Laffitte(Fr) sf *1 Ⓣ RH 1:424 ⒻPrix des Lilas (Listed) Stk 33700 3½ Soumillon C 123 11.00 Marque Royale123nk Ing Ing123nk Polyandry1232½
Timeform rating: 99 *Led,clear 1-1/2f out,headed 100y out,gamely.Winter Solstice*

4May01♦ Toulouse(Fr) sf *1¼ Ⓣ RH 2:08 ⒻPrix Caravelle (Listed) Stk 32700 45½ Soumillon C 123 – Luna Kya1232 Moon Queen1231½ Private Bluff1232
Timeform rating: 92 *Led to 1f out,weaken*

10Mar01♦ Saint-Cloud(Fr) hy *1 Ⓣ LH 2:542 ⒻPrix Ronde de Nuit (Listed) Stk 36800 45½ Soumillon C 121 6.70 L'Emeraude121½ Side of Paradise1215 Snataka121hd
Timeform rating: 92 *Led to over 1f out,lost 3rd on line.Linea d'Ombra*

14Nov00♦ Saint-Cloud(Fr) hy *1 Ⓣ LH 1:521 ⒻPrix Saint-Roman-G3 Stk 47600 56 Soumillon C 123 6.00 Perfect Plum1301 La Vita E Bella1232½ Blushing Bride1232½
Timeform rating: 92 *Rated in 5th,briefly 3rd 2f out,lost 4th on line.She'llBeFirst*

9Oct00♦ Lyon-Parilly(Fr) yl *1 Ⓣ LH 1:391 Criterium de Lyon (Listed) Stk 31700 2¾ Soumillon C 120 3.20 Casual Fame123¾ Polyandry1205 Verdi123½
Timeform rating: 99 *Tracked leaders,bid with winner,second best.Latina 5*

11Sep00♦ Chantilly(Fr) gd *1 Ⓣ RH 1:424 ⒻPrix d'Aumale-G3 Stk 47600 32¾ Soumillon C 121 7.00 Green Minstrel121¾ Winter Solstice1212 [D]Polyandry121½
Timeform rating: 99 *Trckd in 3rd,veered left 150y out.DQ'd,plcd 5th.Choc Ice plcd 3*

3Aug00♦ Deauville(Fr) yl *6f Ⓣ Str 1:122 Prix de Cabourg-G3 Stk 50300 52¼ Mosse G 120 7.00 Crystal Castle123½ Euribor123nk Lunasalt1231
Timeform rating: 94 *Towards rear,brief bid over 1f out,hung.Panis 4*

WORKS: Jly14 Bel 4f fst :49 B *14/49* Jly5 Bel 4f fst :491 B *13/31* Jun13 Bel 4f fst :494 B *18/25* Jun6 Bel 4f fst :50 B *8/15* May26 Bel 4f fst :491 B *24/51* May4 Bel 4f fst :492 B *30/73*

TRAINER: 31-60Days(164 .18 $1.34) Turf(429 .23 $1.70) Routes(471 .22 $1.64) Alw(231 .24 $1.74)

11. Cozie Advantage She had won her career debut at Saratoga by 3¾ lengths at 29-1 in a 1 1/16-mile maiden race on grass before switching barns from Gary Contessa to John Kimmel. In five grass starts for Kimmel, she had two seconds, a close third by half a length (finishing a head behind Supposedly) at 4-5, a fifth in a stakes, and a seventh. She was adding blinkers today. John Velazquez kept the mount.

11 Cozie Advantage
Own:Red Oak Stable
White, Red Dots And Collar, Red Sleeves,
VELAZQUEZ J R (—) 2002:(775 160 .21)

Ch. f. 3 (Apr) OBSMAR01 $75,000
Sire: Tactical Advantage (Forty Niner) $8,500
Dam: Cozie Keri(Meadowlake)
Br: Cashel Stud Inc (Fla)
Tr: Kimmel John C (—) 2002:(263 57 .22)

Blinkers ON

L 116

Life	7	1	2	1	$49,490	89	
2002	5	0	2	1	$22,970	89	
2001	2	1	0	0	$26,520	76	
Sar Ⓣ	1	1	0	0	$25,200	76	
D.Fst	0	0	0	0	$0		
Wet(335)	1	0	0	0	$1,320		
Turf(195)	6	1	2	1	$48,170		
DstⓉ(285)	2	0	1	1	$14,260		

7Jly02-4Bel fm 1¼ [T] :492 1:132 1:373 2:01 3↑ ⒻAlw 46000N1X 85 3 78¼ 68 42 42½ 3½ Velazquez J R L117 *.95 86-15 Terri's Toy122½ **Supposedly**117hd Cozie Advantage117hd Wide throughout

27May02-4Bel fm 1¼ [T] :494 1:132 1:372 2:014 3↑ ⒻAlw 46000N1X 89 1 66 65 34 33½ 2hd Velazquez J R L115 3.00 83-17 Duchcov121hd Cozie Advantage1151½ Sunstone1211 Game finish outside

7Apr02-7GP fm 1⅛ Ⓣ :491 1:132 1:364 1:482+ ⒻVia Borghese75k 75 3 75¾ 710 78 69 56½ Santos J A L116 10.40 86-17 CellarsShiraz1222 DameSylvieguilhem116hd KathyKD1182¾ Empty stretch

21Feb02-7GP fm *1 1/16 Ⓣ :243 :502 1:14 1:451 ⒻAlw 34000N1X 73 2 75 75½ 75¾ 98¼ 74½ Velazquez J R L117 *1.60 72-18 MnhttnSkyln121¾ AlwysContry119nk KtKrtz1171½ Steadied leaving chute

16Jan02-6GP fm *1 Ⓣ :24 :491 1:14 1:39 ⒻAlw 34000N1X 83 7 88¼ 77 76½ 31 22¾ Prado E S L117 2.80 75-24 PartyQueen1212¾ CozieAdvntge117hd SmrtGrce1172½ Svd grnd, up for 2nd

21Sep01-5Bel gd 1 ⊗ :231 :46 1:103 1:361 ⒻAlw 44000N1X 36 1 610 612 513 523 525¼ Arroyo N Jr 120 4.40 61-15 Riskaverse120nk Tempo West1187½ I Will Survive1184 Ducked in start

Previously trained by Contessa Gary C

24Aug01-6Sar fm 1 1/16 Ⓣ :224 :464 1:112 1:423 ⒻMd Sp Wt 42k 76 2 1012 1013 96¾ 2hd 13¾ Arroyo N Jr 118 29.25 83-17 CozieAdvntge1183¾ Don'tPennyMe118nk ReelLss1184½ 6 wide sweep, clear

WORKS: Jly19 Bel tr.t 4f fst :493 B *9/15* Jun30 Bel 5f fst 1:013 B *6/14* Jun23 Bel 4f fst :501 B *43/69* Jun12 Bel 4f fst :501 B *38/47* ●May23 Bel [T] 4f fm :48 B (d) *1/7* May17 Mth 5f fst 1:02 B *6/33*

TRAINER: 1stBlink(34 .03 $0.16) Turf(204 .17 $1.90) Routes(460 .20 $1.90) Alw(341 .24 $1.91)

12. Time for Faith The final 4-year-old in the field, she had raced just once since December, finishing a close fifth at 15-1 in an allowance race at Belmont Park.

12 Time For Faith	B. f. 4		Life 9 1 1 0 $41,430 86 / D.Fst 1 0 0 0 $0 35
Own:Literary Lion Farm	Sire: Gilded Time (Timeless Moment) $20,000		2002 1 0 0 0 $1,380 85 / Wet(360) 1 0 0 0 $1,230 48
Purple/orange Quarters, Orange	Dam: Beloved Bea(Personal Flag)	L 121	2001 6 1 1 0 $36,360 86 / Turf(265) 7 1 1 0 $40,200 86
RROYO N JR (—) 2002:(507 73 .14)	Br: Helen Brann & Flora Roberts (Ky)		Sar Ⓣ 1 1 0 0 $25,200 86 / DstⓉ(320) 1 0 0 0 $2,760 85
	Tr: O'Brien Leo (—) 2002:(88 8 .09)		

Jun02-8Bel fm	1	Ⓣ :231 :462 1:111 1:341 3↑	ⒻAlw 46000N1X	85	2	83½	85¼	72¾	53	51¾	Santos J A	L121	15.50	87–15	Ms. Rapunzel121¾ Prime Queen121no Hottentot115½	Good finish inside 10
Dec01-7Aqu fst	170	⊡ :234 :481 1:13 1:431 3↑	ⒻAlw 44000N1X	35	5	88¼	99¼	88¾	1020	1026¾	Rocco J S Jr	L117	15.30	51–23	*Rift Valley*1172 Rapunzell1162 Tomorrows Angel1172¼	Wide trip, tired 10
Nov01-6Aqu fm	1	Ⓣ :23 :473 1:131 1:372 3↑	ⒻAlw 44000N1X	76	8	922	917	96¼	86	64½	Santos J A	L116	3.60	86–14	Starboard Stinger1162½ Ready116nk T C Kiss116no	Inside, no impact 9
Oct01-9Bel fm	1	Ⓣ :233 :47 1:12 1:351 3↑	ⒻAlw 44000N1X	71	10	3½	31½	2hd	3½	97½	Espinoza J L	L118	5.80	74–18	Vespers116½ *Lngoureuse*1161¾ AmericnDremer1162	Bumped start, 3 wide 10
Oct01-7Bel fm	1¼	Ⓣ :471 1:122 1:371 2:011 3↑	ⒻAlw 46000N2X	85	2	47	49½	52¼	31½	43½	Velazquez J R	L116	5.40	81–15	Alida116¾ Bring Plenty1161½ Speed Of Thought1211¼	Inside trip, no rally 6
Aug01-9Sar fm	1⅛	Ⓣ :474 1:122 1:373 1:494 3↑	ⒻMd Sp Wt 42k	86	10	82¾	73½	51½	1hd	12¾	Velazquez J R	L117	*2.20	87–14	Time ForFaith1172¾ Atherbest117½ *FiveToFour*1178½	3 wide move, driving 12
Jly01-1Bel fm	1	Ⓣ :231 :47 1:104 1:344 3↑	ⒻMd Sp Wt 42k	81	7	73½	41½	21	21½	21¾	Velazquez J R	L117	5.00	82–12	PicturePalce1171¾ *TimeForFith*1176¾ Atherbest1173¼	4 wide move, gamely 9
Aug00-2Sar my	6½f	:214 :453 1:12 1:19	ⒻMd Sp Wt 41k	48	7	1	65½	53½	55½	511¾	Smith M E	118	5.80	67–19	WeekendGold1182¼ CocktilSuce1182 WesternJustice1182½	4 wide run turn 7
Jly00-2Bel fm	6f	Ⓣ :221 :451 :564 1:083	ⒻMd Sp Wt 41k	65	9	6	611	79¾	79¾	46¾	Velazquez J R	117	18.50	94–02	MarqOfBeuty117no *Killistos*1175¾ RuthlessLdy1171	Some interest outside 9

ORKS: Jly18 Bel 5f fst 1:033 B *11/13* May21 Bel 4f fst :494 B *27/47* May5 Bel 4f fst :50 B *44/67*
RAINER: 31-60Days(71 .14 $1.76) Turf(202 .12 $2.34) Routes(243 .11 $2.01) Alw(134 .12 $2.08)

The selections? Dynamic Lady, Bluebird Day, Risotto, Hangingbyamoment, and Time for Faith seemed overmatched. The jockey switch from Prado to Carrero made Another Storm unattractive. Polyandry fit the profile of an overbet chronic loser with her 1-for-13 grass record.

FIFTH RACE
Saratoga
JULY 24, 2002

1⅜ MILES. (Turf)(1.513) ALLOWANCE. Purse $48,000. (Up To $9,312 NYSBFOA) For Fillies and Mares Three Years Old And Upward Which Have Never Won A Race Other Than Maiden, Claiming, Or Starter Or Which Have Never Won Two Races. Three Year Olds 118 lbs.; Older 123 lbs. Non-winners of a race at a mile or over on the turf since June 12 allowed, 2 lbs. (Races where entered for $50,000 or less not considered in allowances). (Preference by condition eligibility). (Registered New York Breds allowed 3 lbs.).

Value of Race: $48,000 Winner $28,800; second $9,600; third $5,280; fourth $2,880; fifth $1,440. Mutuel Pool $597,915.00 Exacta Pool $597,690.00 Trifecta Pool $392,403.00

Last Raced	Horse	M/Eqt.	A.Wt	PP	St	¼	½	¾	Str	Fin	Jockey	Odds $1
26Jun02 4Bel1	Wonder Again	L	3 118	5	3	3½	3½	4hd	31½	1nk	Prado E S	9.60
28Jun02 5Bel1	Showlady	L	3 118	6	4	5½	4½	3½	1hd	22	Bailey J D	2.45
7Jly02 4Bel2	Supposedly	b	3 116	4	2	7½	71½	5hd	22½	31¾	Castellano J J	17.80
21Jun02 6Bel2	Polyandry-IR	L	4 121	10	7	101½	9hd	7½	4½	4½	Santos J A	4.60
9Jun02 7CD2	Boana-GE	L	4 121	7	12	115	113	10½	5½	53¾	Meche D J	3.50
7Jly02 4Bel3	Cozie Advantage	Lb	3 116	11	11	9hd	8hd	8hd	7hd	6nk	Velazquez J R	8.00
20Jun02 7Bel7	Dynamic Lady	Lb	3 116	1	9	12	12	12	106	7½	Bridgmohan S X	53.25
12Jun02 6Bel7	Bluebird Day-IR	L	3 116	3	1	4hd	6hd	91½	9½	82	Samyn J L	29.00
20Jun02 7Bel10	Hangingbyamoment	L	3 116	9	5	22½	2½	2hd	8hd	9½	Chavez J F	45.75
9May02 5Pim4	Risotto	L	3 116	8	6	11	12	1½	6hd	101½	Day P	26.25
20Jun02 7Bel4	Another Storm	L	3 111	2	8	8hd	102	112½	118	1114	Carrero V5	11.50
5Jun02 8Bel5	Time For Faith	L	4 121	12	10	6½	5hd	6½	12	12	Arroyo N Jr	28.50

OFF AT 3:09 Start Good. Won driving. Course yielding.
TIME :231, :482, 1:131, 1:38, 1:553 (:23.31, :48.42, 1:13.27, 1:38.13, 1:55.69)

$2 Mutuel Prices:			
6–WONDER AGAIN	21.20	8.50	6.50
1–SHOWLADY		4.50	3.80
5–SUPPOSEDLY			9.40

$2 EXACTA 6–1 PAID $74.00 $2 TRIFECTA 6–1–5 PAID $738.00

B. f, (Feb), by Silver Hawk–Ameriflora, by Danzig. Trainer Toner James J. Bred by Phillips Racing Partnership & John Phillips (Ky).

WONDER AGAIN raced close up inside while in hand, saved ground, angled out entering the stretch, responded when roused, finished strongly from the outside and was along in time, driving. SHOWLADY raced close up in hand, advanced three wide on the second turn, reached the front nearing the stretch, turned back a bid from SUPPOSEDLY in midstretch then dug in gamely but could not hold off the winner late. SUPPOSEDLY was rated along between rivals, put in a three wide run turning for home and weakened in the final furlong. POLYANDRY (IRE) was rated along while between rivals, came wide approaching the stretch and lacked a solid finishing kick. BOANA (GER) was outrun early, put in a wide run on the second turn and had little left for the stretch run. COZIE ADVANTAGE was outrun early, put in a five wide run on the second turn and had nothing left for the drive. DYNAMIC LADY was outrun early, came wide into the stretch and offered a mild rally outside. BLUEBIRD DAY (IRE) was rated along inside and had no rally. HANGINGBYAMOMENT raced with the pace from the outside and tired in the stretch. RISOTTO quickly showed in front, set the pace for three quarters and tired. ANOTHER STORM had no rally. TIME FOR FAITH chased four wide and tired.

Owners— 1, Phillips Joan G & John W; 2, al Maktoum Mohammed b; 3, Lerman Roy S; 4, de Rothschild Edouard; 5, Tanaka Gary A; 6, Red Oak Stable; 7, C K Woods Stable; 8, Humphrey G W Jr; 9, Flying Zee Stable; 10, Augustin Stable; 11, Alnoff Stable; 12, Literary Lion Farm

Trainers—1, Toner James J; 2, McLaughlin Kiaran P; 3, Lerman Roy S; 4, Clement Christophe; 5, Asmussen Steven M; 6, Kimmel John C; 7, Badgett William Jr; 8, Arnold George R II; 9, Serpe Philip M; 10, Sheppard Jonathan E; 11, Bond Harold James; 12, O'Brien Leo

Scratched— Colonella (3Jly02 6MTH1), Wishful Splendor (5Jly02 6BEL5), Miss Halory (4Jly02 6BEL5), Dubai Fall (22Jun02 10MTH2)

Given Toner's talent for developing grass fillies, Wonder Again made absolute sense among the remaining five contenders. She had beaten Showlady and been favored over her in their one encounter and won her last start emphatically despite an outside post and a wide trip. Supposedly had stepped up dramatically in her last start, but didn't show any works, always a concern. Showlady was an obvious threat, but would offer little betting value thanks to Bailey. I picked Wonder Again first, Supposedly second, and Showlady third. I made Cozie Advantage my saver.

The odds? Wonder Again had gone off at 7-2 and Showlady 7-1 when Wonder Again beat her at Belmont. At Saratoga this day, Showlady went off at 2-1 and Wonder Again at 9-1. Supposedly was 17-1. Wonder Again won by 2½ lengths and paid $21.20. Showlady finished second and Supposedly third. The exacta paid $74 and the triple $738. The triple would obviously have been much higher had Supposedly run second and Showlady third.

ANOTHER NEW YORK TRAINER who is sometimes underplayed at the windows is Hall of Famer Phil "P.G." Johnson, as good a grass trainer as there is. "I like to run horses on turf," he said. "They last longer and it's safer."

P.G. has his own theory about grass racing, one that contrasts with a couple popular conceptions. "A lot of people say horses like to turf because they don't like getting dirt in the eye on the main track," he said. "That's a fallacy. In our dry summers, when we race horses on turf, we have to wash their eyes after a race. Those grass clods come back and hit them in the eye. Any trainer will tell you that's the truth. And, as far as the conformation of the feet, I don't buy into that much."

P.G. has studied turf races on film. He said, "In super slow motion, a horse extends on dirt so much that when his front foot hits the ground, the pastern flexes and the ankle drops and practically hits the ground. Then the feet will slide an inch or two forward before his next stride. Racing on dirt does two things. It tends to make the horse use more energy to get the foot back in the air, so it tires him quicker or discourages him quicker. Number two, if a horse has any ligament problem, the overflexion of those joints could bring on the pain sooner.

"Then the horse gets on turf. When his hoof hits the ground, there is hardly any slide forward. Consequently, there's less flexion and less extension, so his foot gets back in action sooner. It helps the horse who loses his confidence from the first situation on dirt. It's like you're running in deep sand on the beach. It's a real strain. If you see a horse showing speed on the dirt and backing off for no reason, when that horse makes his first appearance on turf, I'd be very interested. He may improve a lot."

Long before the world discovered Volponi, Johnson's 43-1 romping winner in the $4 million Breeders' Cup Classic on dirt in 2002, the son of Cryptoclearance showed considerable talent on turf. He remains one of the few contempory horses in North America who have won graded stakes on both grass and dirt.

olponi
n: Amherst Stable & Spruce Pond Stable

B. c. 4 (Apr)
Sire: Cryptoclearance (Fappiano) $20,000
Dam: Prom Knight(Sir Harry Lewis)
Br: Amherst Stable (Ky)
Tr: Johnson Philip G (—) 2002:(162 21 .13)

126

Life	22	6	7	3	$668,976	113	D.Fst	13	4	5	1	$379,670	113
2002	7	2	3	1	$309,200	110	Wet(335)	0	0	0	0	$0	–
2001	10	3	2	0	$266,176	113	Turf(225)	9	2	2	2	$289,306	110
AP	0	0	0	0	$0	–	Dst(205)	1	0	0	0	$0	93

t02-8Med	fst	1⅛		:464 1:102 1:353 1:484	3↑ Med Cup H-G2	106	3	64¾	66	62¼	31½	2¾	Bridgmohan S X	L 116	*2.10	82-19	Burning Roma115¾ Volponi1161¼ Windsor Castle112nk	6wd bid,closed	9
p02-6Bel	fm	1⅛	T	:481 1:112 1:35 1:463	3↑ Belmont BCH-G2	103	2	11½	1½	1½	1½	2¾	Santos J A	L 117	*.85	95-06	Startac116¾ Volponi1172 Dr. Kashnikow1151¼	Set pace, gamely	6
g02-9Sar	fm	1½	T	:471 1:113 2:002 2:24	3↑ SwordDancrH-G1	106	3	21½	2½	1hd	21	32	Santos J A	L 115	8.70	110-06	*With Anticipation*120hd *Denon*1181¾ Volponi115nk	Stayed on gamely	11
y02-8Sar	fm	1⅛	T	:484 1:124 1:362 1:482	3↑ B Baruch H-G2	109	1	11	1½	1½	2½	2nk	Bridgmohan S X	L 116	3.25	96-17	DelMrShow120nk Volponi116no ForbiddenApple1212	Set pace, gamely rail	7
y02-8Bel	fm	1	(T)	:224 :451 1:081 1:321	3↑ Poker H-G3	110	4	32½	31½	3½	2hd	12¼	Bridgmohan S X	L 115	9.30	99-05	Volponi1152¼ Saint Verre112nk Navesink117¾	Speed 3 wide, driving	7
y02-8Bel	fst	1		:224 :451 1:091 1:343	4↑ Alw 56000N$mY	95	2	42	42½	42¾	47½	47	Bridgmohan S X	L 123 b	*.40	89-18	OpenSesm116½ WildSummr1163¾ CountryBGold1162¾	4 wide, no response	7
y02-6Bel	fst	7f		:23 :452 1:093 1:222	4↑ Alw 54000C	105	5	3	2½	2½	12½	11	Bridgmohan S X	L 121 b	*.85	91-15	Volponi1211 Cherokee Beau1173½ *Tarek*1155	Speed outside, driving	5
w01-8Aqu	fst	1		:232 :453 1:092 1:331	3↑ Cigar MileH-G1	108	8	5¾	41¾	52½	54	45	Bridgmohan S X	L 115 b	5.60	96-16	*Left Bank*1203¼ Graeme Hall118hd Red Bullet1181¾	Bumped start, chased	9
t01-8Med	fst	1⅛		:451 1:084 1:34 1:462	Pegasus H-G2	113	2	42¼	42	41½	2hd	12¾	Bridgmohan S X	L 114 b	4.10	95-14	Volponi1142¾ BurningRoma119½ GiantGentlemn1169½	Duel,clear final 1/16	6
t01-2Bel	fst	1		:234 :463 1:11 1:361	3↑ Alw 46000N2X	108	4	2½	2½	2½	1½	13¾	Bridgmohan S X	L 116 fb	1.50	86-21	*Volponi*1163¾ Pure Prize1202¼ Harley Quinn11911	Bumped start, driving	5
p01-5Bel	fst	1 1/16		:23 :451 1:094 1:431	3↑ Alw 46000N2X	93	6	53¼	42	4¾	2hd	2no	Migliore R	L 118 b	*.80	81-14	*Dayton Flyer*116no *Volponi*1185 Even TheScore118¾	Bumped start, 4 wide	7
g01-10Sar	fst	1¼		:473 1:111 1:354 2:012	Travers-G1	93	2	84	87	76½	715	716½	Migliore R	L 126 b	13.70	81-02	Point Given1263½ **E Dubai**1261¼ ***Dollar Bill***126¾	Wide, no response	9
y01-9Sar	fst	1⅛		:472 1:114 1:354 1:482	3↑ Alw 44000N1X	110	3	52	41½	3nk	110	113½	Migliore R	L 116 b	*2.70	99-01	Volponi11613 Personable Pete1161¼ Carefree1203	Quick 3 wide move	12
y01-8Bel	fm	1¼	T	:473 1:111 1:343 1:584	Lexington-G3	88	2	44½	57	64¾	67¾	45¾	Samyn J L	L 118	7.50	91-12	ShrpPrfrmnc1141 PckgStr1144¼ Whtmr'sCnn114½	Between rivals stretch	8
n01-7Bel	fm	1⅛	T	:474 1:113 1:354 1:481	Hill Prince-G3	92	2	66	75	85½	44	42	Samyn J L	L 120	6.60	86-18	Proud Man122nk Package Store114hd *Navesink*1181¾	Shuffl back far turn	10
y01-8Haw	fm	1⅛	(T)	:503 1:151 1:39 1:502	Haw Derby-G3	84	4	21	21	21	43½	54½	Velazquez J R	L 113	2.30	79-15	Kalu119¾ *Proud Man*1191 Rahy's Secret1151½	Tired	7
r01-7Aqu	fst	6½f		:223 :454 1:094 1:16	3↑ Alw 43000N1X	83	6	5	55	54	26	25¼	Samyn J L	L 115	7.90	91-09	Stake Runner1155¼ Volponi1152¾ Home Silver121¾	Game finish for place	8
t00-9Bel	fm	1⅛	T	:464 1:114 1:36 1:48	Pilgrim-G3	90	7	78	74¾	61¾	1½	12	Velazquez J R	L 115	9.90	88-16	Volponi1152 Baptize1224¼ Strategic Partner1151¼	Quick outside move	10
t00-6Bel	fst	6f		:223 :453 :57 1:102	Md Sp Wt 41k	74	7	6	84¾	73½	45½	34¼	Samyn J L	L 118 b	*1.65	82-17	LittlBoldSwp1183½ TurnBckThTim118¾ *Volpon*1183¼	Inside move, gamely	9
p00-3Bel	fst	1		:224 :462 1:113 1:371	Md Sp Wt 42k	69	4	52	41½	43	39	29	Samyn J L	L 120	*1.55	70-19	Dayton Flyer1209 Volponi1206½ Broad Initiative120½	Second best	9
g00-2Sar	fst	7f		:221 :452 1:114 1:252	Md Sp Wt 41k	73	8	2	66	55¾	22½	22	Samyn J L	L 118	*2.70	76-19	Hero'sTribute1182 Volponi1184¾ BroadInititive1183¾	Game finish outside	9
y00-2Bel	fm	6f	(T)	:22 :453 :574 1:102	Md Sp Wt 41k	59	2	7	78	86¾	54½	31	Velazquez J R	L 117	*1.15	91-06	*Baptize*117no Heroic Sight1171 Volponi1171¼	Came wide, game finish	12

RKS: Oct15 **Bel tr.t 4f fst :48 B** *2/179* ●Oct2 **Bel tr.t 3f fst :36 B** *1/14* ●Sep24 **Bel 5f fst :593 B** *1/9* ●Sep7 **Bel 6f fst 1:134 B** *1/6* Sep1 **Bel 5f fst 1:004 B** *3/13* Aug27 **Sar tr.t 4f fst :501 B** *7/37*
INER: Dirt(161 .09 $1.41) Routes(233 .12 $1.45) GrdStk(14 .14 $2.20)

Volponi began his career on grass as a 2-year-old, July 14th, 2000, at Belmont Park. Sent off the 1.15-1 favorite in a six-furlong maiden race, Volponi closed powerfully from eighth to finish third by a length to Baptize, a subsequent multiple grass stakes winner who earned more than half a million dollars.

After running second twice and third once on dirt, Volponi was put back on grass in a demanding spot, the Grade 3 Pilgrim Stakes at Belmont Park at $1\frac{1}{8}$ miles, an eighth of a mile longer than his longest dirt race. Normally, a maiden appearing in a graded stakes might be viewed skeptically, but P.G. didn't get into the Hall of Fame by putting his horses in spots that are ridiculously over their heads. And the betting reflected that. In the field of 10, Volponi went off at 9-1. Under John Velazquez, Volponi made a powerful move on the turn and drew off to win by two lengths, paying $21.80.

As a 3-year-old, Volponi made three consecutive grass starts in Grade 3 stakes, finishing fifth in the Hawthorne Derby and fourth in the Hill Prince and Lexington. Switched back to dirt, Volponi won four of his next eight starts, including the Grade 2 Pegasus Handicap at The Meadowlands by $2\frac{3}{4}$ lengths under Shaun Bridgmohan.

After sustaining a minor injury during his second start as a 4-year-old when he finished fourth at 2-5 in an allowance race at Belmont Park, May 30, 2002, Volponi came back five weeks later in the Grade 3 Poker Handicap on grass at one mile at Belmont. Sent off again at 9-1, Volponi ran the best race of his life, winning by $2\frac{1}{4}$ lengths under Bridgmohan after running a mile in a sensational $1:32\frac{1}{5}$, earning a 110 Beyer Speed Figure. He paid $20.60.

In his next start, at Saratoga, Volponi ran a huge race, finishing second by a neck at 3-1 in the Grade 2 Bernard Baruch Handicap to Del Mar Show, a nose ahead of multiple graded stakes winner Forbidden Apple.

Volponi raced twice more on grass before last year's Breeders' Cup, finishing third by two lengths at 8-1 to With Anticipation in the $1\frac{1}{2}$-mile, Grade 1 Sword Dancer Handicap at Saratoga and second by three-quarters of a length to Startac in the Grade 2 Belmont Breeders' Cup Handicap as the 4-5 favorite.

That gave Volponi a turf record of two wins, two seconds, and two thirds in nine grass starts. He'd lost at odds of 4-5, 1-1, 2-1, 6-1, 7-1, and 8-1 and won twice at 9-1.

What happens when a grass horse changes trainers? Usually, you'd be hard pressed to find a positive change on any horse leaving the barn of Hall of Fame trainer D. Wayne Lukas. But everything is relative. Lukas is a solid turf trainer, but Bill Mott is the absolute best.

So when the powerful closer Zafonic's Song showed up for a nonwinners-of-three allowance race at Saratoga on August 12, 2001, showing a change from Lukas to Mott, you would have been inclined to believe the odds would drop. But when you also factor in a jockey change from Jorge Chavez, who is good on grass, to Bailey, who is No. 1, you'd think Zafonic's Song would be absolutely pounded at the windows. Then factor in that he was stretching out from 1¼ miles in his last start at Belmont Park to 1½ miles at Saratoga.

In his previous start in the same class, at 1¼ miles at Belmont, he was bet down to 4-5 and finished seventh by 5¼ lengths.

At Saratoga, he went off at 4.40-1. Despite getting checked on the second turn, he won by a neck, paying $10.80.

SEVENTH RACE
Saratoga
AUGUST 12, 2001

1½ MILES. (Inner Turf)(2.23^1) ALLOWANCE. Purse $46,000. (Up To $8,924 NYSBFOA). For Three Year Olds And Upward Which Have Never Won Two Races Other Than Maiden, Claiming, Starter, Or Restricted Or Which Have Never Won Three Races. Three Year Olds 118 lbs.; Older 122 lbs. Non-winners of $26,000 over a mile since June 29 allowed, 2 lbs. (Races where entered for $60,000 or less not considered in allowances). (Preference by condition eligibility).

Value of Race: $46,000 Winner $27,600; second $9,200; third $5,060; fourth $2,760; fifth $1,380. Mutuel Pool $785,560.00 Exacta Pool $713,102.00 Trifecta Pool $478,913.00

Last Raced	Horse	M/Eqt.	A.Wt	PP	¼	½	1	1¼	Str	Fin	Jockey	Odds $1
21Jly01 ^{7}Bel^7	Zafonic's Song-FR	L	4 120	4	$8^{1\frac{1}{2}}$	$8^{3\frac{1}{2}}$	$2^{\frac{1}{2}}$	$1^{\frac{1}{2}}$	1^2	1^{nk}	Bailey J D	4.40
1Jly01 ^{4}WO^4	Lodge Hill	L	4 120	7	7^3	$6^{\frac{1}{2}}$	$6^{2\frac{1}{2}}$	$3^{\frac{1}{2}}$	$3^{1\frac{1}{2}}$	$2^{2\frac{1}{4}}$	Migliore R	3.75
4Jly01 ^{9}Hol^7	Glyndebourne-IR	Lb	4 120	1	$3^{\frac{1}{2}}$	$4^{3\frac{1}{2}}$	$5^{\frac{1}{2}}$	$6^{1\frac{1}{2}}$	$4^{\frac{1}{2}}$	3^{nk}	Prado E S	2.75
3Aug01 ^{10}Cnl^1	Mcdynamo	L	4 120	5	$2^{1\frac{1}{2}}$	$2^{1\frac{1}{2}}$	$3^{1\frac{1}{2}}$	2^{hd}	2^{hd}	$4^{\frac{1}{2}}$	Day P	11.10
18Jly01 ^{7}Bel^1	Jeeves		3 118	10	4^{hd}	$5^{1\frac{1}{2}}$	7^1	7^2	5^1	5^4	Arroyo N Jr	11.30
9Jly01 ^{3}Crc^2	Alkarnak	L	4 120	11	$6^{1\frac{1}{2}}$	$7^{\frac{1}{2}}$	$10^{5\frac{1}{2}}$	$9^{\frac{1}{2}}$	8^{hd}	6^{hd}	Chavez J F	37.25
4Aug01 ^{10}Sar^1	Top C Jim	L	5 120	2	11	10^{hd}	8^{hd}	$10^{2\frac{1}{2}}$	10^6	7^{nk}	Castellano J J	21.60
22Jly01 ^{3}Del^7	Blue Goblin	Lf	7 120	3	$9^{\frac{1}{2}}$	9^2	$9^{1\frac{1}{2}}$	$5^{\frac{1}{2}}$	$6^{2\frac{1}{2}}$	$8^{1\frac{1}{2}}$	Rocco J S Jr	36.25
16Jly01 ^{4}Del^3	Addinson	Lb	5 120	9	$5^{\frac{1}{2}}$	3^{hd}	4^{hd}	$8^{\frac{1}{2}}$	9^{hd}	9^3	Samyn J L	20.00
10Dec00 ^{6}Hol^1	Quiet One	Lb	5 120	8	1^{hd}	$1^{1\frac{1}{2}}$	1^{hd}	$4^{1\frac{1}{2}}$	7^{hd}	$10^{\frac{3}{4}}$	Velazquez J R	5.30
29Jly01 ^{8}Sar^5	Papa M And M	L	3 116	6	10^1	11	11	11	11	11	Guidry M	24.25

OFF AT 4:18 Start Good. Won driving. Course good.
TIME :24^3, :48^3, 1:13^4, 1:39^1, 2:03^3, 2:28^3 (:24.61, :48.73, 1:13.99, 1:39.25, 2:03.73, 2:28.73)

$2 Mutuel Prices:			
4-ZAFONIC'S SONG-FR	10.80	5.10	3.50
7-LODGE HILL		4.50	3.30
2-GLYNDEBOURNE-IR			3.30

$2 EXACTA 4-7 PAID $48.40 $2 TRIFECTA 4-7-2 PAID $158.00

Dk. b. or br. c, by Zafonic–Savoureuse Lady*GB, by Caerleon. Trainer Mott William I. Bred by Du Mezeray Har. (Fr).

ZAFONIC'S SONG (FR) was rated inside, was checked hard along the inside on the second turn, advanced quickly from the outside, drew clear in the stretch then dug in and held off LODGE HILL under a drive. LODGE HILL was rated along inside, rallied three wide on the second turn and finished gamely outside. GLYNDEBOURNE (IRE) was rated along inside, saved ground and stayed on well through the stretch. MCDYNAMO raced with the pace and stayed on stubbornly through the stretch. JEEVES put in a run along the inside on the final turn, came wide into the stretch and finished well outside. ALKARNAK raced wide and had no rally. TOP C JIM raced wide throughout and had no rally. BLUE GOBLIN had no response when roused. ADDINSON chased outside and tired. QUIET ONE raced with the pace and tired after one mile. PAPA M AND M was outrun.

Owners— 1, Padua Stables; 2, Eugene Melnyk Laura Melnyk & Iris B; 3, Liang Dr Thomas T S; 4, Moran Michael J; 5, Parsons William & Howe David S Jr; 6, Buckram Oak Farm; 7, Ingrassia John A & O'Reilly Patrici; 8, Thomas Theresa; 9, Hudson River Farms; 10, Goldfarb Sanford; 11, Conway Dee

Trainers—1, Mott William I; 2, England Phillip; 3, Biancone Patrick L; 4, Moran Michael J; 5, O'Brien Leo; 6, Moubarak Mohammed; 7, Nevin Michael; 8, Thomas Teresa; 9, Sheppard Jonathan E; 10, Dutrow Richard E Jr; 11, Zito Nicholas P

Scratched— Doubly Devious (22Jly01 ^{9}BEL^5)

$2 Pick Three (11-2-4) Paid $783.00; Pick Three Pool $120,640.

Here are the grass records of America's top trainers:

TRAINER	RECORD	PERCENTAGE
Frank Alexander	17-105	16.19
Tom Amoss	92-433	21.24
Joe Aquilino	4-42	9.52
*George Arnold	17-128	13.28
Steve Asmussen	124-857	14.46
Leo Azpurua	8-100	8.00
Billy Badgett	21-152	13.81
Bob Baffert	53-318	16.66
Bobby Barbara	16-114	14.03
Patrick Biancone	6-95	6.31
*Jim Bond	16-84	19.04
Frank Brothers	26-192	13.54
Julio Canani	60-300	20.00
Dale Capuano	57-325	17.53
Gary Capuano	9-43	20.93
*Del Carroll	4-36	11.11
*Richard Ciardullo	19-72	26.38
Christophe Clemente	176-808	21.78
Gary Contessa	41-358	11.45
Buddy Delp	16-86	18.60
Laura De Seroux	13-87	14.94
*Craig Dollase	15-94	15.95
*Wally Dollase	18-86	20.93
*David Donk	12-95	12.63
Neil Drysdale	95-450	21.11
Anthony Dutrow	6-39	15.38
Richard Dutrow Jr.	16-128	12.50
Ron Ellis	27-133	20.30
*Scott Everett	3-18	16.66
Bernie Flint	19-134	14.17
Steve Flint	9-46	19.56

Bobby Frankel	220-890	24.71
Dominic Galluscio	9-86	10.46
Phil Gleaves	8-76	10.52
*John Glenney	8-46	17.39
Mike Gorham	8-126	6.34
*Phil Hauswald	7-71	9.85
Bruce Headley	0-19	0.00
Mark Hennig	32-343	9.32
*Timothy Hills	26-160	16.25
Jerry Hollendorfer	79-558	14.15
Stanley Hough	15-83	18.07
Neil Howard	25-123	20.32
Mike Hushion	11-102	10.78
Alan Iwinski	30-258	11.62
Allen Jerkens	18-140	12.85
James Jerkens	13-78	16.66
Phil Johnson	35-263	13.30
*David Kassen	5-28	17.85
*Pat Kelly	4-82	4.87
John Kimmel	48-351	13.67
Frank Laboccetta Jr.	1-13	7.69
Scott Lake	46-274	16.78
Bruce Levine	7-118	8.47
*D. Wayne Lukas	16-85	18.82
Richard Mandella	95-493	19.26
*Dennis Manning	7-63	11.11
Greg Martin	1-24	4.16
*Michael Matz	15-102	14.70
Ron McAnally	66-579	11.39
Shug McGaughey	18-149	12.08
Kenny McPeek	28-220	12.72
*Kathy Mongeon	2-34	5.88
Graham Motion	72-380	18.94
Bill Mott	234-1,061	22.05

Jeff Mullins	30-138	21.73
*Leo O'Brien	9-134	6.71
Niall O'Callaghan	19-248	7.66
Joe Orseno	10-103	9.70
Jennifer Pedersen	1-25	4.00
Larry Pilotti	6-45	22.22
Todd Pletcher	114-607	18.78
*Ed Plesa Jr.	18-147	12.24
Faustino Ramos	2-31	6.45
Anthony Reinstedler	12-127	9.44
Pat Reynolds	16-132	12.12
Timothy Ritvo	34-322	10.55
Dale Romans	36-278	12.94
Jenine Sahadi	49-295	16.61
John Salzman	15-115	13.04
*Randy Schulhofer	23-92	25.00
Gary Sciacca	58-585	9.91
Mark Shuman	7-87	8.04
*Ron Spatz	5-95	5.26
Albert Stall	40-284	14.08
Dallas Stewart	27-234	11.53
*Howie Tesher	0-26	0.00
Billy Turner	9-64	14.06
*Harvey Vanier	10-96	10.41
Darrell Vienna	45-283	15.90
Elliott Walden	75-393	19.08
*Kelly Walsh	2-43	4.65
*William White	13-112	11.60
Ralph Ziade	38-323	11.76
Nick Zito	6-107	5.60

Source: *DRF Simulcast Weekly* (March 20, 2000, through March 19, 2003)

Daily Racing Form (January 1, 2002, through March 19, 2003)

8

YOUNG AND IMPROVING

SOME HANDICAPPERS DISDAIN MAIDEN or first-level allowance races. I can't get enough of them, especially on grass, where you can frequently rule out more horses with no chance in a race and cash in by identifying ideal situations for trainers who routinely win with young horses in maiden races and/or maiden winners moving up to nonwinners of two. Wonder Again, who was profiled in Chapter 7, was a perfect example.

Here's another from a filly who faced Wonder Again in the summer of 2002. Sobrina del Rey had an awful lot going for her when she stepped into the gate for her second American start, a maiden grass race at $1\frac{1}{16}$ miles at Belmont Park, July 3, 2002.

The 4-year-old filly, now being trained by Angel Penna Jr., was imported from Chile, where she had finished second in 4 of 5 starts in 2001. In her last race as a 3-year-old, she was entered in a $29,400 Grade 1 race. She finished second by $1\frac{3}{4}$ lengths at 37.40-1 in a field of 18, quite a performance for a 3-year-old filly making her fifth lifetime start and stretching out to $1^1/_{16}$ miles for the first time.

Brought to the United States, she made her 4-year-old debut for Penna in a $1^1/_8$-mile maiden race at Belmont Park under Edgar Prado, May 31. Sent off at 5-to-1 from post 8 in a field of nine, she raced three wide, as indicated by her comment line, and finished a late-tiring third by $3^1/_4$ lengths. The second-place finisher was none other than Wonder Again, who then came back to win a maiden race on June 26 at Belmont by $3^1/_4$ lengths at 7-5.

If that was not enough inducement to back Sobrina del Rey in her second U.S. start, consider that she was cutting back a sixteenth of mile in distance. Prado was back on board off a fantastic work-out on dirt. On June 29 at Belmont, she breezed four furlongs in $47^2/_5$ seconds, the second-fastest of 95 workouts at that distance that day.

Her odds? How about 5.30-1? She was actually the fourth choice that day. She won by a length to pay $12.60.

For another example, let's take a look at this nonwinners-of-two allowance for fillies and mares at about $1^1/_{16}$ miles on the grass at Gulfstream Park, the ninth race on January 17, 2003. Scratches left a field of 10. In post-position order:

1. **Hydration** She'd raced four times for trainer Thomas Proctor. Her first two starts were on dirt at Arlington Park and Gulfstream Park and they were dreadful: 10th by $17^1/_4$ lengths at 10-1 and seventh by $28^1/_4$ lengths at 30-1, respectively. But then Proctor sent her to Tampa Bay Downs and put her on grass. The daughter of Unbridled out of Good Picker, by Damascus, was bet down to 4.40-1 and romped wire to wire by $3^1/_4$ lengths. The result was typical of Proctor's success on grass. He had won with an astounding 24 percent of his 46 starters, according to the trainer stats in the *Daily Racing Form*.

    Hydration was then off exactly nine months, returning in a six-furlong dirt allowance race at Tampa Bay. Though she'd shown nothing on dirt previously, she was fourth at 9-2.

1 Hydration Ch. f. 4 (May)
Own:Glen Hill Farm Sire: Unbridled (Fappiano)
Red Orange & Black Halves, White Belt, Black Dam:Good Picker(Damascus)
Br: Glen Hill Farm (Ky)
FIRES E (4 0 0 1 .00) 2002:(382 43 .11) Tr: Proctor Thomas F(3 2 0 0 .67) 2002:(132 34 .26)
L 117

Life 4 1 0 0 $6,570 66 | D.Fst 3 0 0 0 $870 46
2002 3 1 0 0 $6,570 66 | Wet(400) 0 0 0 0 $0 –
2001 1 M 0 0 $0 37 | Turf(270) 1 1 0 0 $5,700 66
GP Ⓣ 0 0 0 0 $0 – | DstⓉ(340) 1 1 0 0 $5,700 66

19Dec02-7Tam fst 6f :222 :453 :582 1:12 3↑ⒻAlw 11000N2L 46 3 1 42½ 56½ 57½ 48 Castanon J L L 116 4.80 82-13 Rahab1182½ Story Book Love1161½ SisterPonche1164 Well placed, no rally 10
19Mar02-4Tam fm 1 1/16 Ⓣ :231 :474 1:124 1:432 ⒻMd Sp Wt 9k 66 7 11 11 13 16 13¼ Castanon J L L 120 4.40 81-18 Hydration1203¼ *Supposedly*1201½ *Something Ventured*1202½ Ridden out 10
17Feb02-5GP fst 6f :223 :47 :593 1:123 ⒻMd Sp Wt 32k 16 3 3 63½ 85¾ 816 728¼ Fires E L 121 30.10 48-21 In Full Bloom1211¼ Pieria1212½ Witch Tradition1216¾ Outrun 8
31Aug01-9AP fst 6f :224 :464 :59 1:111 ⒻMd Sp Wt 38k 37 5 5 84¼ 94¾ 912 1017¼ Fires E L 119 10.50 73-12 Argentina1192 Leeward City119¾ *Flick*1198½ Outrun 10
WORKS: Jan7 Tam 5f fst 1:034 B *4/11* Jan1 Tam 4f my :484 B *1/2* Dec11 Tam 5f gd 1:041 Bg *7/11* Dec4 Tam 6f fst 1:152 B *1/3* ●Nov28 Tam 5f fst 1:031 B *1/4* Nov22 Tam 5f fst 1:04 B *1/1*
TRAINER: Dirt/Turf(15 .13 $1.08) Sprint/Route(13 .31 $2.92) Turf(46 .24 $2.31) Routes(62 .26 $2.68) Alw(56 .27 $1.68)

2. **Unbridled's Pride** Another 4-year-old daughter of Unbridled, out of the Pleasant Colony mare Seewillo, she had raced exclusively on turf, posting a win and two thirds in six starts in 2002. She would be making her first start since October 9, when she finished third by 1½ lengths at Belmont Park at 7.70-1 with the addition of blinkers. In today's race, she had a new trainer, Ed Plesa Jr., and a new rider, with Jorge Chavez replacing Jose Santos. In one previous try at running fresh, in 2002, she was last in a field of six off a four-month layoff. This layoff was three months and a week.

2 Unbridled's Pride B. f. 4 (May) KEEJUL00 $500,000
Own:Carrion Jaime S Sire: Unbridled (Fappiano)
White Gold, Brown Braces & C, Gold Band Dam:Seewillo(Pleasant Colony)
Br: Meriwether/Leahy (Ky)
CHAVEZ J F (52 7 6 5 .13) 2002:(1196 223 .19) Tr: Plesa Edward Jr(12 0 1 0 .00) 2002:(430 70 .16)
L 117

Life 6 1 0 2 $29,660 83 | D.Fst 0 0 0 0 $0 –
2002 6 1 0 2 $29,660 83 | Wet(410) 0 0 0 0 $0 –
2001 0 M 0 0 $0 – | Turf(275) 6 1 0 2 $29,660 83
GP Ⓣ 2 1 0 0 $19,540 74 | DstⓉ(345) 4 1 0 2 $29,660 83

Previously trained by Alexander Frank A
9Oct02-4Bel fm 1 1/16 [T] :243 :49 1:131 1:432 3↑ⒻAlw 48000N1X 83 1 85¾ 83½ 83½ 74¾ 31½ Santos J A L 118 b 7.70 87-17 FlotAndSting1181 MrqutRnt118½ Unbrdld'sPrd118hd Good finish outside 8
21Sep02-10Bel fm 1¼ [T] :491 1:14 1:38 2:02 3↑ⒻAlw 48000N1X 79 6 87 73¾ 76¾ 85¾ 84½ Luzzi M J L 117 19.80 77-13 CozieAdvntge1171½ WonderWomn119nk **AztecPrl**119½ Inside trip, no rally 11
14Aug02-7Sar fm 1 [T] :231 :461 1:11 1:354 3↑ⒻAlw 48000N2L 67 4 69 69½ 66 611 69 Velazquez J R L 117 8.40 80-16 Title Nine119¾ *Sightseek*1171¼ Marquet Rent1175¼ Broke through gate 6
13Apr02-6Aqu fm 1 1/16 Ⓣ :234 :491 1:133 1:45 3↑ⒻAlw 44000N1X 81 5 94½ 103 94¾ 67¼ 31¾ Castellano J J L 115 6.00 77-19 SmrtGrce1141 PrimeQuen121¾ Unbridld'sPrid115½ 5 wide move, gamely 10
9Mar02-7GP gd *1 1/16 Ⓣ :243 :511 1:153 1:464 ⒻAlw 34000N1X 69 9 82¾ 53 31½ 45 67¾ Coa E M 121 10.10 60-32 Weepnomoremyldy1171¾ KtieKritz117¾ *Mlizios*1212¾ Steadied early, tired 10
15Feb02-6GP fm *1 1/16 Ⓣ :241 :512 1:162 1:481 ⒻMd Sp Wt 32k 74 5 64¾ 64½ 42½ 43½ 1¾ Velazquez J R 121 9.60 61-33 Unbridled'sPride121¾ CstleSpring1211 HighMintnnc1211 4 wide, up late 10
WORKS: Jan14 Crc 4f gd :494 B *5/22* Jan6 Crc 5f fst 1:022 B *6/22* Nov29 GP 5f fst 1:014 H *1/3* Nov20 Bel 5f fst 1:023 B *12/13* Nov9 Bel 5f fst 1:034 B *23/24* Nov1 Bel 5f fst 1:013 B *9/12*
TRAINER: 1stW/Tm(23 .30 $1.57) 61-180Days(40 .18 $1.81) Turf(130 .13 $1.68) Routes(197 .16 $1.61) Alw(74 .14 $1.01)

3. **Haley's Classic** This French-raced filly had made three U.S. starts for new trainer Jonathan Sheppard, all in this allowance class of nonwinners of two. She finished sixth at 7-2 at Delaware Park, second by half a length at 8-1 at Keeneland, and third by 2¼ lengths at 7-10 at Churchill Downs sporting front bandages for the first time. Her second and third U.S. turf starts had been run on yielding courses. Sheppard is successful

with a staggering 25 percent of his layoff horses for 61-180 days. This layoff was two months and a week. Pat Day, who had ridden Haley's Classic in her final 2002 start, was back on board for her return, but she showed only three works, on December 3, December 15, and January 14.

3 Haley's Classic
Own: Marablue Farm
Blue — Blue, White Belt, White Band On Sleeves,
DAY P (42 7 3 5 .17) 2002:(1155 258 .22)

B. f. 4 (Jan)
Sire: Sky Classic (Nijinsky II) $20,000
Dam: Proud Nova(Proud Birdie)
Br: Marablue Farm (Fla)
Tr: Sheppard Jonathan E(5 0 1 0 .00) 2002:(421 51 .12)

L 117

Life	8	1	1	2	$28,089	87	D.Fst	0	0	0	0	$0	–
2002	6	1	1	1	$23,767	87	Wet(410)	0	0	0	0	$0	–
2001	2	M	0	1	$4,322	–	Turf(300)	8	1	1	2	$28,089	87
GP Ⓣ	0	0	0	0	$0	–	DstⓉ(320)	1	0	0	0	$300	71

10Nov02-10CD yl 1⅛ Ⓣ :484 1:143 1:41 1:541 3↑ ⒻAlw 42140N1X **84** 2 54¼ 46½ 21½ 21½ 32¼ Day P L 114 f *.70 63–33 Elway Uran1141¾ *Synergistic*118½ Haley's Classic1142¾ 5w bid,empty late 10
13Oct02-9Kee yl 1⅛ Ⓣ :481 1:134 1:392 1:522 3↑ ⒻAlw 45845N1X **87** 9 64 54½ 3nk 1½ 2½ Perret C L 116 8.60 74–31 *VoodooLdy*118½ Hly'sClssic1161 *WhnIGrowUp*1212 6w,bid,led,outgamed 10
1Oct02-5Del gd *1$\frac{1}{16}$ Ⓣ :24 :482 1:131 1:451 ⒻAlw 44800N1X **71** 8 116½116½ 107½ 76 64½ Bartram B E L 117 3.90 84–13 Navarena117¾ Sounds Fishy122hd Risotto117¾ Taken back,hand urging 11
Previously trained by John Hammond
16Jun02♦ Lion dAngers(Fr) gd *1$\frac{7}{16}$Ⓣ LH ⒻPrix Urban Sea (Listed) Stk 36400 74½ Poirier M 123 – Ivy League123½ Arlesienne123nk Bonne Gargotte1231½ 9
Timeform rating: 88 — *Never a factor.Time not taken*
13May02♦ Saint-Cloud(Fr) gd *1$\frac{5}{16}$Ⓣ LH 2:151 ⒻPrix Cleopatre-G3 Stk 60200 56¼ Take Y 121 11.00 Turtle Bow1212 Totally Cosmic121nk Behreyma1211½ 6
Timeform rating: 98 — *Rated in last,never threatened*
13Apr02♦ CroiseLroche(Fr) gd *1$\frac{5}{16}$Ⓣ LH 2:142 ⒻPrix Allez France Alw 15900 1nk Gillet T 121 *1.20 Haley's Classic121nk Kaer Gwell121no Red Stella121½ 8
Trailed slow pace to halfway,sharp late run to lead near line
28Sep01♦ Saint-Cloud(Fr) sf *1 Ⓣ LH 1:46 Prix Aethelstan-EBF Alw 20000 34½ Take Y 120 3.50 Martaline1233 Erna1141½ Haley's Classic120¾ 13
Timeform rating: 74 — *Unhurried in mid-pack,finished well without threatening*
5Sep01♦ Chantilly(Fr) sf *1 Ⓣ RH 1:42 ⒻPrix de Sandricourt-EBF Mdn (FT)13200 45¾ Take Y 126 5.50 Sue Generoos1265 Entretenue120¾ Download126hd 13
Timeform rating: 74 — *Missed break,trailed to 1-1/2f out,finished well.Ombre Legere 5th*
WORKS: Jan14 GP 5f sly 1:023 B *2/4* Dec15 GP 5f fst 1:021 B *7/24* Dec3 GP 5f fst 1:02 B *4/9*
TRAINER: 61-180Days(65 .25 $1.54) Turf(242 .12 $1.27) Routes(326 .13 $1.01) Alw(166 .09 $0.92)

4. Snowrun The 5-year-old mare was an uncoupled stablemate of Haley's Classic in Sheppard's care and also had not raced in a while. Her last start had been in a maiden grass race at Philadelphia Park, when she was steadied and finished second by 1¼ lengths out of the 11 post at even money. She was placed

4 Snowrun
Own: Augustin Stable
Yellow — White & Green Halves White Sleeves
GUIDRY M (48 5 3 5 .10) 2002:(1030 156 .15)

Ch. m. 5
Sire: Rahy (Blushing Groom*Fr) $100,000
Dam: Snowbowl(Northjet*Ire)
Br: George Strawbridge Jr (Pa)
Tr: Sheppard Jonathan E(5 0 1 0 .00) 2002:(421 51 .12)

L 117

Life	8	1	3	1	$23,108	63	D.Fst	0	0	0	0	$0	–
2002	2	1	0	1	$18,600	63	Wet(315)	0	0	0	0	$0	–
2001	6	M	3	0	$4,508	–	Turf(345)	8	1	3	1	$23,108	63
GP Ⓣ	0	0	0	0	$0	–	DstⓉ(355)	1	1	0	0	$15,960	63

6Oct02-4Pha fm 1$\frac{1}{16}$ Ⓣ :234 :484 1:134 1:47 3↑ ⒻMd Sp Wt 25k **63** 11 94¼ 73¾ 42½ 42 21¼ Molina V H L 122 f *1.00 72–25 ⒹSweetDrminSuzy1191¼ Snowrun122nk Joni'sSwtP122½ Steadied stretch 12
Placed first through disqualification.
16Jly02-5Cnl fm 5f Ⓣ :22 :452 :572 3↑ ⒻMd Sp Wt 24k **59** 1 8 63¾ 55 33½ 33½ Pino M G 122 *1.90 89–07 French Silk1172 Spring Kitten1171½ *Snowrun*1224½ Std'd ins,angled,bid 13
Previously trained by Jonathan Pease
28Oct01♦ LyonVllrbnne(Fr) sf *1$\frac{3}{16}$Ⓣ RH Prix Marcel Guillermain Hcp 11000 67¾ Champagne F 124 – Rose Sea1281 Maison Chaude1191½ Prince Solon123nk 8
Never a factor.Time not taken
15Oct01♦ Saint-Cloud(Fr) sf *1 Ⓣ LH 1:483 ⒻPrix de la Hauquerie Hcp 16600 104 Take Y 122 8.50 Spring Girl113hd Dryades1301 Tremiere126hd 19
Towards rear,mild late gain in traffic
3Oct01♦ Lyon-Parilly(Fr) yl *1 Ⓣ LH 1:434 Prix du Jardin Alpestre Alw 10900 2½ Champagne F 120 – Saonoise124½ Snowrun120¾ Deux Decembre1203 12
Tracked leaders,dueled 1f out,headed near line
3Aug01♦ Clairfntaine(Fr) sf *1⅛Ⓣ RH 1:534 Prix d'Aguesseau Hcp 16100 13 Jarnet T 127 5.20 Madame Rose127½ Guest130nk Escoral119hd 18
4th on rail,weakened 1f out
8Jly01♦ Vitre(Fr) sf *1 Ⓣ RH 1:503 Pr Societe Courses Wissembourg Alw 6700 21½ Stefan C7 117 – Visions on Space1201½ Snowrun117¾ Dinan1283½ 9
Well placed in 3rd,brief rail bid over 1f out,outfinished
10Jun01♦ Lisieux(Fr) gd *1$\frac{3}{16}$Ⓣ RH ⒻPrix de St-Martin-de-la-Lieue Maiden 4900 22 Stefan C7 116 – Anoukit1282 Snowrun116¾ ⒹTango Passion122no 12
Towards rear,progress 3f out,up for 2nd.Time not taken
WORKS: Dec24 GP 4f fst :491 B *34/86* Dec15 GP 5f fst 1:06 B *23/24* Dec3 GP 4f fst :483 B *9/17*
TRAINER: 61-180Days(65 .25 $1.54) Turf(242 .12 $1.27) Routes(326 .13 $1.01) Alw(166 .09 $0.92)

first when the winner was disqualified. That was her eighth attempt to win a race. She, too, showed just three works for her first start in four months, December 3, 15, and 24. That meant she hadn't had a published work in more than three weeks.

5. **Harts Gap** This filly had raced well in all four turf starts, finishing fourth by a neck, second by three-quarters of a length, and then first by a neck in maiden company. Off a near three-month layoff, she had finished third by 2½ lengths at 6-1 in a five-furlong grass sprint for $16,000 claimers. She was stepping up here.

5 Harts Gap
Own: Melnyk Eugene & Laura
Green — Navy Blue, Gold Chevrons, Navy Blue
VELASQUEZ C (61 8 12 11 .13) 2002:(1630 332 .20)

Dk. b or br f. 4 (Jan) FTKJUL00 $285,000
Sire: Saint Ballado (Halo) $125,000
Dam: Special Test (Hawkin's Special)
Br: James P Gallagher (Ky)
Tr: Orseno Joseph (3 0 1 0 .00) 2002:(186 25 .13)

L 117

Life	7	1	1	2	$42,764	76	
2002	7	1	1	2	$42,764	76	
2001	0	M	0	0	$0	–	
GP (T)	0	0	0	0	$0	–	
D.Fst	3	0	0	1	$8,784	56	
Wet(320)	0	0	0	0	$0	–	
Turf(275)	4	1	1	1	$33,980	76	
Dst(T)(335)	3	1	1	0	$31,670	76	

31Dec02-5Crc	fm	5f	(T)	:213 :444 :564	3↑ (F)OClm 16000(16-14)N	74	9	6	97½	95½	66	32½	Velasquez C	L119	6.10	88-09	KittyCtWins1162 It'sACubnThng122½ HrtsGp119½	Closed well, up for 3d	10
8Oct02-4Del	fm	*1 1/16	(T)	:242 :493 1:144 1:454	3↑ (F)Md Sp Wt 40k	73	2	21	2½	2hd	1hd	1nk	Coa E M	L120	*1.50	85-08	HrtsGp120nk RomnticAge123½ LdyFromShnghi123½	Stalked, bid, driving	10
12Sep02-4Med	fm	1 1/16	(T)	:224 :471 1:112 1:423	3↑ (F)Md Sp Wt 29k	73	3	31½	2hd	42½	43	2¾	Coa E M	L117	2.20	90-08	Sounds Fishy117¾ *Harts Gap*1172 *Attaga*/117½	Dueled clear in place	10
3Aug02-5Sar	sf	1 1/16	(T)	:231 :481 1:134 1:454	3↑ (F)Md Sp Wt 46k	76	2	22	2½	2½	1hd	4nk	Chavez J F	L118	18.20	67-24	RompAndStomp113no CozznAlng118no CstlSprng118hd	With pace, gamely	12
30Jun02-4Bel	fst	6f		:22 :453 :572 1:10	3↑ (F)Md Sp Wt 43k	55	9	5	65¼	73¼	810	710¼	Chavez J F	L120	14.60	78-11	Colette115½ Adversity1202¼ *Ridaa*1201¾	4 wide, no response	10
6Jun02-5Bel	fst	7f		:22 :444 1:093 1:233	3↑ (F)Md Sp Wt 43k	56	2	5	37	412	613	413	Chavez J F	L120	5.70	72-11	Dignified Diva1207½ *Amarelle*1203¾ Alluring1201¾	Chased on rail, tired	9
Previously trained by England Phillip																			
6Apr02-7WO	fst	5f		:222 :463 :593	3↑ (F)Md Sp Wt 56k	56	8	8	72½	31	33½	33¾	Husbands P	116	3.65	78-17	Expect A Mint1163¼ Cavalier Billie116½ Harts Gap1161¼	Flattened out	10

WORKS: Dec22 GP 4f fst :51 B *19/24* Dec14 GP 5f fst 1:022 B *23/37* Nov30 Bel tr.t 5f fst 1:022 B *4/30* Nov26 Bel tr.t 4f fst :53 B *60/61* Nov21 Bel tr.t 4f fst :494 B *48/73* Nov9 Bel tr.t 5f fst 1:02 B *8/19*
TRAINER: Sprint/Route (20 .05 $0.30) Turf (87 .10 $1.50) Routes (126 .11 $1.28) Alw (66 .15 $2.02)

6. **Bargain Belle** She'd won a $35,000 claimer at Saratoga, then run second and eighth from difficult outside posts in two allowance tries at Pimlico and Delaware Park in her last three starts. She had been off since October 1.

6 Bargain Belle
Own: P T K Racing Ltd
Black — Green, White Ptk, Green Cap
COA E M (61 14 7 11 .23) 2002:(1367 287 .21)

Dk. b or br f. 4 (Apr) KEESEP00 $4,000
Sire: Strodes Creek (Halo) $6,996
Dam: Risen Starlet (Secretariat)
Br: Arthur B Hancock III (Ky)
Tr: Allen A Ferris III (3 1 0 0 .33) 2002:(727 100 .14)

L 117

Life	20	3	7	4	$80,510	78	
2002	16	3	6	3	$75,910	78	
2001	4	M	1	1	$4,600	45	
GP (T)	0	0	0	0	$0	–	
D.Fst	10	0	4	3	$23,410	63	
Wet(360*)	3	1	1	0	$9,250	49	
Turf(310)	7	2	2	1	$47,850	78	
Dst(T)(365)	5	1	2	0	$32,780	78	

10Oct02-5Del	gd	*1 1/16	(T)	:24 :482 1:131 1:451	(F)Alw 44800N1X	68	11	105¾	106	76	86½	86	Alvarado F T	L122fb	*2.50	82-13	Navarena117¾ Sounds Fishy122hd Risotto117¾	Failed to menace	11
14Sep02-8Pim	fm	1 1/16	(T)	:233 :473 1:121 1:444	3↑ (F)Alw 26000N1X	73	10	911	910	56	3½	21	Jurado E M	L115fb	*1.30	78-24	AllApologies1171 BargainBelle1152¾ PisleyBres1171	4wd move 1/4, game	10
2Sep02-3Sar	fm	1 1/16	[T]	:224 :471 1:12 1:424	(F)Clm 35000	78	9	1210	126	51½	2hd	11¾	Alvarado F T	L118fb	9.00	88-14	BargainBelle1181¾ Slypslydnawy1181¼ Cupsoup1182	5 wide move, driving	12
4Aug02-6Sar	yl	1 1/16	[T]	:234 :483 1:123 1:44	(F)Clm 35000	74	3	77½	65½	65	54½	21	Chavez J F	L119fb	11.80	81-22	MjesticGirl1191 *BrginBell*1191 MythiclBrowni1191	Game finish outside	9
21Jly02-8Cnl	fm	1 1/16	[T]	:252 :502 1:15 1:463	3↑ (F)Clm 25000(25-20)N3L	61	7	13	11½	1½	31	45	Pino M G	L114fb	2.60	67-27	Skip To Savannah117¾ Rakeen Lake1193 Awayo1151¼	Off rail, weakened	7
29Jun02-8Cnl	fm	1⅛	(T)	:501 1:143 1:38 1:522	3↑ (F)Clm 25000(25-20)N3L	63	8	51¾	3½	2hd	22	31½	Pino M G	L114fb	*2.00	73-17	GoneAbrod1171½ Miner'sClementine117hd BrginBelle1144	3wd, weakened	9
15Jun02-5Del	gd	1 1/16	(⊗)	:231 :464 1:12 1:451	(F)Clm 50000(50-45)	44	1	511	59½	710	414	422	Vega H	L118fb	4.20	60-23	Not A Problem1166¼ Devil's Honey1181 Marilina11414	Evenly	7
3Jun02-3Del	fm	1	(T)	:234 :474 1:122 1:373	3↑ (F)Clm 25000(25-20)N2L	76	2	67	68	32	21	12¼	Dominguez R A	L113fb	3.90	88-10	BargainBelle1132¼ BlckItOut1184 BnmiMMe115½	Bid 3w,strong handling	10
24May02-6Pim	fst	1 1/16		:251 :493 1:15 1:49	3↑ (F)Clm 25000(25-20)N2L	42	1	1½	11½	1½	42½	58	Pino M G	L116fb	*.70	54-32	RinkBell1162¼ RkeenVerdict111hd GonAbrod122nk	Steadied 5/16,weakened	7
9May02-2Pim	fst	1 1/16		:252 :504 1:16 1:482	3↑ (F)Clm 25000(25-20)N2L	55	2	31½	42	31½	2½	2½	Pino M G	L116b	*1.00	64-28	FllstonVixen118½ BrginBelle1166¾ KeyRelity1223¼	Boxed rail,angled,hung	6
13Apr02-5Pim	fst	1 1/16		:241 :482 1:133 1:463	(F)Clm 25000(25-20)	63	1	11½	1½	11	23	25½	Pino M G	L117fb	.40e	68-26	Beauty'sImge1175½ BrginBelle1172¾ FrostyNote11722	Rail, pace, weakened	7
23Mar02-9Lrl	fst	1 1/16		:242 :482 1:134 1:471	(F)Clm c-(25-20)	56	1	11	1hd	1½	2hd	25½	Johnston M T	L117b	3.00	67-25	Click On Me1175½ Bargain Belle11714 Aunt Celie1173	Rail, pace, 2nd best	7

Claimed from Gumpster Stable for $25,000, Lake Scott A Trainer 2002 (as of 03/23): (411 87 72 55 0.21)

WORKS: Jan11 PmM 5f fst 1:021 B *6/16* Jan5 PmM 4f fst :493 B *10/25* Dec31 PmM 5f fst 1:023 B *8/25* Dec24 PmM 5f fst 1:03 B *9/25* Dec17 PmM 4f fst :51 B *13/13* ●Nov27 Del 4f my :491 B *1/4*
TRAINER: 61-180Days (23 .04 $0.83) Turf (127 .17 $1.57) Routes (371 .16 $1.86) Alw (151 .13 $1.54)

7. Bluebird Day All her nine races were on grass, and she had one win, by 1½ lengths, in a maiden race at Gulfstream Park in her second career start. In seven ensuing starts, she posted one second by four lengths again colts at Kentucky Downs. She, too, had been idle, not starting since November 8, when she made the lead and tired to be fourth by two lengths at 5.30-1 at Churchill Downs. Rene Douglas accepted the mount today.

7 Bluebird Day (Ire)
Own: Humphrey G W Jr
Orange — Forest Green, White Diamonds, White
DOUGLAS R R (31 2 4 5 .06) 2002:(1208 231 .19)

Gr/ro f. 4 (Apr) TATHOU00 $373,269
Sire: Sadler's Wells (Northern Dancer)
Dam: Desert Bluebell(Kalaglow*GB)
Br: Tullamaine Castle Stud and Partners (Ire)
Tr: Arnold George R II(4 1 1 2 .25) 2002:(269 36 .13)

L 117

Life	9	1	1	0	$32,188	83	D.Fst	0	0	0	0	$0	-
2002	9	1	1	0	$32,188	83	Wet(330)	0	0	0	0	$0	-
2001	0	M	0	0	$0	-	Turf(355*)	9	1	1	0	$32,188	83
GP (T)	2	1	0	0	$19,520	71	Dst(T)(365)	1	0	0	0	$320	70

8Nov02-10CD	fm	1⅛ (T)	:473 1:124 1:382 1:51	3+ (F)Alw 41300N1X	82	4	22½	25½	22½	11	42	Albarado R J	L 114	5.30	79-19	FlyingMarlin114hd Boana1171¾ RutledgeDncer116nk	Chased,led,weaken,4w	10
23Sep02-5KD	fm	1½ (T)	:503 1:183 2:061 2:334	3+ Alw 32000N1X	76	5	2½	2hd	1½	1½	24	Lopez J	L 111	*3.10	65-28	ShnnonThCnnon1164 BlbrdDy1111½ LongByDncr1141½	Alternated on pace	11
17Aug02-6Mth	gd	1⅛ (T)	:493 1:132 1:381 1:503	3+ (F)Alw 33000N1X	76	5	42	51¾	51¾	62½	53¼	Bush W V	L 114	9.00	75-21	Polyandry120½ Countessa1221½ *E Mail Pat*120½	Exchanged bumps start	10
24Jly02-5Sar	yl	1 3/16 (T)	:482 1:131 1:38 1:553	3+ (F)Alw 48000N1X	71	3	44	63½	92½	95½	89	Samyn J L	L 116	29.00	71-19	*Wonder Again*118nk *Showlady*1182 *Supposedly*1161¾	Rated inside, no rally	12
12Jun02-6Bel	fm	1⅛ [T]	:491 1:14 1:381 1:493	3+ (F)Alw 46000N1X	77	9	21	21	2½	66	76½	Prado E S	L 115	5.80	74-22	SonataCosmos1213 MissPlybill117½ SkyCover1211¼	Speed outside, tired	9
27May02-4Bel	fm	1¼ [T]	:494 1:132 1:372 2:014	3+ (F)Alw 46000N1X	83	6	33½	33	21½	23	42½	Prado E S	L 115	4.20	80-17	Duchcov121hd Cozie Advantage1151½ Sunstone1211	3 wide move, faded	7
19Apr02-5Kee	fm	1⅛ (T)	:474 1:134 1:382 1:501	(F)Alw 55580N1X	75	6	31	33½	3½	52½	54½	Day P	L 120	3.40	81-14	AffirmedDncer1201½ Disygo123nk *TrnishdLdy*1202¼	Tracked,4w,flatten out	10
22Mar02-10GP	fm	*1⅛ (T)	:511 1:154 1:42 1:541+	(F)Md Sp Wt 32k	71	8	32½	31	1½	11½	11½	Prado E S	L 121	*.90	67-30	Bluebird Day1211½ Glowing Halo1212½ *Dizzy*121no	3 wide, prevailed	8
10Jan02-7GP	fm	*1 1/16 (T)	:23 :481 1:141 1:474	(F)Md Sp Wt 32k	70	8	96½	912	106½	83¼	54	Day P	121	*1.90	59-40	*MnhttnSkylin*121nk TrnishdLdy1212½ Dvid'sDoll1211	Blocked, taken up str	10

WORKS: Jan12 GP 4f fst :49 B *6/36* Dec31 GP 4f fst :50 B *51/72* Dec24 GP 4f fst :49 B *24/86* Dec13 GP 4f fst :50 B *14/31* Nov3 CD 3f fst :371 B *7/11* Oct27 CD 4f fst :492 B *17/55*

TRAINER: 61-180Days(39 .13 $1.19) Turf(109 .13 $2.38) Routes(194 .14 $1.99) Alw(113 .14 $2.11)

8. American Dreamer In her last start, November 29 at Calder, she'd shown speed and tired to finish fifth at 8.10-1 behind Victorious Vicki, who was third. That made American Dreamer 1 for 14 on grass with four seconds and three thirds. She'd been a beaten favorite in three of her last seven starts at odds of 3-2, 2.30-1, and 5-2.

8 American Dreamer
Own: Woods Karen
Pink — Green, Pink Dot Sash, Pink Cap
SANTOS J A (52 12 8 5 .23) 2002:(1160 176 .15)

B. m. 5
Sire: Quest for Fame*GB (Rainbow Quest)
Dam: Reflection(Sunshine Forever)
Br: Palides Investments N V Inc (Ky)
Tr: Azpurua Leo Jr(3 1 0 0 .33) 2002:(169 14 .08)

L 117

Life	16	1	4	3	$68,545	87	D.Fst	1	0	0	0	$1,980	48
2002	6	0	0	1	$7,110	71	Wet(320*)	1	0	0	0	$1,290	6
2001	9	1	3	2	$57,920	87	Turf(305)	14	1	4	3	$65,275	87
GP (T)	1	1	0	0	$20,400	71	Dst(T)(340)	6	1	2	2	$41,065	82

29Nov02-4Crc	fm	1 1/16 (T)	:23 :472 1:112 1:424	3+ (F)Alw 24000N2L	68	3	2hd	2½	1hd	31	54	Castellano A Jr	L 122 b	8.10	78-14	GoHelenGo119nk StrshipWondr1161½ **VictoriousVicki**1221	Vied, gave way	8
13Oct02-8Del	wf	1 (X)	:232 :47 1:134 1:40	3+ (F)Alw 43000N1X	6	1	11	21½	46½	518	536	Martin C W	L 118 b	5.30	46-21	LdyAndromed1186½ **SpiceIslnd**1176¾ ProprPudding1187½	Gave way readily	5
Previously trained by Pletcher Todd A																		
17Aug02-6Mth	gd	1⅛ (T)	:493 1:132 1:381 1:503	3+ (F)Alw 33000N1X	70	8	1hd	1½	1½	2hd	85¾	Coa E M	L 120 fb	5.30	72-21	Polyandry120½ Countessa1221½ *E Mail Pat*120½	Pace,dueled,weakened	10
3Aug02-4Mth	fst	1 1/16 (X)	:232 :464 1:12 1:471	3+ (F)Alw 33000N1X	48	3	31	31½	31	45	46¾	Coa E M	L 120 f	*2.50	65-15	Pat1141½ Kathie's Sibiling1204 I P O Pat1141¼	Bore out 1/4,drifted	6
14Jly02-5Mth	fm	1 1/16 (T)	:23 :462 1:11 1:414+	3+ (F)Alw 33000N1X	71	9	53	55½	2½	2½	33	Coa E M	L 120 f	*2.30	89-09	Lojo1152½ Kthie'sSibiling120½ AmericnDremer120½	Outside bid,willingly	11
21Jun02-6Bel	fm	1 (T)	:23 :454 1:093 1:341	3+ (F)Alw 46000N1X	67	7	53	53½	54	610	710½	Castellano J J	L 121 f	11.70e	79-15	Sandra's Song121no Polyandry121½ *Prime Queen*121hd	No response	9
17Nov01-6Aqu	fm	1 (T)	:23 :473 1:131 1:372	3+ (F)Alw 44000N1X	80	2	39½	37	2½	22½	42¾	Velazquez J R	L 116 f	*1.50	88-14	Starboard Stinger1162½ Ready116nk T C Kiss116no	Middle move, no punch	9
3Nov01-8Aqu	fm	1 1/16 (T)	:232 :483 1:133 1:444	3+ (F)Alw 44000N1X	82	8	31½	42½	41½	3½	21½	Velazquez J R	L 116 f	2.85	78-15	PeanutGallery1191½ AmericnDremer1161¼ TCKiss116no	Game finish inside	10
19Oct01-9Bel	fm	1 (T)	:233 :47 1:12 1:351	3+ (F)Alw 44000N1X	83	3	42	42	52	5¾	32¼	Velazquez J R	L 116	5.30	80-18	Vespers116½ *Langoureuse*1161¾ American Dreamer1162	Stayed on well	10
3Sep01-8Med	fm	1 (T)	:231 :464 1:111 1:361	3+ (F)Alw 40000N1X	78	11	83¾	3½	2hd	2½	2¾	Coa E M	L 114	6.30	89-10	PrsmdInnocnt119¾ AmrcnDrmr114½ RdsHrtnt1191	Game try,outfinished	11
8Aug01-6Sar	fm	1⅜ [T]	:464 1:113 1:363 2:14	3+ (F)Alw 44000N1X	64	7	2½	2½	22½	108	1013	Velazquez J R	L 116	10.00	81-06	ChezCherie120½ Yanseeni1161 *SpeedOfThought*1202	Chased pace, tired	10
11Jly01-8Bel	fm	1 1/16 (T)	:241 :474 1:113 1:413	3+ (F)Alw 44000N2L	79	7	2½	2½	2hd	1hd	33¼	Velazquez J R	L 116	7.30	85-11	LovN'KssS.1182¾ ChrokPrms118½ AmrcnDrmr116no	Vied 3 wide, stayed on	10

WORKS: Jan5 GP 4f fst :503 B *29/39* Nov23 GP 4f fst :49 B *3/9*

TRAINER: 31-60Days(41 .12 $0.83) Turf(72 .08 $1.05) Routes(92 .07 $0.73) Alw(44 .09 $1.40)

9. Victorious Vicki She'd won 1 of 12 grass starts with three thirds, the last when she beat American Dreamer by 2¼ lengths at Calder at nearly the same odds, 8.60-1. She'd been off since that race, too.

(racing past performance chart for Victorious Vicki)

10. Bubbles Cachet She was idle since November 28, when she was steadied on the far turn and finished sixth by six lengths as the 8-5 favorite. In her previous start, she won a maiden race by 6¼ lengths at 3-5 at Delaware. Edgar Prado rode today.

(racing past performance chart for Bubbles Cachet)

Analysis: There were eight fillies in here who would have to be gauged by how well they handled layoffs. Of those eight, Snowrun seemed an easy toss. American Dreamer and Victorious Vicki both had that one-win-for-too-many-starts profile and were further compromised by outside posts. Of the remaining five layoff fillies, Haley's

Classic and Bargain Belle made the most sense. Unbridled's Pride had lost five straight and had not run well off a layoff previously. Bluebird Day had lost seven straight. Bubbles Cachet was adding Prado off a troubled return, but was hampered by the 10 post.

What of the two who had run recently? It was tough to recommend Harts Gap, who had finished third in a $16,000 claimer at 6-1 at Calder, over Bargain Belle, who'd won a $35,000 claimer at Saratoga. Harts Gap was next to go.

What about Hydration? She had won her lone grass start "ridden out," according to the comment in the *Form,* had a useful dirt prep for this race, and broke from the rail, a decided advantage. While she was obviously facing better horses at Gulfstream than she had in her grass debut at Tampa Bay, she was also trained by a man who was winning 24 percent on his turf races from a sizable sample. She also was the lone speed in the race. Of the 58 other grass past-performance lines showing for the competition, only two revealed one of today's fillies in front at the first call. American Dreamer had been first by half a length in a $49^3/5$ half, and Bubbles Cachet was first by a head in a $48^3/5$ half. Hydration had run a half in $47^4/5$ in her successful lone grass start. She had as much right as any to succeed.

What happened on the tote board? Haley's Classic went off the 8-5 favorite. Unbridled's Pride was 9-2, Bubbles Cachet and Bluebird Day both 5-1, and Harts Gap 9-1. Bargain Belle was 14-1. Hydration went off at 16.50-1, almost the same price as Snowrun, who had never finished first in a race, at 18.40-1.

Hydration shot to the lead under Earlie Fires and held off Haley's Classic by half a length, paying $35 to win. The exacta came back $155 with the 8-5 favorite running second. Harts Gap finished third for a $1,158.40 trifecta, and Bluebird Day completed the superfecta worth $5.404.

NINTH RACE

Gulfstream

JANUARY 17, 2003

ABOUT 1$\frac{1}{16}$ MILES. (Turf Chute)(1.40[1]) ALLOWANCE. Purse $34,000 For Fillies and Mares Four Years Old And Upward Which Have Never Won A Race Other Than Maiden, Claiming, Or Starter Or Which Have Never Won Two Races. (Condition Eligibility) Weight 121 lbs. Non-winners of a race other than claiming at a mile or over since November 15 allowed, 2 lbs. Such a race since October 15, 4 lbs. (Rail at 15 feet).

Value of Race: $34,000 Winner $20,400; second $6,120; third $3,740; fourth $1,700; fifth $340; sixth $340; seventh $340; eighth $340; ninth $340; tenth $340. Mutuel Pool $336,316.00 Exacta Pool $294,863.00 Trifecta Pool $249,445.00 Superfecta Pool $90,067.00

Last Raced	Horse	M/Eqt.	A. Wt	PP	St	$\frac{1}{4}$	$\frac{1}{2}$	$\frac{3}{4}$	Str	Fin	Jockey	Odds $1
19Dec02 7Tam4	Hydration	L	4 117	1	1	1^4	1^3	11$\frac{1}{2}$	1^2	1$\frac{1}{2}$	Fires E	16.50
10Nov02 10CD3	Haley's Classic	Lb	4 117	3	4	7$\frac{1}{2}$	6^1	6^{hd}	2^{hd}	2^1	Day P	1.60
31Dec02 5Crc3	Harts Gap	L	4 117	5	2	2$\frac{1}{2}$	3^1	3^{hd}	3^2	3^1	Velasquez C	9.80
8Nov02 10CD4	Bluebird Day-IR	L	4 117	7	9	8$\frac{1}{2}$	8^2	5$\frac{1}{2}$	4$\frac{1}{2}$	4^1	Douglas R R	5.40
9Oct02 4Bel3	Unbridled's Pride	Lb	4 117	2	7	10	10	8^1	6^2	5$^{2}\frac{1}{2}$	Chavez J F	4.90
29Nov02 4Crc5	American Dreamer	Lb	5 117	8	5	3$\frac{1}{2}$	2$\frac{1}{2}$	2$\frac{1}{2}$	5^1	6^2	Santos J A	29.50
6Oct02 4Pha2	Snowrun	L	5 117	4	3	4$1\frac{1}{2}$	7$\frac{1}{2}$	9^2	8$\frac{1}{2}$	7^{hd}	Guidry M	18.40
1Oct02 5Del8	Bargain Belle	Lbf	4 117	6	10	6^1	4^1	41$\frac{1}{2}$	7^1	8$\frac{3}{4}$	Coa E M	14.20
29Nov02 4Crc3	Victorious Vicki	Lb	5 117	9	8	9^2	9^1	10	9$\frac{1}{2}$	91$\frac{3}{4}$	Aguilar M	47.80
28Nov02 7Crc6	Bubbles Cachet	Lb	4 117	10	6	5^{hd}	5^{hd}	71$\frac{1}{2}$	10	10	Prado E S	5.30

OFF AT 4:55 Start Good. Won driving. Course firm.

TIME :24, :49^4, 1:14, 1:39^2, 1:45^3 (:24.92, :49.89, 1:14.14, 1:39.45, 1:45.66)

$2 Mutuel Prices:

1–HYDRATION	35.00	11.40	8.80
3–HALEY'S CLASSIC		3.60	2.80
5–HARTS GAP			5.60

$2 EXACTA 1–3 PAID $155.00 $2 TRIFECTA 1–3–5 PAID $1,158.40 $2 SUPERFECTA 1–3–5–7 PAID $5,404.00

Ch. f, by Unbridled–Good Picker, by Damascus. Trainer Proctor Thomas F. Bred by Glen Hill Farm (Ky).

HYDRATION sprinted to a clear lead along the rail, made the pace into the stretch, then was fully extended to last over HALEY'S CLASSIC. The latter, bumped with BARGAIN BELLE and steadied on the first turn, saved ground while advancing into contention around the far turn, eased outside HYDRATION for the drive and was gaining on the winner at the finish. HARTS GAP chased the pace into the stretch and couldn't gain late. BLUEBIRD DAY (IRE) reserved early, advanced between horses on the far turn, then closed with a mild response. UNBRIDLED'S PRIDE steadied in tight quarters leaving the chute, was trailing when checked to avoid running up on rivals on the first turn, then passed tired rivals in the drive without threatening. AMERICAN DREAMER chased the pace to nearing the stretch and tired. SNOWRUN fractious being loaded into the gate, rated of the pace, was steadied from tight quarters on the far turn and faltered. BARGAIN BELLE bumped with HALEY'S CLASSIC and steadied on the first turn, made a run to loom a threat three wide on the far turn, then gave way. VICTORIOUS VICKI was always outrun. BUBBLES CACHET was through after a half mile.

Owners— 1, Glen Hill Farm; 2, Marablue Farm; 3, Melnyk Eugene & Laura; 4, Humphrey G W Jr; 5, Carrion Jaime S; 6, Woods Karen; 7, Augustin Stable; 8, P T K Racing Ltd; 9, Ersoff Stanley M; 10, Robins Gerald & Weiss Jay

Trainers—1, Proctor Thomas F; 2, Sheppard Jonathan E; 3, Orseno Joseph; 4, Arnold George R II; 5, Plesa Edward Jr; 6, Azpurua Leo Jr; 7, Sheppard Jonathan E; 8, Allen A Ferris III; 9, Ersoff Stanley M; 10, Blengs Vincent L

Scratched— Takealetter (29Nov02 4CRC6), Aztec Pearl (14Nov02 5CRC2), Royal Alba (30Dec02 5CRC2), Spice Island (19Dec02 8CRC5)

$2 Pick Three (1–6–1) Paid $1,477.60; Pick Three Pool $29,555.

9

TRIPS

ONE OF THE MOST difficult aspects of handicapping grass races is distinguishing between significant bad trips that compromised a horse's chances to win a race and bad trips that did not matter.

In any grass race, half the field may get carried wide or run into traffic jams. That does not mean each one of those horses could have won the race had he not encountered trouble. It doesn't matter if a horse gets shut off if he wasn't making a meaningful move in the first place.

That's why doing your homework, in this case seeing as many races as you can, translates to an edge.

Race-replay centers at racetracks should be expanded. They are an extremely valuable tool. When you bet a horse in a race, you obviously focus on the horse you bet. But when you encounter a different horse who was in that same race two weeks later, you can go to a replay center, punch up that race, and focus on him. It's amazing how different a race appears when you concentrate on a horse other than the one you bet. You frequently get an entirely different perspective.

The most common bad trips in grass racing are wide trips from outside posts. Accordingly, outside post positions should be evaluated by the length of the run to the first turn, the winning percentages at that turf course for outside post positions, and whether or not a horse has either a good grass jockey and/or sufficient early speed to minimize the damage of the poor post.

Check out Danesfort's first two career grass starts in 2001. In his debut at Pimlico in a nonwinners-of-two allowance at 1¹/₁₆ miles, August 8, he broke from the outside post in a field of nine. He was second much of the way before tiring to fourth, only beaten one length, at odds of 3.60-1. Seventeen days later, Danesfort was entered under the same allowance conditions at Delaware Park at 1¹/₈ miles. Yet off his deceptively good race from a poor post, he was dispatched at odds of 10.80-1. He won by three-quarters of a length.

Hall of Fame jockey Jerry Bailey, possibly the best grass rider of all time, shared his opinions on turf trips in a 2003 interview. "Basically, if turf courses are in normal condition, not a soft bog and not as hard as a rock, horses that can relax and make a late run generally can win," Bailey said. "I don't care what their position is."

Getting position in a turf race, however, is decidedly more diffi-cult from an outside post on an inner turf course, such as those at Belmont Park and Saratoga. "Without a doubt," Bailey said. "It's worse when you have a course starting inside the circumference of the other turf course. You have tighter turns and you're starting closer to the turns. You have to either go forward or take back very quickly. You have to have a game plan.

"The outside post at Gulfstream is horrible. Saratoga is the same way on the inner course. But at a mile and three-eighths at Saratoga or Gulfstream, even though you break on the turn, it's easier because it's a longer race. You can tuck in. It becomes less of a problem because you have the longer distance to make up the discrepancy."

At every racetrack in North America, there is a line of demar-cation separating the poor post positions from the nearly impossi-ble ones.

The winter meet at Santa Anita from December 26, 2002, through March 27, 2003, provided a telling example.

In grass sprint races, horses from post position 9 were 5 for 38. Post-position 10 horses were 3 for 20; post 11 horses 0 for 12, and post 12 horses 0 for 6. A horse breaking from the 10 post was at a severe disadvantage, but posts 11 and 12 were even worse. Handi-cappers who noticed horses coming out of a race from one of those three post positions should have factored that into their analysis. If a horse was extremely wide from the 11 or 12 post, or even the 10, he should have been given the benefit of the doubt if his post posi-tion was better the next time. Conversely, if a horse had a good post position and raced poorly, then drew an extreme outside post in his next race, you could have tossed him. Any improvement in form probably would not have been sufficient to overcome the bad-post disadvantage.

What about route grass races at the 2002-2003 Santa Anita win-ter meet? Post 8 horses were 8 for 53. Those in post 9 were 5 for 35. But posts 10, 11, and 12 were a combined 3 for 44. Post 10 horses were 3 for 24, those in post 11 were 0 for 14, and post 12 horses were 0 for 6. Again, use the bias of an awful grass post in evaluating a horse's chances in the future. If he was stuck in post 10, 11, or 12, he was up against it. If he raced well from such a disadvantageous starting point, give him more credit than you routinely would, especially if he raced wide.

At Gulfstream Park's 2003 winter meet from January 3 through April 21, the line of demarcation was the 10 post. Horses with post position 8 were 17 for 160, those in post 9 were 10 for 153, and post 10 horses were 10 for 112. Post 11 horses went 1 for 6, and post 12 horses 0 for 5.

It was pretty much the same story at Fair Grounds' meet from November 28, 2002, through March 27, 2003. Horses from post 9 went 8 for 71, and from post 10 they were 4 for 43. From post 11, the numbers were 1 for 29, even worse than the 12 post, which was 2 for 14.

How about other tracks? In a 2002 sample at The Meadowlands from September 2 through October 16, post 7 went 9 for 59; post eight, 3 for 52; post 9, 4 for 43; post 10, 5 for 31; post 11, 0 for 13; and post 12, 1 for 5.

In Belmont's 2002 fall meet, a sample from September 6 through October 16, the 8 post was the last good one for turf races, with 13 of 74 winners. Post 9 horses were 5 for 57; post 10, 5 for 48; post 11, 2 for 19; and post 12, 2 for 17. Look at it this way. Horses from the 8 post were 13 for 74, while horses from posts 9 through 12 were a combined 14 for 141.

At Monmouth Park's 2002 summer meet from May 11 through August 29, the 9 post was the last good one, with a 12-for-88 success rate. Posts 10 through 12 were a combined 4 for 54, with post 10 going 3 for 36; post 11, 1 for 15; and post 12, 0 for 3.

At the Delaware Park 2002 meet from April 27 through October 15, post 8 was 9 for 11; post 9, 3 for 89; post 10, 4 for 69; post 11, 1 for 32; and post 12, 2 for 16.

Now what about trips from races you haven't seen?

On January 10, 2003, Alice From Marigny showed up in a

$30,000 turf claimer for Louisiana-breds at Fair Grounds at $7\frac{1}{2}$ furlongs. The 5-year-old had raced three times previously on turf. His first two grass races didn't show up in his past performances. But his last did. In a near-identical $25,000 turf claimer for Louisiana-breds at $7\frac{1}{2}$ furlongs, sent off at 21-1, he had raced third early and weakened to seventh, $4\frac{1}{4}$ lengths behind Spend a Web, who was also in today's race. But Alice From Marigny's comment line from that race said "Steadied, checked," and he had been moved up from seventh to sixth on the disqualification of the second-place finisher, Right On The Mark.

What can we deduce? Well, two separate trouble comments are unusual in one comment line, so his trouble must have been significant. But it was a guess. He'd done nothing in his two previous turf races, but look closer at his past performances. There are 10 PP's showing. Starting from the bottom, the first six races were run with front bandages. When front bandages were removed for two races, Alice From Marigny had raced strongly, finishing first by a head and second by a neck. With fronts back on, he'd been a distant third. In his last start on grass, he had raced without them, a positive indication.

Put all that together, and you might have given Alice From Marigny a shot this day. Sent off at nearly 11-1, he won by a length despite being steadied again.

Another example. Medinaceli was in tight and steadied at the quarter pole when he finished sixth by 4½ lengths at odds of 15.40-1 in a one-mile maiden race at Santa Anita on February 5, 2003, with blinkers added. He cut back to 6½ furlongs for his next start in a grass maiden race and went off at 8.60-1, winning by a length.

SEVENTH RACE **ABOUT 7½ FURLONGS. (Turf)(1.29 1) CLAIMING. Purse $25,500 (includes $3,500 Other Sources) ACCREDITED LA. BRED, FOUR YEAR OLDS AND UPWARD Weight 122 lbs. Non-winners of two races since November 10 allowed, 2 lbs. A race since then, 4 lbs. CLAIMING PRICE $30,000.**

Fair Grounds

JANUARY 10, 2003

Value of Race: $25,500 Winner $15,300; second $5,100; third $2,805; fourth $1,530; fifth $765. Mutuel Pool $158,019.00 Exacta Pool $123,167.00 Quinella Pool $12,999.00 Trifecta Pool $104,765.00 Superfecta Pool $26,273.00

Last Raced	Horse	M/Eqt.	A.Wt	PP	St	¼	½	Str	Fin	Jockey	Cl'g Pr	Odds $1
1Dec02 5FG7	Alice From Marigny	L	5 118	2	4	3hd	41½	32	11	Bourque C C	30000	10.80
3Jan03 10FG4	Xtreme Monique	L	4 118	5	6	41	61	42	21¼	Sellers S J	30000	4.80
3Jan03 10FG5	Early Goer	L	6 120	7	8	9	9	71	31¼	Melancon L	30000	4.80
19Dec02 7FG3	Say First Bid	Lf	6 118	4	5	21½	3hd	2½	4no	Meche L J	30000	15.70
4Jan03 7FG7	Silky Zarb	Lb	6 120	1	2	12½	11½	12½	51	Leblanc K P	30000	2.70
1Dec02 5FG1	[DH]Spend A Web	L	5 120	3	3	71½	5hd	6½	6	Melancon G	30000	2.50
2May02 7EvD7	[DH]Forty Niner Course	L	4 118	6	9	8½	7½	9	61½	Theriot H J II	30000	31.80
19Sep02 9Pim6	Spark Boulevard	Lf	8 114	9	7	51	2hd	5hd	8nk	Terry D M5	30000	25.60
29Dec02 5FG5	Ikkimaani Otoom	Lb	5 118	8	1	6hd	81	8½	9	Albarado R J	30000	8.80

[DH]—Dead Heat.

OFF AT 3:31 Start Good. Won driving. Course firm.
TIME :26 1, :50 3, 1:16 1, 1:35 (:26.20, :50.61, 1:16.31, 1:35.10)

$2 Mutuel Prices:				
	2–ALICE FROM MARIGNY	23.60	8.80	7.00
	5–XTREME MONIQUE		6.60	4.60
	7–EARLY GOER			4.40

$2 EXACTA 2–5 PAID $193.20 $2 QUINELLA 2–5 PAID $79.00 $2 TRIFECTA 2–5–7 PAID $1,076.20 $2 SUPERFECTA 2–5–7–4 PAID $19,704.60

Ch. h, by Wild Gale–Seven From Heaven, by Star Gallant. Trainer Alonzo Howard. Bred by Jake V Morreale (La).

ALICE FROM MARIGNY settled along the inside, steadied midway around the second turn, recovered, angled out turning for home, gained the lead nearing the final sixteenth and proved best under a drive. XTREME MONIQUE allowed to settle off the rail, split foes in upper stretch, eased out a bit and finished gamely. EARLY GOER trailed until nearing the drive, circled foes and rallied late. SAY FIRST BID close up, had no final kick. SILKY ZARB set the pace and then faltered late. SPEND A WEB between foes early, raced inside around the second turn, angled out and had no late kick. FORTY NINER COURSE was outrun. SPARK BOULEVARD forwardly placed off the rail, moved up before the second turn and then weakened. IKKIMAANI OTOOM had no speed and was no threat.

Owners— 1, Bourgeois Elizabeth; 2, Panic Stable; 3, Nolan Tonia; 4, Laviolette Gerald; 5, Angelica Susan & D'Angelo Louis; 6, Franks John; 7, F Lambert & B Byers; 8, Thompson Arcott H & Krzycki Darlene; 9, R Bar S Thoroughbreds

Trainers—1, Alonzo Howard; 2, Smith Jere R Jr; 3, Cathey Bradley J; 4, Laviolette Gerald; 5, Ney Andrew T; 6, Wilson Shane; 7, Bourgeois Keith; 8, Thompson Arcott H; 9, Barnett Bobby C

$2 Pick Three (4–3–2) Paid $707.20; Pick Three Pool $16,977.

1 Medinaceli (Ire)
Own:Brahm H & Miraleste Inc & Taylor
Red Purple/green Halves, Green Da
GARCIA M S (16 2 1 2 .13) 2003:(193 18 .09)

Ch. f. 4 (Apr)
Sire: Grand Lodge (Chief's Crown) $19,650
Dam: Gracious Line*Fr(Fabulous Dancer)
Br: Hinojosa F (Ire)
Tr: Abrams Barry(4 0 1 1 .00) 2003:(138 13 .09)

L 121

Life	13	2	1	1	$77,526	87	D.Fst	0 0 0 0		
2003	6	2	0	0	$70,420	87	Wet(280*)	0 0 0 0		
2002	4	M	1	0	$3,493	53	Turf(435*)	13 2 1 1	$77,52	
Hol ⓣ	0	0	0	0	$0	–	Dstⓣ(445)	8 1 0 1	$40,87	

11Apr03–2SA fm 1 ⓣ :24 1 :47 3 1:11 1 1:34 1 4↑ ⒻOClm 80000N 80 5 54 53½ 43½ 54¾ 46¼ Garcia M S LB 120 b 9.30 85–13 FunHouse118¾ I'mThBusinss1182½ NturllyWild1183 Saved ground to l
21Mar03–3SA fm 1 ⓣ :23 2 :47 2 1:11 2 1:35 1 4↑ ⒻAlw 56000N1X 87 3 64 62¾ 62¼ 5¾ 1no Garcia M S LB 118 b 49.80 86–11 Medinaceli118no Janein118no ViewFromTheTop120hd Blockd, split, up
1Mar03–1SA gd 1⅛ ⓣ :47 2 1:11 2 1:36 2 1:49 4↑ ⒻAlw 59360N1X 81 1 98¼ 99¾ 910 89 46¼ Valdivia J Jr LB 118 b 46.30 78–16 Trekking1184 SereneInSettl1182 KysToThHrt118nk Came out,missed
23Feb03–1SA fm *6½f ⓣ :22 :44 4 1:08 2 1:14 3 4↑ ⒻMd Sp Wt 50k 79 3 5 56 43 22 11 Flores D R LB 122 b 8.60 84–11 Medinaceli1221 Worldly Excess1231 Fast Goat123½ 4wd into lane,ral
5Feb03–6SA fm 1 ⓣ :24 1 :48 2 1:12 3 1:36 2 4↑ ⒻMd Sp Wt 59k 72 7 65¼ 52¼ 73¾ 85½ 64½ Garcia M S LB 121 b 15.40 75–20 Intricate1213 Delavallade123½ Minamala121nk Tight,steadied
5Jan03–2SA fm 1⅛ ⓣ :50 3 1:14 4 1:38 3 1:50 4 4↑ ⒻMd Sp Wt 50k 75 7 64 63 62¾ 63¾ 53 Espinoza V LB 121 13.50 72–25 Honeypenny121½ Sonia121½ *Tifonica*1231 4 wide into stre
Previously trained by Canani Julio C
10Oct02–4SA fm 1 ⓣ :22 2 :45 4 1:10 1 1:36 1 3↑ ⒻMd Sp Wt 45k 53 3 914 911 710 611 712 Nakatani C S LB 119 2.80 69–13 ⒹJitterbug Jan1191 Casting Call119½ Nedra122hd Off slow,stumb
Previously trained by Carlos Laffon-Parias
7Aug02 ♦ Vichy(Fr) sf *1¼ⓣ RH 2:14 Prix Rene Bedel Alw 17400 21½ Blancpain M9 110 5.00 Spirit of Peace1141½ Medinaceli110½ Tekakwhita1271 *Towards rear,late bid,up f*
30Jun02 ♦ Dieppe(Fr) sf *1⅛ⓣ RH ⒻPrix Linabox Alw 10900 63 Fargeat S 128 – Porretta120½ Sandiyla122no Lorigane1281½ *Time not*
18Jun02 ♦ M-Laffitte(Fr) gd *1 ⓣ RH 1:39 2 ⒻPrix Quintette Alw 16200 1010¾ Peslier O 123 22.00 La Belle Simone126¾ Adalgisa1232½ Great Pamela126no *Towards rear,even*
1Dec01 ♦ Saint-Cloud(Fr) hy *1 ⓣ LH 2:00 2 ⒻPrix de Malesherbes Alw 16000 1012½ Bonilla D 121 *2.00 Turtie Doue1221½ Bongo Fury1232 Kaloneka1211½ *Tracked leaders,weakened*
Timeform rating: 62
6Nov01 ♦ M-Laffitte(Fr) hy *1 ⓣ RH 1:46 2 ⒻPrix Hayati-EBF Alw 19600 33 Binot D8 116 6.50 Moly1231 Seditieuse1232 Medinaceli116nk *Wide in 3rd,quickened 3f out,one-pac*
Timeform rating: 84
WORKS: Apr22 SA 4f fst :49 3 H *19/26* **Mar18 SA 4f fst :47 3 H** *7/63*
TRAINER: Turf(120 .10 $2.72) Alw(50 .16 $3.86)

Asked about evaluating bad turf trips, Bailey said, "If you have a horse that needs to be on the lead and you get on a soft course with too much speed, you can tell he's going to have a hard time before you get out of the gate. Or if you have a hard course and you have a horse that comes from behind."

What's crucial is determining how a horse dealt with that difficulty, or with other types of bad trips. Did he show speed from an outside post and cave in immediately when pressured, or did he fight it out to the wire? If he was stopped cold while making a move, did he try to make a second rally?

Let's look at the PP's of Native Desert, a 10-year-old gelding who showed up in the $150,000 TVG Khaled Stakes at 1 1/8 miles at Hollywood Park, April 26, 2003.

Starting at the bottom of his 12 PP's, check out the third race up, the Grade 1 2001 Shoemaker Breeders' Cup Mile at Hollywood. Sent off at 10-1, Native Desert was sixth by 15 lengths before rallying to finish fourth by two lengths. The comment line says "Blocked, steadied upper stretch." When a horse is making a strong rally and gets stopped at the top of the stretch, it's extremely significant. But without seeing the race, it's impossible to tell just from the comment line how bad his trouble was and whether or not he re-rallied after being stopped.

Freshened for his next start in the Grade 1 Eddie Read Handicap at Del Mar, Native Desert was bet heavily off that trouble line, went off at 5.40-1, and rallied three wide for second, a fine performance in a Grade 1 stakes. He won his next two starts, at 3-5 in a dead heat and at 6-5, then concluded his 8-year-old season by running seventh in the Grade 2 Citation Handicap at Hollywood at 12-1.

Exactly four months later, Native Desert began his 9-year-old season in 2002 in the $139,000 Crystal Water Handicap for California-breds at Santa Anita. Sent off as the 2.30-1 favorite, he broke slowly and rallied for third despite encountering traffic problems. His comment line says, "Off slow, boxed past ⅛," which means he was boxed in past the eighth pole with nowhere to go. Again, that's extremely significant trouble.

Sent off as the 2.20-1 favorite in his next start, the 2002 TVG Khaled Stakes at Hollywood, Native Desert rallied four wide under Eddie Delahoussaye and won by a head, beating Hugh Hefner, who had beaten him by two lengths the start before. Shipped north to Bay Meadows for his next start, Native Desert won the $67,000 Foster City by half a length at 5-2.

An ideal scenario is to locate a horse that had significant trouble in his last race and is going off at higher odds in his next start. Some examples:

Honor in War: Honor in War had been freshened for nine weeks by trainer Paul McGee following a fifth-place finish in a $62,500 optional claimer at Churchill Downs, on a yielding course at 9-5, November 10, 2002.

Honor in War, now a 4-year-old, returned to the races at Gulfstream Park in a one-mile grass allowance for nonwinners of four on January 18, 2003. Sent off the 2.10-1 favorite from the rail, Honor in War finished fifth by 2½ lengths. His comment line said "Blocked deep stretch."

4 Honor In War
Own:3rd Turn Stables
ellow Black; Red 3rd In Oval Red Sleeves
ESORMEAUX K J (29 5 4 2 .17) 2003:(202 30 .15)

Ch. c. 4 (Jan) KEESEP00 $140,000
Sire: Lord At War*Arg (General*Fr)
Dam: Catumbella(Diesis*GB)
Br: Mill Ridge Farm Ltd & W Lazy T Ltd (Ky)
Tr: McGee Paul J(6 1 0 1 .17) 2003:(69 7 .10)

L 116

Life	11	4	1	3	$144,993	99	D.Fst	1	1	0	0	$31,850	68
2003	3	1	0	1	$29,420	99	Wet(345)	1	0	0	1	$3,740	89
2002	5	1	1	1	$48,323	94	Turf(425)	9	3	1	2	$109,403	99
Kee Ⓣ	1	0	1	0	$16,785	94	DstⓉ(415)	0	0	0	0	$0	–

Mar03-9GP fm *1 1/16 Ⓣ :232 :474 1:112 1:42 4↑ OClm 100000N 96 2 42 43 41¾ 3nk 32½ Douglas R R L 122 11.70 99-08 Sttemnt1221¾ BsbllChmpion118¾ HonorInWr1221 Bumped twice stretch 9
Feb03-8GP fm 1 Ⓣ :223 :454 1:10 1:334 4↑ Alw 40000N3X 99 9 64¾ 52 52¼ 3½ 11¼ Coa E M L 118 3.50 97-06 Honor In War1181¼ Love TheGame1203¼ SpruceRun1181 Strong hand ride 10
Jan03-9GP fm 1 Ⓣ :241 :484 1:132 1:362 4↑ Alw 38000N3X 88 1 54 63½ 62½ 51¾ 52½ Day P L 118 *2.10 82-12 BttrTlkNow120nk GoodBoySm118hd HndsmGrg118½ Blocked deep stretch 10
Nov02-8CD yl 1 1/16 Ⓣ :251 :503 1:151 1:462 3↑ OClm 62500N 90 1 63 85¼ 76½ 55 53 Day P L 116 *1.80 69-33 Frefourintrnt1172 *BilOutThKing*117nk Tubrok117½ Bmp start,empty late 8
Oct02-7Kee fm 1 Ⓣ :234 :473 1:123 1:362 Storm Cat83k 94 7 31 3nk 11 11½ 2½ Albarado R J L 117 2.90 85-13 FebruryStorm117½ HonorInWr1172 GentlBin117½ Drift out 1/16p,2ndbst 8
Sep02-8AP sly 1 ⊗ :231 :46 1:11 1:372 3↑ Alw 34000N3X 89 7 42 44 3nk 2hd 32½ Sibille R L 118 *1.30 84-17 RockchalkJayhwk1182½ FourthFloor118hd HonorInWr11811 Flattened out 7
Aug02-9AP fm 1 Ⓣ :233 :473 1:12 1:36 Alw 39960N2X 90 4 32½ 21½ 2hd 13 15 Albarado R J L 118 *1.70 98-05 HonorInWar1185 TheGeneral'sBank122½ StormyImpact1203 Ridden out 8
Jan02-7GP fm 1 1/16 Ⓣ :242 :481 1:12 1:433+ Dave Feldman73k 82 5 62¼ 66 42 51¾ 42¾ Court J K L 120 4.20 74-21 WorldlyVictor1181½ ChrmingColony1181¼ LordJubn118no Not enough late 11
Nov01-3CD fm 1 Ⓣ :242 :483 1:132 1:373 Alw 49600NC 84 4 41½ 62½ 62¾ 21 1hd Court J K L 112 4.40 85-14 Honor In War112hd Rylstone1216½ Mystic Storm113nk Angled 6w lane,drv 7
Oct01-5Kee fst 1 1/16 :241 :483 1:141 1:472 Md Sp Wt 51k 68 5 32½ 32½ 32 31 11¾ Court J K L 118 2.90 68-32 *Honor In War*1181¾ Sip'n118nk Odell1182¼ 3-4w, steady drive 10
Sep01-3KD fm 1 Ⓣ :491 1:153 1:403 Md Sp Wt 28k 65 8 74 3½ 31½ 22 32 Peck B D 121 *1.90 70-17 Dell Place1212 Sip'n121hd *Honor In War*1213 No closing bid 8
ORKS: Apr3 Kee Ⓣ 5f fm 1:031 B (d) *2/3* Feb26 GP 5f fst 1:05 B *23/24* Feb19 GP Ⓣ 4f fm :491 B (d) *2/4*
AINER: 31-60Days(102 .14 $1.17) Turf(39 .13 $2.87) Routes(130 .15 $1.87) Alw(137 .16 $2.16)

That's significant. Honor in War's next start was at the same track, in the same allowance condition. He had a jockey change from Pat Day to Eibar Coa and a tougher post, the 9 in a field of 10. But he also figured to move forward in his second start back from a layoff. Sent off at 7-2, Honor in War got a clean trip and won by 1¼ lengths under a strong hand ride.

Trekking: The lightly raced filly from Great Britain was sent off at 3.20-1 in her first U.S. start for trainer Bobby Frankel, February 2, 2003. She dead-heated for fourth in the field of 10 from the 8 post under David Flores. Her comment line said she was shuffled at the quarter pole and steadied late.

Frankel returned Trekking on March 1, 2003, in a nonwinners-of-two allowance race. She had the same post, the 8 in a field of nine, and the same jockey, but went off at 6.30-1. Flores placed Trekking on the lead and it was all over as she cruised to a four-length win.

2 Trekking
Own:Juddmonte Farms Inc
ite Green, Pink Sash, White Sleeves, Pink
ZE T C (332 40 43 45 .12) 2003:(313 38 .12)

Ch. f. 4 (Jan)
Sire: Gone West (Mr. Prospector) $125,000
Dam: Didina*GB(Nashwan)
Br: Juddmonte Farms Inc (Ky)
Tr: Frankel Robert(83 23 16 12 .28) 2003:(92 30 .33)

L 111

Life	6	2	2	0	$47,235	95	D.Fst	0	0	0	0	$0	–
2003	2	1	0	0	$35,840	95	Wet(340)	0	0	0	0	$0	–
2002	4	1	2	0	$11,395	–	Turf(370)	6	2	2	0	$47,235	95
SA Ⓣ	2	1	0	0	$35,840	95	DstⓉ(410)	5	1	2	0	$13,635	83

Mar03-1SA gd 1⅛ Ⓣ :472 1:112 1:362 1:49 4↑ ⒻAlw 59360N1X 95 8 12½ 14 15 13 14 Flores D R LB 118 6.30 84-16 Trekking1184 SerenInSttl1182 KysToThHrt118nk Inside,steady handling 9
Feb03-7SA fm 1¼ Ⓣ :484 1:134 1:373 2:014 4↑ ⒻOClm 40000N 83 8 64¾ 65 65 54 43½↓ Flores D R LB 117 3.20 80-16 Splendeur117½ Absolute Charmer1171½ Java1191½ Shuffled 1/4,stdy late 10
Previously trained by Roger Charlton
Aug02 ♦ Brighton(GB) gd 1¼Ⓣ LH 1:592 3↑ ⒻVirginia Rated Hcp (Listed) Stk 42500 1224½ MacKay J 111 6.50 Averted View1332 Mubkera125no Celtic Ballet1112½ 13 *Rank tracking leaders,weakened 3f out*
Aug02 ♦ Beverley(GB) sf 1¼Ⓣ RH 2:102 Hull Daily Mail Maiden Stakes Maiden 11100 1¾ Darley K 121 *.50 Trekking121¾ Tanaji121¾ Alnahda1213 4 *Led throughout,held well*
Timeform rating: 76+
Jun02 ♦ Newmarket(GB) gd 1¼Ⓣ RH 2:052 Bjorn Again Maiden Stakes Maiden 9600 2no Hughes R 121 *2.75 Distinction126no Trekking1212½ Transit1262 16 *Led for 1f,led again over 2f out,caught on line*
Timeform rating: 82
Jun02 ♦ Newmarket(GB) gd 1¼Ⓣ Str 2:063 ⒻNGK Spark Plugs Maiden Stakes Maiden 11100 22½ Hughes R 123 5.00 Mount Street1232½ Trekking1232½ Ishtak1235 14 *Led or dueled to 100y out,outpaced late by winner*
Timeform rating: 82
ORKS: Apr15 Hol 5f fst 1:013 H *10/14* Apr7 Hol 5f fst 1:042 H *26/29* Apr1 Hol 5f fst 1:014 H *9/16* ●Mar25 Hol 5f fst 1:00 H *1/11* Feb24 Hol 4f fst :49 H *8/37* Feb17 Hol 5f fst 1:002 H *7/52*
AINER: 31-60Days(187 .27 $1.88) Turf(412 .25 $1.79) Routes(457 .26 $1.83) GrdStk(206 .27 $1.86)

Senora Poppy: She raced in a nonwinners-of-two allowance at Hollywood Park on July 12, 2002. Breaking from the rail in a field of 10, she went off at 8.60-1 and rallied from sixth, 10 lengths off the lead, to finish fifth by 3¾ lengths. The comment was, "Steadied ⅞, mild bid." But the mild bid came after she encountered trouble. Returned at the same allowance level at the same distance with the same jockey at Del Mar, August 17, she was 9-1 from the 3 post. She rallied from in between horses and won by a nose.

4 Senora Poppy
Own:Lakin Lewis A
Yellow — Green, Yellow Kj In Red Diamond Frame — $40,000
ALMEIDA G F (117 9 9 10 .08) 2003:(114 9 .08)

B. m. 5
Sire: El Gran Senor (Northern Dancer)
Dam: Tall Poppy(Alydar)
Br: Gallaghers Stud (NY)
Tr: McAnally Ronald(97 12 13 10 .12) 2003:(100 13 .13)

L 118

Life	16	2	4	0	$96,225	90	D.Fst	2	0	0	0	$960	5
2003	2	0	0	0	$3,120	82	Wet(300)	0	0	0	0	$0	-
2002	8	2	2	0	$81,660	90	Turf(350)	14	2	4	0	$95,265	9
SA Ⓣ	3	1	0	0	$33,120	82	DstⓉ(340)	9	1	3	0	$53,780	8

14Mar03-2SA	fm	1	Ⓣ :241 :472 1:111 1:353	4↑	ⒻClm 62500 (62.5-55)	71	1	31	31½	31½	53	56	Almeida G F	LB 118 b	4.80	78-08	ⒹQuFcilCorzon1202½ KissingGirl120½ LndEdr1181	Tight 7/8,lckd room1/8
Placed 4th through disqualification.																		
17Jan03-7SA	fm	1	Ⓣ :232 :461 1:093 1:332	4↑	ⒻOClm 80000N	82	1	77	89½	77½	84½	96¾	Almeida G F	LB 119 b	24.40	88-07	*SeaOfShowers*1191 Revenante1191½ Nanogrm1191½	Saved ground, no rally
21Nov02-7Hol	fm	1	Ⓣ :241 :473 1:111 1:35	3↑	ⒻOClm 80000N	89	1	45½	43½	41½	52½	63	Almeida G F	LB 118 b	27.20	86-13	Adalgisa117hd Nanogram118nk Sweep The Deck115½	Saved ground to 1/4
17Aug02-6Dmr	fm	1 1/16	Ⓣ :243 :50 1:142 1:443	3↑	ⒻAlw 60000N1X	90	3	74¼	74½	51¾	41¼	1no	Almeida G F	LB 121 b	9.00	80-18	SenoraPoppy121no CrmelQueen119nk RunwyPro1162½	Rallied btwn,gamely
12Jly02-6Hol	fm	1 1/16	Ⓣ :241 :481 1:121 1:421	3↑	ⒻAlw 50000N1X	80	1	610	79½	66	64	53¾	Almeida G F	LB 121 b	8.60	80-16	FullyInvstd1192 NorthrnBlu123hd *I'mThBusnss*119hd	Steadied 7/8,mild bid
16Jun02-8Hol	fm	1	Ⓣ :234 :47 1:104 1:353	3↑	ⒻAlw 51000N1X	87	3	75½	65½	74¾	72½	42½	Almeida G F	LB 121 b	34.70	83-16	QuickToPls1212 BlushngRhy119½ I'mThBusnss119hd	Tight 3/8,stdied 5/16
5May02-6Hol	fm	1	Ⓣ :232 :462 1:103 1:342	4↑	ⒻAlw 51918N1X	83	6	55	68¼	63¾	54½	75¾	Solis A	LB 120 b	27.50	86-09	*Surya*1203 BlushingRahy113½ I'mTheBusiness1181	Chased btwn,no rally
17Apr02-2SA	fm	1	Ⓣ :24 :481 1:123 1:37	3↑	ⒻMd Sp Wt 52k	78	3	11½	11	11	12½	12½	McCarron C J	LB 124 b	*1.80	77-16	SenoraPoppy1242½ Delavllde1241 GingerRoo1241	Inside,steady handling
Previously trained by Stewart Dallas																		
8Mar02-10FG	fm	*1	Ⓣ :252 :502 1:17 1:424	3↑	ⒻMd Sp Wt 28k	75	5	31½	3nk	1hd	21	2nk	Melancon L	L 123 b	*1.80	71-27	Executricker123nk *Senora Poppy*1235½ Hot Time1231½	Not good enough
3Feb02-6FG	fm	*1	Ⓣ :242 :49 1:15 1:403	4	ⒻMd Sp Wt 30k	69	5	21½	2hd	2hd	13	2nk	Meche L J	L 122	2.40	82-12	MotownMedley122nk SnorPoppy1221½ *Norm'sLgcy*1222	Took over, failed
27Dec01-6FG	fm	*1	Ⓣ :232 :481 1:151 1:394	3↑	ⒻMd Sp Wt 30k	73	1	33	32	21	11½	21½	Meche L J	L 119	6.20	84-13	*Vauxhall*1191½ Senora Poppy1191½ Skyline1191	Took over, no match
4Nov01-1CD	fst	1 1/16	:234 :474 1:133 1:451	3↑	ⒻMd Sp Wt 41k	53	2	11	11½	1½	46	515	Meche L J	L 118	10.90	69-16	Eden1188¼ Naropa118½ *Restless One*1185¾	Weakened after 3/4s

WORKS: Apr13 SA 5f fst 1:02 H *18/33* Apr8 SA 5f fst 1:002 H *5/40* Mar30 SA 5f fst 1:011 H *33/63* Mar23 SA 4f fst :483 H *15/32* Mar7 SA 6f fst 1:121 H *8/52* Mar1 SA 6f fst 1:134 H *21/47*
TRAINER: 31-60Days(164 .16 $2.38) Turf(277 .12 $1.41) Claim(53 .15 $1.77)

Marine: Sent off the 1.30-1 favorite from the 5 post in the Grade 3 Ascot Handicap at Bay Meadows on June 10, 2001, she was sixth in midrace and then did not finish. The comment was "Impeded, pulled up." There cannot be any more trouble than that.

12 Marine (GB)
Own:Englander Richard A
Lime — Green Green Rae 18 On White Diamond — $80,000
VALENZUELA P A (450 87 90 75 .19) 2003:(424 84 .20)

Dk. b or br h. 5
Sire: Marju*Ire (Last Tycoon*Ire)
Dam: Ivorine(Blushing Groom*Fr)
Br: Juddmonte Farms (GB)
Tr: Mullins Jeff(85 28 25 8 .33) 2003:(85 28 .33)

L 118

Life	20	5	1	3	$252,799	100	D.Fst	0	0	0	0	$0
2003	1	0	0	0	$1,040	95	Wet(309*)	0	0	0	0	$0
2002	4	1	1	0	$55,360	100	Turf(375)	20	5	1	3	$252,799
SA Ⓣ	5	1	1	0	$69,849	95	DstⓉ(400)	11	2	1	2	$129,871

13Mar03-3SA	fm	1	Ⓣ :233 :471 1:104 1:341	4↑	Clm c-(62.5-55)	95	4	76	75	51¼	51½	51½	Nakatani C S	LB 118 b	2.30	89-11	*BitOfLuck*118½ TimberBron118½ *RodToSlew*118½	4-5wd into lane,no bi
Claimed from Juddmonte Farms Inc for $62,500, Frankel Robert Trainer 2003(as of 03/13): (55 14 12 6 0.25)																		
28Nov02-7Hol	fm	1	Ⓣ :234 :463 1:101 1:341	3↑	Alw 58000N$mY	94	5	410	416	49½	47	43	Valenzuela P A	LB 116 b	2.70	90-09	River Rush1181 Lugny116hd Master Belt1162	Came out,closed ga
1Nov02-7SA	fm	1	Ⓣ :242 :49 1:124 1:361	3↑	OClm 80000	95	7	64	63¾	73¾	62¾	2½	Valenzuela P A	LB 118 b	*2.00	80-20	Motto118½ Marine118no R. Baggio118½	Blocked lane,stdie
4Oct02-3SA	fm	1	Ⓣ :241 :481 1:113 1:35	3↑	OClm 100000	95	5	74¾	73¼	63¼	63¼	41¼	Valenzuela P A	LB 118 b	4.30	86-14	*NightLife*118no ByouTheMoon118hd *DukeOfGren*1181	Cameo out,late bi
24Aug02-3Dmr	fm	1	Ⓣ :232 :47 1:102 1:341	3↑	Clm 80000 (80-70)	100	5	54	52¼	41¼	31	1nk	Valenzuela P A	LB 119 b	2.60	94-04	Marine119nk Motto1192½ Macaneo1192	3wd into lane,gamel
26Dec01-8SA	fm	1	Ⓣ :233 :473 1:114 1:361		Sir Beaufort77k	82	7	89¾	78¼	54½	45	45½	Desormeaux K J	LB 122 b	4.00	80-13	Orientate1222 Sigfreto1221½ Blue Steller1222	Rail move,no late bi
3Sep01-8Dmr	fm	1⅛	Ⓣ :473 1:11 1:36 1:474		Del Mar Dby-G2	84	8	96½	99½	1011	96½	85½	Nakatani C S	LB 121 b	*2.10e	89-14	Romnceishope1211 *IndygoShiner*121nk *BlueStellr*1211½	Split foes,no rall
11Aug01-7Dmr	fm	1 1/16	Ⓣ :232 :473 1:113 1:413		La Jolla H-G3	95	8	87¾	76¼	74	51¾	1nk	Nakatani C S	LB 117 b	7.60	97-03	Marine117nk *Romanceishope*1182 *MisterApprovl*113nk	Waited,split,rallie
10Jun01-8BM	fm	1 1/16	Ⓣ :242 :49 1:123 1:44		Ascot H-G3	—	5	74	87	67½	—	—	Blanc B	LB 120 b	*1.30	— 10	SirAlfred114¾ Hoovergetthekeys121nk SeaToSee1182	Impeded, pulled u
20May01-8Hol	fm	1⅛	Ⓣ :482 1:12 1:354 1:482 +		Cinema H-G3	92	5	77¼	76½	77¼	54	32½	Delahoussaye E	LB 119 b	*1.90	84-15	Sligo Bay1181 Learing At Kathy1171½ Marine119¾	Off bit slow,late 3r
20Apr01-7Hol	fm	1	Ⓣ :242 :481 1:104 1:35		WillRogers-G3	88	2	54	62¾	52¼	42	51½	Delahoussaye E	LB 121 b	*1.90	88-10	DH MdMogl116 DH Dr.Prk117hd LrngAtKthy1161¼	Moved btwn,no late bi
31Mar01-8SA	fm	1	Ⓣ :232 :47 1:11 1:351		Ⓡ La Puente83k	95	6	87	66	31	2hd	1½	Delahoussaye E	LB 116 b	4.70	91-14	Marine116½ DH River God118 DH *Media Mogul*1141	4wd into lane,gamel

WORKS: Apr12 SA 5f fst 1:00 H *11/64* Apr4 SA 5f fst 1:024 H *38/40* Mar28 SA 4f fst :511 H *32/33* Mar9 Hol 4f fst :492 H *15/23* Mar3 Hol 6f fst 1:144 H *8/21* Feb24 Hol 6f fst 1:141 H *2/11*
TRAINER: 1stClaim(33 .27 $2.39) 31-60Days(71 .25 $3.05) Turf(72 .21 $2.83) Claim(139 .27 $2.70)

She was freshened and returned to the races two months later in a Grade 3 stakes, the La Jolla Handicap, at the same distance, 1¹/₁₆ miles. Corey Nakatani replaced Brice Blanc from the 8 post. She won by a neck at 7.60-1.

Storm Signal: At Bay Meadows on June 9, 2001, Storm Signal was sent off as the 2.20-1 favorite in a nonwinners of two from post 3. The gelding finished seventh by four lengths in the field of eight with the comment "Steadied at the eighth pole."

Five weeks later, Storm Signal was entered in the same allowance level—for a bigger purse—at Hollywood Park with a new trainer, Simon Bray, and a new jockey, Victor Espinoza. Breaking from the 7 post in the field of nine, he won by half a length at odds of 30.80-1.

10

ON SHAKY GROUND

WHEN YOU BET GRASS races over wet courses labeled soft and/or yielding, you're adding a volatile variable to your handicapping. In a way, betting such grass races is even more difficult than betting horses on wet dirt tracks. Everybody pretty much has a handle on the difference between sloppy, muddy, and wet-fast racetracks. But when grass courses get bogged down, it's nearly impossible to gauge how soft or yielding they might be, and how yielding courses at different tracks compare. A horse who has performed well on a yielding course at Churchill Downs might be uncomfortable on a yielding course at Belmont Park.

A turf course is labeled yielding when it contains a considerable amount of moisture and horses' hooves sink into it noticeably. A course is labeled soft when there is a large amount of moisture and horses' hooves sink even more deeply into the surface.

Hall of Fame trainer Phil Johnson tries to avoid sending inexperienced grass horses out on a soft or yielding course for their first grass race. "If you introduce a horse to turf on a soft course, you're making a mistake. It's a struggling course. You can hurt a tendon or a suspensory. You can ruin him for life. You also can't get a straight line on him. I always make a point of, if I introduce a horse to turf racing, I do it on a firm course."

Johnson said yielding courses can improve a front-runner because the horses behind him have to run over ground that he may have already torn up.

A sample of races from major tracks around the country for five weeks in March and April 2003 discovered only one grass race run on a soft course. That race, at Bay Meadows, was won by a closer sent off at 2.40-1.

Ten other races in that sample were conducted over yielding courses at Golden Gate Fields, Bay Meadows, Keeneland, Santa Anita, and Fair Grounds. Three of the 10 came in the space of 90 minutes on the afternoon of April 17 at Keeneland. The first winner, Honor in War, closed from last in a field of four to win by half a length at odds of 2.10-1. In the next grass race, Californian came from last in the field of nine to win by $3\frac{1}{4}$ lengths at 13-1. The final turf race was taken by Jester, a 59.30-1 longshot who stalked the early pace from third and fourth and won by a nose.

The very next day at Keeneland, two more races were contested over that same yielding course. Affirmed Dancer won his race by three-quarters of a length at 7-5 after dueling on the front end almost the entire way, opening a clear lead and holding on. The other grass race was won wire to wire by Ocean Drive at odds of 2-1.

Of the 10-race sample, three were won wire to wire or virtually wire to wire, three by stalkers, two by midpack closers, and two by closers from well off the pace. Six of the 10 winners were 5-2 or lower. The others were 5-1, 7-1, 13-1, and 59-1.

What about performance on soft and yielding courses by top turf horses? Twenty-six horses who competed in the 2002 Breeders' Cup Filly and Mare Turf, Breeders' Cup Mile, and Breeders' Cup Turf had run on soft or yielding courses in Europe or the United States.

Of the 26, the combined European horses' record was 14 for 35 on yielding courses and 12 for 32 on soft courses. In North America, those same European grass horses were a combined 5 for 9 on yielding courses and 2 for 4 on soft courses. Obviously, as is already widely known, European grass horses tend to do well on soft and yielding courses in North America. One of the most interesting examples is Starine, who was only 2 for 7 on yielding courses in Europe, but won her lone North American start on a yielding course convincingly at Arlington Park in the 2002 Breeders' Cup Filly and Mare Turf.

Courses labeled heavy and/or good are an entirely different matter. What is termed good at one track may be labeled firm at another. So look for horses that have at least shown success on the same type of course at the same track they're competing at today. If that information is unavailable, focus on past-performance lines with the exact same condition at other tracks that horse had previously competed on.

But the reality is that you are playing with too many unknowns unless you are focusing on a single track you know well. Be cautious if you're betting on simulcasts of grass races being run on "off" turf at other tracks. It's hard enough to handicap and bet winners when the track condition is a constant.

However, when a horse who has raced well on firm footing runs poorly on a soft or yielding course, throw the race out, much as you would a bad showing by a dirt horse who had been racing well on dry tracks, then performed poorly on a sloppy or muddy one.

A perfect example was the outstanding grass filly Graceful Darby. After going 1 for 9 on dirt, the daughter of Darby Creek Road out of the His Majesty mare Graceful Touch won her first three grass starts, one of them a stakes, and all of them on firm turf. She then ran third twice in stakes on courses labeled soft and yielding. When she showed up for the 1987 Nijana Stakes at Saratoga, she was sent off at 7-2 over firm turf. She won by two lengths. That made her 4 for 4 on firm turf.

How about a more recent example? "Awful" would be a kind word to describe Pimlico Race Course after unrelenting rain pelted Baltimore on the day before and day of the 2003 Preakness Stakes, May 17. It was amazing that the Grade 2, $200,000 Dixie Stakes was kept on the grass, but it was. Officially, the soggy course was labeled soft for the $1^1/8$-mile stakes.

Scratches reduced the field to six, with the obvious favorite being Del Mar Show, trained by Bill Mott and ridden by Jerry Bailey. Del Mar Show had finished second by $2^1/2$ lengths in the 2002 Dixie, which had been contested on a yielding course, in his 5-year-old debut, then won the Grade 3 New Hampshire Sweepstakes and the Grade 2 Bernard Baruch Handicap.

Del Mar Show had also won his 6-year-old debut, an allowance race at Keeneland, by two lengths at even money. He was 1 for 31 on yielding courses in his PP's and would go off at 9-10 this day.

What about the competition?

Sardaukar, whose only win in 11 starts the last two years was in an allowance race at Delaware Park, appeared overmatched. He was third in allowance company in his only PP on a soft or yielding course.

Strategic Partner was a classy grass horse through 2001, accumulating more than $160,000 in earnings. But he raced just three times since, posting a pair of thirds. He'd run well in his last start, finishing third by $1^1/2$ lengths in the Grade 3 Canadian Turf Handicap. He showed three starts in his PP's in yielding courses, finishing second, seventh, and fifth.

Perfect Soul would be the 1.70-1 second choice, stepping up off a $5^1/4$-length allowance win for nonwinners of four (three other than) at 2-1 in his 5-year-old debut. He had finished second, fourth, eighth, and sixth in four stakes tries. Two were Grade 1 stakes on yielding courses. In the Canadian International, he was fourth by $6^3/4$ lengths at 7-1. In the Breeder's Cup Turf, he was last by 20 lengths in the field of eight at 33-1.

Loup Masque exited the same allowance race at Keeneland, having finished fourth behind Perfect Soul at 6-1. Previously in Europe, he had won 1 of 4 starts on soft courses.

Dr. Brendler's last start was a different allowance race for non-winners of four at Keeneland, a race he won by three-quarters of a length at 3-1. That was his top PP showing. His bottom PP was intriguing. In the only PP showing a soft or yielding course, Dr. Brendler had finished fourth by $3^{1}/_{2}$ lengths in the 2002 Dixie Stakes, beaten all of one length by Del Mar Show at odds of 34-1.

Any horse within a length of Del Mar Show had to be considered a contender, but Dr. Brendler also showed he was in good form off his last race and had displayed an ability to run on a soft course right here at Pimlico in the very same stakes.

After cashing maybe one ticket the previous two days, I bet pick threes concluding with Funny Cide and Peace Rules in the Preakness. The Dixie was the first leg, and I used two horses, Del Mar Show and Dr. Brendler. I used several horses in the middle leg and caught the winner, Windsor Castle, at 9-2, but the horse who made the $2 pick three worth $652.40 was Dr. Brendler, who won the Dixie by half a length at 18-1, paying $39.40.

Was it a fluke? Not really. Dr. Brendler followed his Dixie victory with another fine performance on a soft course, this time the Grade 1 Manhattan Handicap, on the Belmont Stakes undercard June 7. Sent off at 22-1, Dr. Brendler finished third, verifying his class, form, and ability to handle soggy grass.

11

A PERFECT SIX

FOR A PUBLIC HANDICAPPER, it was the chance of a lifetime. How many times will any handicapper be on the threshold of selecting an entire pick six straight, let alone one at Saratoga Race Course, arguably the most difficult meet to handicap in the country?

Yet as the field of six headed into the starting gate for the eighth race at Saratoga, August 15, 2002, that was the opportunity in front of me. And we weren't talking about a pick six worth a couple of hundred dollars; rather, I estimated, at least a thousand dollars. Maybe two or three.

The odd thing about that Thursday afternoon was that my day couldn't have started on a worse note. My first-race selection in the *Daily Gazette* (of Schenectady, New York) was the favored 8-5 entry in a steeplechase allowance. But one half of the entry, Cairo Express, did something I'd never seen in 30 years of watching steeplechase racing at Saratoga. He stood there. He just stood there.

Eventually, his rider walked him up the length of the course. His entrymate, Miles Ahead, finished second. I thought maybe the entry would have been declared a scratch, but that did not happen.

In the second race, the first-time starter I'd selected in a 2-year-old New York-bred maiden race, Manny's Gold Maker, came from far back to win by a neck, paying $8.30.

In the third, the first leg of the pick six, I had settled on the 9-5 favorite, Talk's Cheap. Fifty yards from the finish, he looked hopelessly beaten as Wild Imagination continued his attempt to wire the field. Just before the last jump, Talk's Cheap got within a nose-bob of Wild Imagination. But I, as well as most everyone in the press box, thought Wild Imagination had held on. He had not. Talk's Cheap won by a head. Then I won the fourth with 6-5 favorite Roses for Sonja.

The fifth race was a $60,000 claimer for 3-year-olds at $1\frac{1}{8}$ miles on grass. Three scratches reduced the field to eight. In post-position order:

1. **Wild Goose** He and the No. 3 horse, Wild Maple, were coming out of the same race, a $60,000 turf claimer at $1\frac{1}{16}$ miles at Saratoga. At 14-1, Wild Goose had beaten Wild Maple by a head, continuing a remarkable run since being claimed for $10,000 on February 18 at Gulfstream Park by W. Paschal Bignault. Wild Goose finished second by seven lengths when he was claimed, but won a $12,500 claimer by $6\frac{3}{4}$ lengths for his new connections. Bignault decided to try the son of Prenup out of the Sharpen Up mare Clarity on grass in the $37,000 Fabulous Frolic Stakes at Calder. Wild Goose finished fourth at 24-1. After finishing second in an off-the-turf race and fourth in a nonwinners of two on grass, Wild Goose won a stakes race at Colonial Downs for Virginia-breds by $6\frac{1}{2}$ lengths. After finishing third in a $40,000 claimer at Calder that had been taken off the turf, Wild Goose switched barns. Trainer Timothy Ritvo brought Wild Goose to Saratoga and

spotted him well in the $60,000 claimer he gamely won under Victor Carrero, who kept the mount today. An obvious threat.

Wild Goose Dk. b or br g. 3 (Apr)
Own: Michael C Hanafin Robert Killian — Sire: Prenup (Smarten) $3,500
Cream, Green Shamrock, Cream/green $60,000 — Dam: Clarity(Sharpen Up*GB)
Br: Melville Church III (Va)
ARRERO V (97 4 11 19 .04) 2002:(465 52 .11) — Tr: Ritvo Timothy(14 2 0 1 .14) 2002:(315 37 .12)
L 117⁵

Life	18	4	4	4	$79,899	83	D.Fst	9	2	2	3	$18,945 67
2002	10	3	3	2	$69,064	83	Wet(321)	5	0	2	1	$8,730 71
2001	8	1	1	2	$10,835	49	Turf(295)	4	2	0	0	$52,224 83
Sar Ⓣ	1	1	0	0	$25,200	83	DstⓉ(310)	0	0	0	0	$0 –

Jly02-6Sar fm 1 1/16 Ⓣ :233 :482 1:123 1:43 Clm 60000 (60-50) 83 2 31½ 41 44½ 42 1hd Carrero V5 L 117 14.80 87-13 Wild Goose117hd **Wild Maple**119hd FineAndDandy1191½ Split rivals, driving 8
Previously trained by Bignault W Paschal
Jly02-5Crc sly 1 1/16 ⊗ :232 :473 1:132 1:473 Clm 40000 (40-35) 71 7 65 65½ 33 33 31¼ Toribio A Jr L 119 3.20e 73-25 Mar Rojo117½ Plausible115¾ *Wild Goose*1197¾ Boxed in into stretch 8
Jun02-7Cnl fm 1 1/16 Ⓣ :233 :481 1:131 1:444 Ⓢ John D Marsh40k 77 6 55¼ 53¾ 42 12½ 16½ Karamanos H A L 115 *1.70 81-23 Wild Goose1156½ Charles115½ Chain1152¾ Rated,4wd sweep,drivng 6
Jun02-9Crc fm 1 1/16 Ⓣ :231 :481 1:122 1:441 Alw 24000N1X 71 8 3nk 31 31 3½ 44¾ Nunez E O L 117 3.00 70-25 Valid Action1171½ *Mar Rojo*1171¾ Suave King1171½ 3 wide, bid, weakened 10
May02-8Crc sly 1 1/16 ⊗ :231 :48 1:142 1:493 Alw 24000N1X 67 4 65¼ 63¼ 32½ 32½ 25¼ Nunez E O L 119 6.40 59-26 Noble Jester1195¼ Wild Goose119¾ Suave King1193¼ Steadied far turn 10
May02-8Crc fm 1 1/16 Ⓣ :241 :492 1:124 1:42 FabulousFrol37k 80 7 11 11 1½ 2½ 44¼ Nunez E O L 114 24.00 82-10 *Lord Juban*1212 Class Of Seventy118¾ Bernie B1161½ On rail, weakened 7
Apr02-1GP fst 7f :232 :472 1:122 1:252 Clm 12500N2L 67 1 1 2hd 1½ 14 16¾ Toribio A Jr L 122 *1.80 80-12 WildGoose1226¾ TroubleNPrdise122½ *GentlemnJrry*1228 Inside, drew off 6
Feb02-3GP fst 1 1/16 :232 :473 1:134 1:474 Clm c-(10-9) 55 1 54 46 42½ 33½ 27 Toribio A Jr 120 *1.40 62-31 *LiberlMedi*1207 *WildGoose*1201 TheRedAppl1203 Saved grnd, up for 2nd 8
Claimed from Hale Kay for $10,000, Hale Robert A Trainer 2002(as of 02/18): (235 45 30 35 0.19)
Feb02-3GP fst 170 :234 :484 1:152 1:471 Clm 9000 (10-9) 62 5 3½ 31 31 1hd 2hd Toribio A Jr 118 *1.30 65-36 SuvKng122hd ⒹWldGoos1182¾ BrgndyTowr12010 Bounced around stretch 5
Disqualified and placed third
Jan02-1GP fst 1 1/16 :25 :504 1:162 1:50 Clm 9000 (10-9) 51 6 21½ 21½ 3½ 1hd 33½ Toribio A Jr 118 8.10 54-31 Super Editor1201 ⒹStone Ledge1132½ Wild Goose118nk In tight 1/16 pole 9
Placed second through disqualification.
Dec01-6Crc fst 7f :232 :474 1:14 1:273 Clm 10500 (12.5-10.5)N2L 46 7 3 53½ 31½ 33½ 43 Toribio A Jr 118 4.70 73-21 MinngCsh120½ Murry'sD.J1181 TroublNPrds1201½ Bumped bkstr, no rally 7
Dec01-3Crc fst 1 :242 :49 1:142 1:414 Clm 10500 (12.5-10.5) 49 2 1hd 1hd 1hd 2½ 35½ Toribio A Jr 118 4.80 76-19 *There'sHopeSir*113nk FabulousFlir1155¼ WildGoose1186 Vied on rail, tired 5
ORKS: Aug9 Sar tr.t 4f fst :512 B *8/10* Jly7 Crc 5f fst 1:024 B *6/15* Jun15 Crc 5f sly 1:05 B (d) *9/12*
RAINER: Turf(198 .10 $1.14) Routes(301 .11 $1.14) Claim(347 .11 $1.32)

2. **Gleam Supreme** Off five months since winning a maiden claimer dirt race at Gulfstream Park. The race before he was fifth in a maiden claimer, his third grass start without a win. Next.

Gleam Supreme Dk. b or br c. 3 (Mar) KEESEP00 $360,000
Own: Marceda Michael — Sire: Mt. Livermore (Blushing Groom*Fr) $40,000
Red, Green Star, Green Chevrons $60,000 — Dam: Glimmer of Gold(Slew o' Gold)
Br: LJH Farm (Ky)
AMYN J L (31 3 4 4 .10) 2002:(310 40 .13) — Tr: Russo Sal(3 1 0 0 .33) 2002:(27 4 .15)
118

Life	6	1	1	1	$17,850	77	D.Fst	1	1	0	0	$10,200 71
2002	2	1	0	0	$10,440	71	Wet(365)	2	0	0	1	$2,730 50
2001	4	M	1	1	$7,410	77	Turf(290)	3	0	1	0	$4,920 77
Sar Ⓣ	0	0	0	0	$0	–	DstⓉ(325)	0	0	0	0	$0 –

Previously trained by Mott William I
Mar02-10GP fst 170 :22 :453 1:121 1:434 Md 45000 (45-40) 71 5 59 38 3nk 1½ 17¼ Bailey J D 122 b *1.60 82-14 GlemSuprm1227¼ PkbbuBoy1228¼ *StormyRomn*122nk Steadied st, drew off 9
Jan02-10GP fm *1 1/16 Ⓣ :24 :493 1:141 1:464 Md 62500 (62.5-57.5) 64 1 53 54½ 64½ 33½ 54 Bailey J D 122 b *1.20 64-32 Dungeon1221¼ Dinner Bound1221 *Admiration*1201 Lacked late response 10
Dec01-9Crc gd 1 1/16 ⊗ :234 :484 1:144 1:49 Md Sp Wt 26k 50 4 51¾ 53 21½ 32 34 Douglas R R 120 b *.90 72-19 Classical Hunter120½ Acting Class1203½ Gleam Supreme12020 Weakened 6
Nov01-2Crc fm 1 1/16 Ⓣ :223 :474 1:123 1:452 Md Sp Wt 24k 77 10 56 54 32 3½ 2½ Douglas R R 118 b 3.00 68-28 PrgmticPursuit118½ GlemSuprem1182¾ Midwtch1183½ Off slowly, gamely 10
Oct01-4Bel gd 1 Ⓣ :234 :48 1:131 1:381 Md Sp Wt 42k 62 7 82 83½ 83¾ 66¾ 57¾ Castellano J J 118 b .80e 59-25 Royalton118¾ Orchard Park1182¾ Market Floor118½ Inside trip, no rally 10
Aug01-2Sar my 7f :23 :463 1:114 1:244 Md Sp Wt 41k 10 9 1 94¾ 67¼ 820 830¼ Castellano J J 118 b 5.70e 51-17 LighteningDeher1181½ PowrConnction1185¼ *FinlTbl*1181 4 wide trip, tired 9
ORKS: Aug10 Sar 4f fst :48 H *2/50* Jly27 Sar 4f fst :50 B *31/49* Jly21 Bel 4f fst :493 B *25/44*
RAINER: 1stW/Tm(4 .25 $1.85) 61-180Days(3 .33 $15.53) Dirt/Turf(6 .33 $27.77) Turf(13 .31 $14.63) Routes(27 .15 $7.04) Claim(28 .14 $2.77)

3. **Wild Maple** Though 0 for 4 on grass, he'd been second twice and third once. The lone miss was a close fifth in an $80,000 claimer at Gulfstream in his grass debut. He'd been 7-1 under Edgar Prado in his head loss to Wild Goose in his last start, but Prado departed to ride Charming Colony. Jorge Chavez picked up the mount.

3 Wild Maple
Own:Johnston Mrs S K
Orange, Brown Sash/j, Brown $60,000
CHAVEZ J F (98 13 19 9 .13) 2002:(789 151 .19)

Dk. b or br g. 3 (Mar) FTFFEB01 $72,000
Sire: Wild Again (Icecapade) $50,000
Dam: Maple Heart(Woodman)
Br: Hermitage Farm LLC & Walter Freeman (Ky)
Tr: Connors Robert F(4 0 1 1 .00) 2002:(96 19 .20)

L 118

Life	13	1	3	2	$50,100	83	D.Fst	9	1	1	1	$29,240
2002	8	1	3	1	$44,060	83	Wet(360)	0	0	0	0	$0
2001	5	M	0	1	$6,040	60	Turf(305)	4	0	2	1	$20,860
Sar Ⓣ	1	0	1	0	$8,400	83	DstⓉ(335)	0	0	0	0	$0

28Jly02-6Sar fm 1 1/16 Ⓣ :233 :482 1:123 1:43 Clm 60000 (60-50) 83 1 65½ 52 32 3½ 2hd Prado E S L 119 b 7.00 87-13 **WildGoose**117hd WildMaple119hd FineAndDndy1191½ 3 wide move, gamely
22Jun02-9Del fm *1 1/16 Ⓣ :234 :481 1:132 1:464 3↑ Alw 40500N1X 75 7 1014 918 68 31 3¾ Dominguez R A L 112 b 2.70 79-20 Star Captain112no *In The Clear*112¾ Wild Maple112¾ Blockd,split h,outfin
9Jun02-4Del fm 1 1/16 Ⓣ :234 :474 1:114 1:432 Alw 39900N1X 77 4 87¾ 86 72½ 1hd 21¼ Dominguez R A L 118 b *2.20 89-12 Skate Away1231¼ Wild Maple1182¼ Mt. Moran118½ Rated,bid,gamely
5May02-8Del fst 170 :231 :471 1:12 1:422 Alw 39500N1X 62 9 88 74¼ 53 58 612½ Caraballo J C L 116 b 7.30 76-17 JimThirdsBolero116½ InTheClear116¾ InHalo'sImge1167¼ Brushed,no bid
3Apr02-7GP fst 1 1/16 :241 :481 1:13 1:46 Alw 34000N1X 78 4 43 53 51¼ 31½ 22¾ Coa E M L 118 b 3.60 75-28 Catlike Move1182¾ Wild Maple118hd Star Captain1186¼ Drifted out,placed
2Mar02-8GP fm 1 1/16 Ⓣ :241 :484 1:13 1:441+ Clm 80000 (80-75) 75 9 74¾ 66½ 55 44¼ 51¾ Chavez J F L 120 b 6.90 72-23 ClssOfSeventy122nk TmeNtive118nk DinnerBound120nk Slow start, gaining
6Feb02-8GP fst 170 :244 :491 1:132 1:424 Alw 34000N1X 68 1 51¾ 41 51¾ 44 46 Chavez J F L 118 b 13.90 81-13 Personal Reward118½ Quest Star1223¼ Marasca1182¼ Steadied 1st turn
24Jan02-1GP fst 1 1/16 :243 :49 1:144 1:492 Md 62500 (62.5-57.5) 64 6 44 41¾ 31 13 18½ Chavez J F L 122 b 4.20 61-36 WildMaple1228½ JamicnJustice1223½ ResidentRogue1221¼ 3 wide, drew off
24Oct01-2Del fst 170 :221 :461 1:14 1:471 Md Sp Wt 30k 40 5 58¼ 56½ 42¼ 57 515 Beckner D V L 120 b 5.20 50-34 *SetOpn*1208¼ PowrConnction120nk Hlo'sHonour1204¾ Bid far turn, stopped
9Oct01-1Med fst 1 :23 :454 1:104 1:363 Md Sp Wt 44k 52 3 64½ 57 45½ 48 315 Beckner D V L 118 b 6.50 74-16 *Soul Of The Tiger*1187¼ AugustSong1187¾ WildMaple118nk Mild stretch bid
8Sep01-1Del fst 6f :22 :454 :591 1:13 Md Sp Wt 46k 27 11 1 73½ 96½ 87½ 816 Delgado A L 119 11.10 62-15 CapnWunnerful114no *FuzzyStar*1191½ *MazoolianGhost*1192 Through early
25Aug01-3Sar fst 6f :223 :46 :581 1:111 Md Sp Wt 41k 56 4 9 79½ 73½ 77 69¾ Bridgmohan S X L 118 25.50 78-08 BrntEmbr1182 Esyfromthgtgo1181¼ *BoldTrth*1185 Bumped start, greenly
WORKS: Jly24 Del 4f fst :513 B *47/60* May31 Del 3f fst :362 B *2/10* May16 Del 4f fst :49 B *2/17*
TRAINER: Turf(76 .12 $0.91) Routes(137 .15 $1.21) Claim(64 .17 $1.31)

4. Wild Buddy In his very first grass start, he'd finished fifth by three lengths behind Charming Colony at 7-1 in a nonwinners-of-two allowance at this distance at Calder on December 22, 2001. Charming Colony that day was 19-1. Wild Buddy subsequently won 1 of 7 turf starts, by a head at 4-5, in a nonwinners of two. On June 1, 2002, he was fourth by 7¼ lengths at 13-1 in the $75,000 Simply Majestic Stakes on a yielding course at Calder at 1 1/16 miles.

More recently, he'd been given two months off by trainer Edward Plesa Jr. Wild Buddy returned to action in a nonwinners of three at Saratoga at one mile on a soft course. He was dead on the board at 23-1 despite the addition of new rider Robbie Davis, one of the better grass riders in New York. Though he gained five lengths in the stretch, he finished sixth by eight lengths.

4 Wild Buddy
Own:Thorobeam Farm
Hunter Green Silver Triangular Panel $60,000
DAVIS R G (40 2 6 2 .05) 2002:(419 60 .14)

B. g. 3 (Feb)
Sire: Line In The Sand (Mr. Prospector)
Dam: Island Capitol(Manila)
Br: Farnsworth Farms (Fla)
Tr: Plesa Edward Jr(8 1 1 1 .13) 2002:(219 34 .16)

L 118

Life	11	2	3	1	$51,130	83	D.Fst	3	1	1	0	$12,140
2002	8	1	2	1	$39,100	79	Wet(275)	0	0	0	0	$0
2001	3	1	1	0	$12,030	83	Turf(275)	8	1	2	1	$38,990
Sar Ⓣ	1	0	0	0	$0	78	DstⓉ(280)	2	0	0	1	$3,630

3Aug02-10Sar sf 1 Ⓣ :242 :481 1:122 1:364 3↑ Alw 50000N2X 78 1 86½ 86¼ 87¾ 613 68 Davis R G L 117 b 23.70 76-24 River Rush1213½ YankeeGentleman1171¾ FebruaryStorm117no Had no ra
1Jun02-6Crc yl 1 1/16 Ⓣ :234 :491 1:131 1:451 SimplyMajest75k 79 10 43 41¾ 73¾ 64½ 47¼ Beasley J A L 115 b 13.80 63-30 Lord Juban1223½ Noble Jester115¾ Erv's Creek1133 Lacked late respo
11May02-12Crc fm 1 1/16 Ⓣ :231 :471 1:11 1:42 Alw 24000N1X 79 3 43½ 44½ 44 3½ 1hd Beasley J A L 117 b *.80 86-12 WildBuddy117hd *FoolishPride*117½ Absolutly1171 Bumped late, prevai
13Apr02-10GP fm 1 1/16 Ⓣ :233 :474 1:114 1:42 + Alw 34000N1X 76 7 55¾ 66 52½ 54 63 Garcia J A L 118 b 5.30 82-15 ClssOfSeventy118½ BernieB118nk NobleJester118hd Lacked late respo
24Mar02-10GP fm 1⅛ Ⓣ :473 1:113 1:36 1:48 + Alw 34000N1X 77 4 75½ 63¾ 72¾ 32½ 35½ McCarthy M J L 118 b 7.90 88-10 Legisltor1224¼ *SquirrlnutZippr*1201¼ WildBuddy1181½ Stdy early & far t
2Mar02-12GP fm 1 1/16 Ⓣ :232 :482 1:13 1:442+ Clm 80000 (80-75) 78 8 711 86½ 63½ 51¾ 2hd Velazquez J R L 120 *3.10 73-23 FunnySoldier120hd WildBuddy120¾ TrueGnius120hd 4 wide, gaining slo
4Feb02-6GP gd *1 Ⓣ :23 :471 1:113 1:363 Clm 80000 (80-75) 76 9 68 55 53¼ 31½ 2no Douglas R R L 120 4.60 90-12 Bernie B118no Wild Buddy1201½ Tammany Star120¾ Led late, just fai
19Jan02-9GP fst 7f :221 :451 1:103 1:233 Alw 34000N1X 73 2 7 74¼ 65½ 58½ 514 Prado E S L 118 10.90 75-22 Speed Hunter1183 Saint Appeal1221¾ *Charioteer*1228 Off slowly, out
22Dec01-3Crc fm 1⅛ Ⓣ :484 1:13 1:374 1:494 Alw 28000N1X 66 1 41½ 42½ 51¾ 53½ 53 Karamanos H A L 117 7.20 77-15 **Charming Colony**117½ Moonluck117nk BernieB117½ Lacked late respo
1Dec01-4Crc fst 6f :222 :46 :583 1:114 Clm c-(40-35) 83 7 1 52½ 43½ 23 2nk Coa E M L 117 4.90 85-15 Sure You Can120nk Wild Buddy1171¾ Powder Keg115½ 3 wide, gain
Claimed from Sherman Michael H for $40,000, Salinas Angel Trainer 2001(as of 12/01): (250 39 40 34 0.16)
23Nov01-4Crc fst 5f :224 :471 1:002 Md 20000 (20-18) 63 5 5 56 53½ 53¼ 11¾ Velasquez C L 120 6.30 87-18 Wild Buddy1201¾ Mr. Jenks1202¼ *Banj*1203¼ Drew clear la
WORKS: Jly5 Crc 1 fst 1:481 B *1/1* Jun14 Crc 4f gd :501 B *17/32* ●May23 Crc 5f fst 1:012 H *1/16*
TRAINER: Turf(229 .12 $1.18) Routes(286 .14 $1.33) Claim(220 .19 $1.81)

5. Onlycook Half Ofit After finishing second in a pair of nonwinners-of-two allowance races at Churchill Downs, Onlycook Half Ofit was shipped to Saratoga by trainer Charles Simon and ran third in a $75,000 claimer against Charming Colony at the same 1⅛-mile distance. With Pat Day aboard, Onlycook Half Ofit went off at 6.80-1. He pressed the pace early, then tired to third, 4¾ lengths behind the wire-to-wire winner, He's Crafty, and 1¾ lengths behind Charming Colony in second.

5 Onlycook Half Ofit
Own:Ramsey Kenneth L & Sarah K
White, Red 'r,' Red Sleeves, White Hoop, **$60,000**
AILEY J D (109 30 13 12 .28) 2002:(564 152 .27)

Ch. g. 3 (Mar) FTKJUL00 $80,000
Sire: Siphon*Brz (Itajara)
Dam: Quarrel Over(One for All)
Br: Bwamazon Farm (Ky)
Tr: Simon Charles(14 2 2 1 .14) 2002:(183 31 .17)

L 118

Life	6	1	2	1	$35,410	85
2002	6	1	2	1	$35,410	85
2001	0	M	0	0	$0	-
Sar Ⓣ	1	0	0	1	$5,060	84
D.Fst	2	1	0	0	$12,990	75
Wet(305)	1	0	0	0	$0	55
Turf(260)	3	0	2	1	$22,420	85
DstⓉ(270*)	1	0	0	1	$5,060	84

1Jly02-4Sar fm 1⅛ Ⓣ $:47^1$ $1:10^3$ $1:35^2$ $1:48^1$ Clm 75000(75-65) **84** 6 2^2 2^{hd} 2½ 3$3\frac{1}{2}$ $34\frac{3}{4}$ Day P L119 b 6.80 83-16 H'sCrfty119^3 **ChrmngColony**$119^{1\frac{3}{4}}$ OnlyckHlfOft$119^{2\frac{3}{4}}$ With pace, no rally 7

0Jun02-9CD fm 1 Ⓣ $:24^1$ $:47^3$ $1:12^3$ $1:37^1$ Alw 42600N1X **82** 6 2^2 2^1 2½ $2^{1\frac{1}{2}}$ $2^{2\frac{1}{4}}$ Melancon L L116 b 4.10 84-14 Enttlmnt$123^{2\frac{1}{4}}$ OnlycookHlfOft$116^{\frac{1}{2}}$ MjstcThf$118^{\frac{3}{4}}$ Drift out bmp start,4w 9

2Jun02-8CD fm $1\frac{1}{16}$ Ⓣ :23 $:46^3$ $1:11^2$ $1:43^1$ Alw 43180N1X **85** 5 2^4 $3^{3\frac{1}{2}}$ 2^2 $1^{1\frac{1}{2}}$ 2^1 Court J K L115 b 10.90 87-11 CmpDvid115^1 OnlycookHlfOfit$115^{\frac{3}{4}}$ GoldShdd117^1 Drift out start,2ndbst 7

8May02-2CD fst 1 $:22^1$ $:44^4$ 1:10 $1:37^3$ 3↑ Md c-(30-20) **75** 9 $4^{2\frac{1}{2}}$ 4^2 $2^{1\frac{1}{2}}$ $1^{1\frac{1}{2}}$ 1^4 Martinez W 115 fb 9.10 79-18 OnlyckHlfOft115^4 WstrnDrms$115^{3\frac{1}{4}}$ SAccnts$113^{\frac{1}{2}}$ Angled 5w lane,driving 12

Claimed from Lazy Lane Farms Inc for $30,000, Brothers Frank L Trainer 2002(as of 05/08): (60 5 6 8 0.08)

9Mar02-7FG sly 1^{40} $:23^3$ $:47^3$ $1:13^1$ $1:40^3$ Md Sp Wt 28k **55** 8 $7^{4\frac{1}{2}}$ 7^7 $8^{6\frac{1}{2}}$ 7^{10} $7^{18\frac{1}{4}}$ Perret C 119 9.90 73-14 Wild Horses119^{10} Mark The Shark$119^{\frac{1}{2}}$ High Firm$119^{3\frac{1}{2}}$ Wide trip, outrun 10

8Jan02-10FG fst 6f $:21^3$:45 $:57^2$ $1:10^2$ Md Sp Wt 30k **59** 11 2 $7^{5\frac{1}{4}}$ $6^{7\frac{1}{2}}$ $4^{7\frac{1}{2}}$ 5^{12} Martinez W 120 14.30 77-17 *WorldTrde*120^{10} CowboyCt$120^{\frac{1}{2}}$ Connor'sGlory$120^{1\frac{1}{2}}$ Lacked serious rally 12

VORKS: Jly24 Sar tr.tⓉ 4f fm $:52^1$ B *21/22* **Jly11 CD 4f fst :50 B** *12/26* **May26 CD 4f fst $:48^4$ B** *14/32* **May20 CD 4f fst :49 B** *17/33*

RAINER: Turf(163 .18 $2.20) Routes(252 .19 $2.00) Claim(120 .19 $1.25)

Charming Colony had gone off at 5.30-1. But Day wasn't riding Onlycook Half Ofit today. Jerry Bailey was.

6. Mystic Storm This shipper was trained by Bill Mott, which immediately made me ask, "Why isn't Bailey riding?" Lonnie Meche had ridden Mystic Storm in his two most recent starts as Mott replaced Kenneth Wirth as trainer. In two nonwinners-of-two allowance races at Churchill Downs and Ellis Park,

6 Mystic Storm
Own:Kinsman Stable
Royal Blue, Brown Sash, Brown Hoop **$60,000**
UIDRY M (42 6 7 2 .14) 2002:(725 118 .16)

B. c. 3 (Mar)
Sire: Kingmambo (Mr. Prospector) $200,000
Dam: Am Sensational(Deputy Minister)
Br: Kinsman Farm (Ky)
Tr: Mott William I(51 13 6 5 .25) 2002:(430 102 .24)

L 118

Life	9	1	3	3	$40,971	80
2002	3	0	1	1	$9,051	80
2001	6	1	2	2	$31,920	69
Sar Ⓣ	0	0	0	0	$0	-
D.Fst	3	1	1	1	$22,150	65
Wet(325*)	1	0	0	1	$1,265	62
Turf(370)	5	0	2	1	$17,556	80
DstⓉ(400)	0	0	0	0	$0	-

4Jly02-9EIP fm $1\frac{1}{16}$ Ⓣ $:23^1$ $:46^3$ $1:10^2$ $1:40^1$ 3↑ Alw 23028N1X **80** 10 4^5 $5^{2\frac{1}{2}}$ 2^{hd} $2^{2\frac{1}{2}}$ $2^{4\frac{1}{2}}$ Meche L J L110 5.50 92-03 Mon General$116^{4\frac{1}{2}}$ Mystic Storm$110^{\frac{1}{2}}$ Mr. Krisley$116^{1\frac{1}{2}}$ 5w bid,no match 10

0Jun02-9CD fm 1 Ⓣ $:24^1$ $:47^3$ $1:12^3$ $1:37^1$ Alw 42600N1X **79** 9 9^{10} 9^{10} $8^{8\frac{3}{4}}$ $7^{8\frac{1}{2}}$ $4^{3\frac{1}{2}}$ Meche L J L116 14.20 82-14 Entitlement$123^{2\frac{1}{4}}$ **OnlycookHlfOfit**$116^{\frac{1}{2}}$ MjesticThif$118^{\frac{3}{4}}$ 5w bid,mild gain 9

Previously trained by Wirth Kenneth B

5Jan02-4Tam gd $1\frac{1}{16}$ ⊗ :23 $:47^3$ $1:13^3$ $1:46^1$ Alw 11500N1X **62** 1 10^{13} 10^9 $6^{6\frac{1}{4}}$ 4^{13} 3^{17} Castanon J L L118 2.10 71-20 *Bunk N Ted*118^{12} Coahoma118^5 Mystic Storm$118^{\frac{3}{4}}$ Failed to sustain bid 10

3Dec01-8Tam gd *1 Ⓣ :24 $:49^3$ $1:15^1$ 1:41 Alw 13500N1X **65** 4 9^8 $7^{7\frac{1}{4}}$ 7^5 5^3 $2^{3\frac{1}{4}}$ Allen M 118 *.40 76-20 AwolSoldier$118^{3\frac{1}{4}}$ MysticStorm118^1 Coahom$118^{2\frac{1}{4}}$ Wide, outfinished rest 9

5Nov01-3CD fm 1 Ⓣ $:24^2$ $:48^3$ $1:13^2$ $1:37^3$ Alw 49600NC **69** 3 3^1 2^{hd} 4^2 6^5 $3^{6\frac{1}{2}}$ Perret C L113 9.80 78-14 Honor In War112^{hd} Rylstone$121^{6\frac{1}{2}}$ Mystic Storm113^{nk} 4w,no closing bid 7

Previously trained by Tammaro John J III

10Oct01-8Pim fst $1\frac{1}{16}$ $:23^4$ $:48^1$ 1:13 1:46 Alw 26000N1X **65** 1 $3^{1\frac{1}{2}}$ $4^{2\frac{1}{2}}$ 2^3 $2^{5\frac{1}{2}}$ 3^4 Wilson R L120 f 3.10 79-23 *Outstnder*$115^{3\frac{1}{2}}$ OffThGlss$115^{\frac{1}{2}}$ MysticStorm$120^{1\frac{1}{2}}$ Chased inside,outfinsh 8

1Sep01-9Mth fm 1 Ⓣ $:23^1$:47 $1:11^4$ $1:36^3$ ContntalMile50k **62** 6 $7^{3\frac{1}{2}}$ $7^{3\frac{3}{4}}$ $6^{1\frac{3}{4}}$ $4^{3\frac{1}{4}}$ $4^{5\frac{3}{4}}$ Alvarado R Jr L117 f 6.00 80-11 Hunter Cruise$120^{2\frac{1}{4}}$ Fine And Dandy$120^{\frac{1}{2}}$ Dr Gold117^3 No stretch bid 8

6Aug01-2Pim fst $1\frac{1}{16}$:25 $:49^1$ 1:14 1:47 Md Sp Wt 24k **56** 2 1^1 1½ $1^{1\frac{1}{2}}$ 1^5 $1^{8\frac{3}{4}}$ Dominguez R A L120 f *.60 78-16 MysticStorm$120^{8\frac{3}{4}}$ Cryptobeat$120^{\frac{1}{2}}$ ClenBrek120^1 Towards ins,ridden out 5

7Jly01-1Cnl fst 5½f $:22^3$ $:46^3$ 1:00 1:07 Md Sp Wt 24k **46** 4 4 $5^{7\frac{1}{4}}$ $5^{6\frac{1}{4}}$ $4^{1\frac{1}{4}}$ 2^{hd} Goodwin N L118 *.60 81-19 Thomas Cat118^{hd} *Mystic Storm*$118^{2\frac{1}{4}}$ FashionAward$118^{\frac{3}{4}}$ Rallied five wide 6

VORKS: Aug11 CD 4f fst $:49^4$ B *13/20* **Aug4 CD 4f fst $:48^1$ B** *6/12* **Jly28 CD 4f fst $:49^4$ B** *11/20* **Jly6 CD 4f fst $:51^4$ B** *27/29* **Jun30 CD 4f fst $:51^2$ B** *45/49* **Jun14 CD 5f fst $1:01^4$ B** *9/20*

RAINER: 31-60Days(358 .27 $1.84) Turf(583 .23 $1.72) Routes(821 .23 $1.65) Claim(64 .19 $1.13)

Mystic Storm had finished a good closing fourth at 14-1 at one mile and a tiring second by 4½ lengths at 5.50-1 at 1 1/16 miles. Previously on grass, Mystic Storm had finished fourth, third, and second. He also had never raced farther than 1 1/16 miles. Mark Guidry took the mount.

7. Charming Colony Charming Colony was an interesting study whom I had picked in his prior start. His grass record was three wins, three seconds, and one third in 11 starts, but only nine grass starts were showing his past performances today. By using

the power of subtraction, I deduced that Charming Colony had finished first and second in his two absent grass PP's.

His first grass PP showing today was 1⅛-mile nonwinners-of-two allowance race at Calder, a race he won by half a length at 19-1 under Rene Douglas.

Trainer Vinnie Blengs moved Charming Colony up to stakes company for three starts at Gulfstream, and he finished second in the Dave Feldman at 31-1, seventh at 6.20-1 in the Grade 3 Palm Beach to the very talented Orchard Park, and fifth in the Gravesline Stakes, also to Orchard Park, at 6.40-1.

Charming Colony raced at Pimlico in his next three starts, running third by a nose in an optional $20,000 claimer at 6-5, sixth in the $75,000 Woodlawn Stakes at 7.80-1, and fourth at 4.40-1 in another optional $20,000 claimer.

Blengs gave Charming Colony almost seven weeks of rest and he returned to racing in a $50,000 claimer at Delaware, winning by a neck at even money under Ramon Dominguez.

I thought Charming Colony had some back class and picked him in his last start, a $75,000 claimer at Saratoga at 1 1/8 miles with Edgar Prado aboard. Sent off at 5.30-1, Charming Colony made a powerful rush on the outside on the far turn as if he'd blow past front-running He's Crafty, but He's Crafty's jockey, Jerry Bailey, had been playing coy, and He's Crafty surged to a three-length win. Charming Colony saved second, beating Onlycook Half Ofit by 1 3/4 lengths.

Charming Colony was dropping to $60,000 claimers here, and Prado gave up Wild Maple to stick.

8. Honiara Honiara's first two turf starts were a one-length maiden win at Belmont Park at 41-1 and a seventh by 7 1/2 lengths in the $83,000 Pilgrim Stakes at Aqueduct. After a poor December 7 performance on dirt, Honiara was out of action until his last race. On July 12 at Belmont in a nonwinners-of-two allowance on grass at 1 1/16 miles, Honiara was sixth by 5 1/4 lengths at 11-1 with the addition of Lasix. Chavez rode him at Belmont,

9 Honiara
Own:Cohn Seymour
Purple/white Blocks White Sleeves **$60,000**
BRIDGMOHAN S X (60 6 8 7 .10) 2002:(722 110 .15)

B. c. 3 (Feb) FTSAUG00 $170,000
Sire: Honor Grades (Danzig) $15,000
Dam: Da Bounboun(Sunshine Forever)
Br: John Phillips & Kent Sweezey (Ky)
Tr: Hertler John O(13 0 2 2 .00) 2002:(123 11 .09)

L 118

Life	5	1	0	0	$25,200	82
2002	1	0	0	0	$0	82
2001	4	1	0	0	$25,200	73
Sar Ⓣ	0	0	0	0	$0	–
D.Fst	2	0	0	0	$0	40
Wet(340)	0	0	0	0	$0	–
Turf(305)	3	1	0	0	$25,200	82
DstⓉ(330)	1	0	0	0	$0	73

12Jly02-5Bel fm	1 1/16 Ⓣ	$:23^2$	$:47^3$	$1:10^3$	$1:40^2$	Alw 46000N2L	**82**	7	4^8	4^8	$6^{4\frac{3}{4}}$	$7^{5\frac{1}{2}}$	$6^{5\frac{1}{4}}$	Chavez J F	L120	11.00	91 –	Peppermint Kid$120^{1\frac{3}{4}}$ *DeelitefulGuy*$120^{\frac{1}{2}}$ Getiton$122^{2\frac{1}{4}}$	Inside trip, no rally 7
7Dec01-7Aqu fst	1 ⊡	$:23^3$	$:47^2$	$1:12^3$	1:38	Alw 44000N1X	**40**	5	8^{19}	8^{23}	8^{18}	7^{30}	7^{28}	Galarza N^7	114	40.00	60-22	SoulOfTheTiger119^1 D'Coch$117^{6\frac{1}{2}}$ *OneTuffFox*$114^{3\frac{3}{4}}$	Stumbled badly start 8
6Nov01-8Aqu fm	1⅛ Ⓣ	:49	$1:13^3$	$1:38^3$	$1:50^4$	Pilgrim83k	**73**	3	$9^{8\frac{1}{2}}$	8^{11}	8^{12}	7^9	$7^{7\frac{1}{2}}$	Smith A E	117	27.50	77-14	Miesque'sApprovl119^{nk} Finlity$117^{2\frac{1}{2}}$ ReglSnction115^1	Inside trip, no rally 9
18Oct01-9Bel fm	1 1/16 Ⓣ	:23	$:46^4$	1:12	$1:44^1$	Md Sp Wt 42k	**71**	4	$10^{7\frac{3}{4}}$	$10^{6\frac{3}{4}}$	$7^{3\frac{1}{2}}$	3^3	1^1	Smith A E	118	41.50	75-21	Honiara118^1 Biagio118^{nk} *Clever Louis*118^2	Came wide, driving 10
25Aug01-3Sar fst	6f	$:22^3$	:46	$:58^1$	$1:11^1$	Md Sp Wt 41k	**35**	3	7	9^{20}	9^{12}	9^{14}	9^{18}	Gryder A T	118	83.50	70-08	Burnt Ember118^2 Easyfromthegitgo$118^{1\frac{1}{4}}$ *Bold Truth*118^5	Outrun 9

WORKS: Aug5 Sar tr.t 4f fst $:51^2$ B *16/20* Jun27 Bel 5f fst $1:02^2$ B *7/12* Jun18 Bel 4f fst $:49^2$ B *47/80*
TRAINER: 31-60Days(58 .09 $1.91) Turf(104 .05 $1.61) Routes(167 .08 $1.99) Claim(26 .04 $0.49)

but Shaun Bridgmohan was up today, not a good grass-rider switch.

Analysis: Gleam Supreme was an easy toss, and Honiara was next. Wild Buddy's dull return at huge odds was a turn-off. That left five. Wild Goose and Wild Maple had finished a head apart. Since I thought Prado's decision to get off Wild Maple was important, and those two had been so close, my next step was to eliminate both from my top three picks. Mystic Storm was interesting except for Bailey's absence on a horse trained by Mott. That meant I had to pick Mystic Storm third. Charming Colony had just beaten Onlycook Half Ofit, so I went with Charming Colony. Charming Colony won by 3¼ lengths at 2.20-1, paying $6.20.

That gave me the first half of the pick six, races three through five. But I'd gone against Persian Deputy, the 6-5 favorite in the sixth, a maiden race for 2-year-olds, in favor of a first-time starter trained by John Veitch named Vasquez. Eight of the nine 2-year-olds, including Persian Deputy and Vasquez, were first-time starters. Veitch, now training for John Ed Anthony's Shortleaf Stable, had not won a race at Saratoga since 1996. But Vasquez made a furious rally and finished in a tight photo with Western Rush, the 7-2 second choice, who had added blinkers in his third lifetime start. Vasquez had won by a nose at 6-1, paying $15.20.

There was no way I could continue to ignore the prospect of hitting the pick six.

In the seventh, I needed Svea Dahl, part of the 3-5 favored entry in a field of just five. Svea Dahl needed the entire length of the stretch to get past Lifebythedrop and win by a neck.

I had spent more than half an hour the day before handicapping the eighth race, a $52,000 allowance at one mile on grass. I had gone back and forth several times trying to resolve whether or not two obvious speed horses in the race, Tap the Admiral and River Rush, would duel each other into the ground, setting the race up for a closer.

Initially, I thought they would. But that was the coward's way out, I had told myself. It was too easy to look at these two front-runners and reach that conclusion, especially if you had only glanced at each horse's most recent past performance, which we don't. We read PP's from the bottom up, and this race was a perfect example of why we do that.

The scratches of Jaki's Magic and For Love and Honor would reduce the field to six.

2 Aslaaf
Own:Al Maktoum Sheik Maktoum b
Royal Blue White Triangular Panel
DAY P (82 12 8 4 .15) 2002:(741 162 .22)

B. c. 4
Sire: Quiet American (Fappiano)
Dam: Ville d'Amore(Irish River*Fr)
Br: Gainsborough Farm Inc (Ky)
Tr: McLaughlin Kiaran P(15 4 5 2 .27) 2002:(57 16 .28)

Blinkers ON **L 121**

Life	18	3	5	4	$133,575	100	D.Fst	9	2	1	2	$59,415	81
2002	5	1	1	0	$24,973	96	Wet(365)	1	0	1	0	$8,800	91
2001	9	2	4	2	$96,962	100	Turf(275)	8	1	3	2	$65,360	100
Sar Ⓣ	3	1	2	0	$46,000	100	DstⓉ(325)	3	0	1	2	$19,080	96

Race	Running line	Jockey	Wt	Odds		Finishers	Comment	
31Jly02-7Sar fm 1 1/16 Ⓣ :24 :48 1:121 1:413 4↑ Alw 52000N3X	**96** 6 31 2½ 2½ 31 21½	Bailey J D	L 117	*2.25	86-16	Jubileo1191½ Aslaaf117½ **Tap The Admiral**1192½	Game finish for place	6
21Jun02-7Bel fst 1 :222 :442 1:084 1:344 3↑ Alw 50000N3X	**81** 3 53 32½ 33 48½ 512	Bailey J D	L 118 b	*1.85	83-12	SntVrr1181½ **ForLovAndHonor**1184¾ MntIntrpd1175¼	Bumped start, 3 wide	8
26May02-6Bel fm 1⅛ [T] :472 1:104 1:344 1:47 3↑ Alw 50000N3X	**89** 4 2½ 2½ 2½ 32½ 52½	Velazquez J R	L 122 b	3.25	91-08	Harrisand122nk Illusionary1221¼ **TapTheAdmiral**1221	Between rivals, tired	7
7Mar02♦ NadAlSheba(UAE) fst *1 LH 1:37 3↑ Park Avenue Handicap	1½	Hind G	132	-		Aslaaf132½ Walmooh1222¾ Muthaaber130½		10
Timeform rating: 97 Hcp 23100						*Tracked in 4th,lacked room 2-1/2f out,rallied to lead near line*		
3Feb02♦ NadAlSheba(UAE) fst *1¼Ⓣ LH 2:05 4↑ Al Rashidiya (Listed) Stk 95300	726¼	Supple W J	120	-		Musha Merr1201¼ Celtic Silence1206¼ Clodion1216		10
						Mid-pack,3rd 3f out,weakened 2f out.Broche 4th,Nooshman 5th		
29Sep01-8Med fm 1 1/16 Ⓣ :223 :463 1:114 1:432 3↑ Alw 42000N2X	**86** 10 65½ 54 4¾ 1hd 22½	Coa E M	L 114 b	*1.10	80-18	Boastful1162½ Aslaaf1142¾ Baby Poppy114hd	Dueled,weakened 1/16	11
3Sep01-7Sar gd 1 [T] :24 :473 1:113 1:344 3↑ Alw 46000N3L	**96** 8 42 31½ 2½ 21½ 22½	Velazquez J R	L 118 b	3.15	91-13	Krieger1182½ Aslaaf1182¾ French Envoy120hd	Stayed on gamely	9
25Jly01-5Sar fm 1 3/16 Ⓣ :463 1:102 1:35 1:531 3↑ Alw 44000N1X	**100** 1 2½ 21½ 21 11½ 13¾	Velazquez J R	L 116 b	4.30	92-10	Aslaaf1163¾ *Megantic*1161½ *Szczerbiak*1202½	When roused, driving	11
21Jun01-7Bel fm 1 Ⓣ :224 :452 1:093 1:342 3↑ Alw 44000N1X	**92** 1 55½ 65 33 33½ 32¼	Velazquez J R	L 116 b	*2.65	84-19	**River Rush**116no *Krieger*1162¼ *Aslaaf*1161	Saved grd, willingly	12
24May01-9Bel my 1 :223 :453 1:093 1:354 3↑ Alw 44000N2L	**91** 4 2½ 2hd 1½ 2½ 2¾	Bailey J D	L 116 b	*2.55	87-18	Prime Customer121¾ Aslaaf1168¾ Amjaad116nk	3 wide, bumped stretch	6
Previously trained by Saeed Bin Suroor								
14Apr01♦ NadAlSheba(UAE) fst *1⅛ LH 1:472 Al Bastikiya (Prestige) Stk 200000	311¼	Carroll J	120 b	-		E Dubai1209 Dubai To Dubai1202¼ Aslaaf120		10
Timeform rating: 87						*Tracked leaders,one-paced through last quarter.Bakhoor 4th*		
24Mar01♦ NadAlSheba(UAE) fst *1⅛ LH 1:47 UAE Derby-G3 Stk 2000000	1020½	Carroll J	122 b	-		Express Tour122hd Street Cry1226 Lido Palace1283½		14
						Tracked in 3rd,weakened over 2f out.Tapatio 6th		

WORKS: Jly28 Sar 4f fst :502 B *32/38* Jly21 Sar 4f fst :491 B *15/30* Jly14 Sar tr.t 4f fst :51 B *4/10* Jun17 Bel 4f fst :481 B *17/79* Jun11 Bel 4f fst :49 B *10/36* Jun9 Bel 4f fst :49 B *24/101*
TRAINER: BlinkOn(12 .17 $2.84) Turf(64 .22 $1.70) Alw(57 .23 $2.29)

5 Tap The Admiral
Own:Pont Street Stable
Violet/pink Diamonds, Pink Sleeves
LUZZI M J (44 2 2 7 .05) 2002:(634 67 .11)

Ch. c. 4 KEESEP99 $32,000
Sire: Pleasant Tap (Pleasant Colony) $25,000
Dam: Polish Buck(Polish Navy)
Br: Highland Farms Inc (Ky)
Tr: Carroll Del W II(8 0 2 1 .00) 2002:(97 11 .11)

L 121

Life	21	3	6	6	$158,880	95	D.Fst	7	0	1	2	$13,830	78
2002	5	1	1	3	$54,100	95	Wet(350)	2	0	1	1	$10,710	72
2001	14	2	5	3	$102,320	93	Turf(290)	12	3	4	3	$134,340	95
Sar Ⓣ	3	0	0	1	$8,360	95	DstⓉ(325)	2	0	2	0	$18,400	94

Race	Running line	Jockey	Wt	Odds		Finishers	Comment	
31Jly02-7Sar fm 1 1/16 Ⓣ :24 :48 1:121 1:413 4↑ Alw 52000N3X	**95** 4 1½ 1½ 1½ 1hd 32	Luzzi M J	L 119	7.40	86-16	Jubileo1191½ **Aslaaf**117½ Tap The Admiral1192½	Set pace, weakened	6
29Jun02-8Bel fm 1 Ⓣ :233 :482 1:111 1:36 3↑ Alw 50000N3X	**94** 6 2½ 2½ 1½ 1½ 2no	Davis R G	L 118	3.10	80-14	Zoning118no Tap The Admiral1181¼ *Celtic Sky*117hd	Gamely rail, lost nod	6
26May02-6Bel fm 1⅛ [T] :472 1:104 1:344 1:47 3↑ Alw 50000N3X	**92** 3 1½ 1½ 1½ 1½ 31½	Luzzi M J	L 122	8.20	92-08	Harrisand122nk Illusionary1221¼ Tap The Admiral1221	Set pace, gamely	7
4May02-10Aqu yl 1 1/16 Ⓣ :244 :494 1:134 1:46 3↑ Alw 46000N2X	**93** 4 21 2½ 2hd 1hd 1½	Luzzi M J	L 122	*2.65	74-26	TpTheAdmirl122½ BlltCritic122hd CrdiffArms122no	Speed outside, driving	10
19Apr02-8Aqu fm 1⅛ Ⓣ :51 1:15 1:39 1:51 4↑ Alw 48000N3X	**95** 4 1hd 1½ 1½ 1hd 3¾	Luzzi M J	L 117	8.00	82-19	Whtmor'sConn120½ WlkngArond117nk *TpThAdmrl*117nk	Set pace, gamely	9
10Nov01-7Aqu fm 1⅛ Ⓣ :484 1:13 1:381 1:503 3↑ Alw 44000N1X	**93** 8 76 72½ 64½ 3nk 12	Luzzi M J	L 116	2.65	85-06	TpThAdmrl1162 DcnsStrm114nk DnglnNmbrs119½	Bumped start, driving	12
28Oct01-3Bel fm 1 1/16 [T] :242 :473 1:12 1:413 3↑ Alw 44000N1X	**91** 6 46½ 23½ 2½ 1hd 21	Luzzi M J	L 116	4.20	89-14	Accept1181 *Tap The Admiral*1162 *Jubileo*1192	Dug in gamely stretch	8
13Oct01-8Bel fm 1⅛ [T] :474 1:111 1:352 1:472 3↑ Alw 44000N2L	**89** 8 61½ 41¾ 3½ 1hd 21¼	Luzzi M J	L 116	5.20	91-10	WintrGlittr1191¼ TpThAdmirl116hd GoodBoySm119½	4 wide move, gamely	10
25Aug01-4Sar fm 1 1/16 Ⓣ :23 :464 1:10 1:402 3↑ Alw 44000N1X	**88** 4 21½ 2½ 11 2hd 61½	Chavez J F	L 118	4.10e	93-05	*Boastful*118no Jubileo1201 *Qawaqeb*116no	With pace, weakened	12
25Jly01-5Sar fm 1 3/16 Ⓣ :463 1:102 1:35 1:531 3↑ Alw 44000N1X	**83** 4 1½ 11½ 11 21½ 47¾	Chavez J F	L 118	9.30	84-10	**Aslaaf**1163¾ *Megantic*1161½ *Szczerbiak*1202½	Set pace, tired	11
5Jly01-4Bel gd 1¼ [T] :48 1:13 1:381 2:031 3↑ Md Sp Wt 42k	**89** 4 25½ 25½ 1½ 12½ 14	Luzzi M J	L 118	5.30	75-23	TapTheAdmirl1184 LeftOnNelson118hd *Bostful*1184	When asked, driving	8
13Jun01-6Bel fm 1 Ⓣ :224 :46 1:101 1:343 3↑ Md Sp Wt 42k	**88** 2 1½ 11½ 11 12 2no	Espinoza J L	L 117	35.75	85-17	Lots Of Truth117no *TapTheAdmiral*1172¼ Boastful1173¾	Yielded grudgingly	10

WORKS: Jly22 Sar tr.t 4f fst :51 B *17/27* Jly12 Bel tr.t 5f fst 1:013 B *3/7* Jun25 Bel 4f fst :504 B *25/35* Jun17 Bel 5f fst 1:04 B *24/24* Jun8 Bel 4f fst :48 B *3/41* May16 Bel [T] 4f fm :52 B (d)*8/8*
TRAINER: Turf(86 .13 $1.40) Alw(86 .14 $1.33)

7 Peak Dancer
Own:Centennial Farms
Tan, Red Sash, Red Sleeves, Tan/red
BAILEY J D (109 30 13 12 .28) 2002:(564 152 .27)

Ch. h. 5
Sire: Mt. Livermore (Blushing Groom*Fr) $40,000
Dam: Ballerina Princess(Mr. Prospector)
Br: Robert N Clay & Albert G Clay (Ky)
Tr: Mott William I(51 13 6 5 .25) 2002:(430 102 .24)

L 121

Life	9	3	3	1	$111,340	97	D.Fst	7	3	2	0	$97,700	97
2002	1	0	0	0	$1,900	87	Wet(365)	1	0	1	0	$8,800	89
2001	5	2	2	1	$76,040	97	Turf(290)	1	0	0	1	$4,840	86
Sar Ⓣ	0	0	0	0	$0	-	DstⓉ(320)	1	0	0	1	$4,840	86

Race	Running line	Jockey	Wt	Odds		Finishers	Comment	
24Jan02-9GP fst 7f :223 :452 1:103 1:231 4↑ OClm 80000(80-75)N	**87** 7 2 21½ 1hd 31½ 48	Bailey J D	L 120 b	3.10	83-17	*Dream Run*1202¼ *Bowman'sBand*1201½ **WindsorCastle**1204¼	Slim lead, tired	7
21Sep01-8Bel fst 1 :231 :451 1:093 1:354 3↑ Alw 48000N3X	**97** 5 4¾ 4¾ 1½ 1hd 2nk	Bailey J D	L 121 b	*1.20	88-15	Dash'nDance116nk PeakDncer1215¼ Justifiction1192¾	Speed 4 wide, gamely	7
25Aug01-6Sar fst 7f :23 :452 1:101 1:23 3↑ Alw 45000N2X	**94** 4 5 31½ 32 1½ 13	Bailey J D	L 122 b	3.75	90-08	PeakDancer1223 *DaytonFlyer*116¾ BigTlkinMn118nk	3 wide move, driving	9
28Jly01-7Sar fst 7f :222 :451 1:10 1:223 3↑ Alw 43000N1X	**95** 7 7 61½ 51½ 1hd 1½	Bailey J D	L 120 b	4.70	92-06	*Peak Dancer*120½ Amjaad1164 Final Dream120½	Bumped stretch, drive	12
28May01-8Bel my 1⅛ :47 1:13 1:384 1:514 3↑ Alw 44000N1X	**89** 4 1½ 2hd 1½ 2½ 23¾	Bailey J D	L 121	*.85	67-26	Galactic1213¾ *Peak Dancer*1212¾ *Tampa*1164	Stayed on for place	7
9May01-7Bel fm 1 Ⓣ :23 :454 1:092 1:331 3↑ Alw 44000N1X	**86** 5 52 52 42 43 34	Bailey J D	121	*1.40	88-14	*Navesink*1152½ Gasperillo Daze1211½ Peak Dancer121nk	3 wide, weakened	11
26Aug00-1Sar fst 7f :222 :451 1:103 1:232 3↑ Alw 43000N1X	**81** 1 12 4¾ 51¾ 2½ 94¾	Bailey J D	119	4.80	83-09	UncommonVlor119no FmosAgn1171 SmoknChb121hd	Hit rail 1/2 mile pole	12
7Jly00-3Bel fst 1 :231 :461 1:102 1:352 3↑ Md Sp Wt 42k	**94** 6 1½ 2hd 1½ 12½ 14¼	Gryder A T	116	*.45	88-15	PeakDancer1164¼ Mandn1167 ThunderRider1112¼	When asked, ridden out	6
4Jun00-6Bel fst 7f :223 :461 1:114 1:244 3↑ Md Sp Wt 41k	**78** 2 5 31½ 41¼ 21½ 2nk	Bailey J D	116	*.80	79-18	Past Due Account116nk *Peak Dancer*1164¾ Murhif116½	Lugged in stretch	7

WORKS: Aug7 Sar 5f fst 1:031 B *21/30* Jly31 Sar 5f fst 1:01 B *3/10* Jly25 Sar 5f fst 1:033 B *32/34* Jly17 Sar 4f fst :502 B *8/17* Jly9 Sar tr.t 3f fst :381 B *5/18* Jun18 Sar tr.t 4f fst :502 B *10/41*
TRAINER: +180Days(61 .18 $1.12) Dirt/Turf(93 .23 $2.64) Sprint/Route(109 .25 $1.88) Turf(583 .23 $1.72) Alw(452 .24 $1.76)

8 Montecastillo (Ire)

Own: Thayer Stella F
Pink Purple Sleeves Two Pink Hoops
CARRERO V (97 4 11 19 .04) 2002:(465 52 .11)

B. g. 5
Sire: Fairy King (Northern Dancer)
Dam: Arcade*GB(Rousillon)
Br: Baronrath Stud (Ire)
Tr: Connors Robert F(4 0 1 1 .00) 2002:(96 19 .20)

L 116 5

Life	22	3	3	3	$110,877	89	D.Fst	0 0 0 0	$0	–
2002	5	0	0	0	$4,300	89	Wet(289*)	0 0 0 0	$0	–
2001	12	2	2	3	$99,292	–	Turf(285*)	22 3 3 3	$110,877	89
Sar ⓣ	0	0	0	0	$0	–	Dst ⓣ(420)	11 1 3 3	$45,807	81

21Jly02-9Del fm 1 1/16 ⓣ :234 :471 1:111 1:422 3↑ Alw 54800N$mY 89 7 5 5¼ 6 3¾ 5 2¼ 3½ 62 Dominguez R A L 118 b 14.90 93-04 Private Slip118nk Royal Romp118nk Dog Tags123nk Wide bid, needed more 11
25Jun02-5Del fm 1⅛ ⓣ :471 1:112 1:364 1:483 3↑ Alw 46500N3X 77 1 34 35 33 2hd 68½ Martin E M Jr L 118 5.30 89-03 Tm'sTerms1231½ PolishTimes1201 SpectculrLight118½ Stalked,led,g way 10
8Jun02-11Bel gd 7f ⓣ :232 :454 1:10 1:221 4↑ Alw 49000N3X 83 8 10 10 12 108½ 74½ 56½ Bridgmohan S X L 116 16.40 81-12 Quiet One1161½ Point Of America1162¾ Zoning116nk Mild rally outside 11
25May02-3Mth fm 1 ⓣ :241 :472 1:104 1:353 3↑ OClm 50000 (50-45)N 81 7 77¾ 87¼ 76½ 56¾ 55 Lavoy R L 120 8.50 86-14 Flying Retsina Run120nk Szep120hd ⒹFull Brush1202½ Checked near lane 8
Placed 4th through disqualification.
9Feb02-7GP fm *1⅛ ⓣ :502 1:14 1:39 1:503 + 4↑ Alw 38000N3X 86 9 33 33½ 51¾ 42¼ 65 Velasquez C L 120 11.40 80-15 *Full Flow*1201¾ Absaroka120hd River Sounds120nk 3 wide, tired 10
Previously trained by Charles O'Brien
7Oct01♦ Tipperary(Ire) sf 7f ⓣ LH 1:41 3↑ Concorde Stakes-G3 1 1½ O'Shea T P 126 14.00 Montecastillo1261½ Toroca121½ Gaelic Queen121hd 12
Timeform rating: 113 Stk 75800 *Tarry Flynn4th,One Won One5th,D'Anjou(126)6th,Dr. Brendler 11th*
8Sep01♦ Leopardstwn(Ire) gd 7f ⓣ LH 1:293 3↑ Tote Exacta Handicap 45 Kinane M J 124 10.00 D'Anjou131½ Montpelier Street1052½ Provosky1182 18
Timeform rating: 97 Hcp 116000 *Mid-pack,towards rear, over 2f out,up for 4th.One Won One(125)5th*
18Aug01♦ Tipperary(Ire) sf 7f ⓣ LH 1:382 3↑ Andersen Race 1 10 Kinane M J 137 *.80 Montecastillo13710 Double Click1251 Meritocracy1252½ 12
Timeform rating: 107+ Alw 17400 *Tracked in 4th,2nd 4f out,led over 1f out,soon clear,easily*
6Aug01♦ Cork(Ire) fm 1 ⓡ RH 1:352 3↑ Platinum Stakes (Listed) 35½ Murtagh J P 131 12.00 Caumshinaun1283 Avorado1242½ Montecastillo1312 7
Timeform rating: 105 Stk 50400 *Led,clear 3f out,headed 1-1/2f out,soon weakened.Dr. Brendler 5th*
21Jly01♦ Leopardstwn(Ire) gd 1⅛ⓣ LH 1:514 3↑ Marlborough.ie Handicap 61¾ Kinane M J 130 8.00 Right Honorable117 Avorado130 Diamond Trim109 17
Timeform rating: 103 Hcp 77200 *Rated in 12th,progress over 2f out,stayed on*
1Jly01♦ Curragh(Ire) yl 1 ⓣ Str 1:402 3↑ Budweiser Guiness Handicap 31 Kinane M J 129 b 6.00 Osprey Ridge121hd Derivative1221 Montecastillo129½ 16
Timeform rating: 103 Hcp 64500 *Trckd in 5th,3rd 2f out,,bid 1-1/2f out,hung.Silverware(117)10th*
20Jun01♦ Ascot(GB) gd 1 ⓣ Str 1:401 3↑ Royal Hunt Cup Handicap 107¼ Eddery Pat 123 b 25.00 Surprise Encounter1212½ Big Furure119½ Muchea1243½ 30
Timeform rating: 96 Hcp 167000 *Rated towards rear,progress over 2f out,never catching leaders*

WORKS: May21 Del 3f fst :382 B *25/26*
TRAINER: Turf(76 .12 $0.91) Alw(99 .17 $1.68)

6 River Rush

Own: Gold Spur Stable
Black Red Ball Red Seams On Sleeves
MIGLIORE R (65 12 10 8 .18) 2002:(602 97 .16)

Dk. b or br g. 4
Sire: Strodes Creek (Halo) $6,996
Dam: Gracefull Wings(Groovy)
Br: Stonerside Stables Ltd (KY)
Tr: Lewis Lisa L(6 2 0 0 .33) 2002:(51 8 .16)

L 123

Life	14	4	1	1	$114,470	97	D.Fst	5 1 0 0	$18,060	58
2002	2	1	0	1	$35,060	96	Wet(385*)	0 0 0 0	$0	–
2001	7	2	1	0	$63,030	97	Turf(330)	9 3 1 1	$96,410	97
Sar ⓣ	3	1	0	0	$30,000	96	Dst ⓣ(380)	3 2 0 1	$61,460	97

3Aug02-10Sar sf 1 Ⓣ :242 :481 1:122 1:364 3↑ Alw 50000N2X 96 8 13 11½ 11½ 11½ 13½ Migliore R L 121 f 7.50 84-24 RiverRush1213½ YnkeeGentlemn1171¾ FbruryStorm117no Set pace, driving 9
13Jly02-4Bel fm 1 ⓣ :222 :442 1:081 1:334 4↑ Clm 75000 (75-65) 90 2 16 15½ 16 2hd 34¾ Velazquez J R L 120 fb *2.35 86-13 Treasured Gift1203½ Soldotna1161¼ *River Rush*1202¾ Set pace, tired 6
28Oct01-6Bel fm 7f ⓣ :23 :453 1:082 1:203 3↑ Alw 47000N3X 96 1 3 15 11 2hd 21½ Castellano J J L 116 fb 6.10 94-04 Krieger1201½ River Rush1161½ *Prime Pine*118nk Set pace, gamely 6
13Oct01-8Med fm 5f ⓣ :212 :434 :554 Matt Scudder50k 77 3 10 52½ 42½ 45 44¼ Luzzi M J L 114 b 5.10 92-04 Take AchanceOnMe1152¾ Pirate'sGold113½ Rock1221 Brushed gate start 11
25Aug01-5Sar fm 1⅛ Ⓣ :461 1:11 1:353 1:473 3↑ Alw 46000N2X 77 6 16 18 1½ 4½ 118¼ Castellano J J L 116 fb 16.10 90-05 Regal Dynasty1201 Ravaro1201 Deputy Strike1161¼ Long lead, tired 12
7Jly01-5Mth gd 1 1/16 ⓣ :23 :461 1:10 1:414 + LamplighterH75k 82 1 12 13 11½ 2hd 64¼ Coa E M L 113 fb *1.80 89-09 First Spear1141½ *Spruce Run*117½ Tremmor1142 Pace,inside,weakened 6
21Jun01-7Bel fm 1 ⓣ :224 :452 1:093 1:342 3↑ Alw 44000N1X 97 7 11 11½ 11 1½ 1no Chavez J F L 116 fb 7.60 86-19 River Rush116no *Krieger*1162¼ *Aslaaf*1161 Fully extended, gamely 12
5May01-6Aqu fm 1 1/16 ⓣ :224 :461 1:103 1:42 Clm 40000 (50-40) 92 4 16 110 110 112 19¼ Smith M E L 116 fb 5.00 94-04 *RvrRsh*1169¼ HomcookngRby1114½ BnsInThTns118nk Long lead, kept busy 8
17Jan01-3Aqu fst 1 1/16 ⊡ :232 :48 1:13 1:463 Clm 30000 (30-25) 58 3 12 11 1½ 24½ 46¼ Gryder A T L 122 fb 7.30 67-23 Wicklow Warrior1194¼ Max Patch119nk Activate1221¾ Set pace, tired 6
23Dec00-4Aqu fst 6f ⊡ :23 :463 :591 1:112 Alw 43000N1X 26 6 3 42½ 54½ 612 620¾ Bravo J L 116 fb 28.50 64-13 BincoAppl1182½ MgicAndBird118nk WildBndit1187¾ No response from turn 6
24Nov00-5Aqu fst 1 :233 :47 1:121 1:382 Alw 44000N1X 44 2 3½ 33 34½ 510 519 Arroyo N Jr L 118 fb 12.30 57-25 SeekingDaylight1218½ ManalpnAcdemy118½ FstLine1188¼ Tired after 3/4s 7
25Oct00-1Aqu fst 1 :233 :463 1:113 1:38 Md 50000 (50-40) 56 3 11½ 1½ 1hd 12½ 15¾ Luzzi M J L 119 fb 4.30 78-13 RivrRush1195¾ MgcFountn119nk Allgonwththwnd119no Pace, clear, driving 8

WORKS: Jly29 Sar tr.tⓣ 4f fm :491 B *17/24* Jun29 Bel tr.t 5f fst 1:024 B *3/12* Jun19 Bel 4f fst :48 B *14/49* ●May30 Bel Ⓣ 5f fm 1:00 H (d) *1/4* May20 Bel tr.t 4f fst :493 B *11/31*
TRAINER: Turf(55 .18 $2.10) Alw(51 .10 $1.34)

3 Windsor Castle

Own: Dogwood Stable
Green, Yellow Dots/collar, Yellow
VELAZQUEZ J R (112 18 13 16 .16) 2002:(887 178 .20)

B. c. 4 OBSMAR00 $45,000
Sire: Lord Carson (Carson City) $10,000
Dam: Frigidette(It's Freezing)
Br: Windwoods Farm (Ky)
Tr: Alexander Frank A(10 1 2 1 .10) 2002:(92 18 .20)

L 121

Life	16	3	5	2	$322,375	110	D.Fst	12 2 3 2	$263,475	110
2002	6	0	1	2	$64,275	110	Wet(330*)	4 1 2 0	$58,900	96
2001	3	0	2	0	$49,000	97	Turf(310*)	0 0 0 0	$0	–
Sar ⓣ	0	0	0	0	$0	–	Dst ⓣ(325)	0 0 0 0	$0	–

3Aug02-6Sar fst 7f :224 :45 1:094 1:212 3↑ Alw 51000N3X 98 3 3 22½ 21½ 32 44 Day P L 121 8.10 94-10 Voodoo1211¼ Aldebaran1211½ Smooth Jazz1191½ Chased pace, no rally 7
8May02-8Bel fst 1 :222 :442 1:092 1:352 3↑ WestchestrH-G3 96 9 84½ 85½ 51¾ 32 53¼ Davis R G L 113 2.60 89-19 FreeOfLove1141½ DytonFlyr1121 CountryBGold114¾ Altered course turn 9
6Apr02-8Aqu fst 1⅛ :471 1:114 1:363 1:491 3↑ ExclsiorBCH-G3 110 2 58½ 511 52¼ 1hd 2nk Davis R G L 113 3.70 90-14 JohnLittle111nk WindsorCstl1132½ GroundStorm118nk Came wide, gamely 6
10Mar02-10GP fst 1 1/16 :233 :473 1:114 1:422 3↑ CremeFrch H-G3 105 9 97½ 87¼ 87 75½ 32¼ Velazquez J R L 112 9.50 93-16 *Hl'sHope*1122¼ AmericnHlo113nk WindsorCstl112nk Swung wide, up for 3rd 9
25Feb02-8GP fst 1 1/16 :233 :472 1:111 1:424 4↑ OClm 80000 (80-75)N 93 7 54 51¾ 41½ 32½ 46 Velazquez J R L 120 2.20 88-21 Bowman'sBnd120½ GoldBlld1204 RichCelebrtion1201½ 5 wide move, tired 7
24Jan02-9GP fst 7f :223 :452 1:103 1:231 4↑ OClm 80000 (80-75)N 96 1 6 32 41½ 41½ 33¾ Velazquez J R L 120 4.00 87-17 *DremRun*1202½ *Bowmn'sBnd*1201½ WindsorCstl1204¼ Steadied leaving turn 7
9Jly01-8Bel sly 1 1/16 :221 :44 1:074 1:401 Dwyer-G2 96 4 45½ 47 47½ 27 25¾ Davis R G L 119 5.60 90-10 E Dubai1215¾ Windsor Castle1191¼ Hero's Tribute12115 Rallied for place 4
9Jun01-8Bel fst 7f :214 :442 1:082 1:213 Riva Ridge-G2 97 2 6 66 610 46 44¼ Davis R G L 120 17.00 91-05 PutItBack120nk FlmeThrower1202¾ *TouchTone*1231¼ Hustled, no response 6
23May01-4Bel sly 7f :221 :444 1:091 1:222 Alw 48500N$Y 93 3 2 33½ 33 23½ 25¼ Davis R G L 122 2.40 86-19 *Put It Back*1225¼ Windsor Castle1224¾ Fistfite1222¼ Inside trip, gamely 4
25Nov00-7Aqu fst 1⅛ :482 1:134 1:391 1:514 Remsen-G2 92 8 85½ 83¼ 72½ 2½ 12½ Davis R G L 116 7.00 78-17 WindsorCstl1162½ *Ommdon*1222 BuckIDownBn122¾ Swung wide, driving 8
5Nov00-9Aqu fst 1 :23 :462 1:111 1:363 Nashua-G3 97 8 71½ 81½ 52½ 22½ 21¼ Davis R G L 117 11.30 84-24 Ommadon1151¼ *Windsor Castle*1171¾ Griffinite1152¼ 4 wide move, gamely 10
15Oct00-7Bel fst 6½f :222 :45 1:09 1:153 Cowdin-G3 85 1 5 51¼ 62 64¼ 22¼ Prado E S L 119 20.80 92-12 Fistfite1192¼ WindsorCstl119no AmrícnCntury119no Altered course stretch 6

WORKS: Jly27 Sar 5f fst 1:01 B *5/41* Jly13 Bel 5f fst 1:01 B *4/25* Jun29 Bel 4f fst :484 B *26/95* Jun22 Bel 3f fst :363 B *4/11*
TRAINER: 1stTurf(13 .08 $1.63) Sprint/Route(26 .08 $1.56) Turf(44 .20 $2.26) Alw(77 .17 $1.52)

The favorite at 9-5 would be Aslaaf, even though his turf record, 1 for 8, was spotty at best. Of greater interest was that on June 21, 2001, in a turf allowance race at this same distance of one mile, Aslaaf had run third as the 5-2 favorite, beaten $2^1/_4$ lengths by none other than River Rush, who won by a nose at 7.60-1. The horse who finished in between Aslaaf and River Rush was Krieger, a speedster who would develop into a graded stakes winner.

Also of interest in Aslaaf's PP's was that he had faced Tap the Admiral three times on turf, beating him twice, most recently by half a length in his last start when he finished second to Jubileo. Jerry Bailey had ridden Aslaaf in his last two starts, but opted to ride Peak Dancer today for his biggest client, Bill Mott, even though Aslaaf was reacquiring blinkers.

Pat Day replaced Bailey on Aslaaf. Day is a Hall of Fame rider who is not as good as Bailey on grass. There are few jockeys in the history of grass racing that are.

Bailey had jumped ship to ride Peak Dancer, who was a non-threatening third by four lengths in his lone turf try, though it was without the Lasix he'd be racing on today.

But neither Aslaaf nor Peak Dancer was the key to the race. The keys were Tap the Admiral and River Rush.

Tap the Admiral was a hard hitter, showing a record of three wins, four seconds, and three thirds in 12 prior grass starts.

His entire turf record was on display in that day's *Daily Racing Form* because Tap the Admiral had followed modest success on dirt by making his most recent 12 starts on turf.

He'd made the lead 5 of 12 times, never by as much as a length.

In five starts this year, he'd been first by a head, second by a length, first by half a length, second by half a length, and first by half a length. But the half-mile times of those five races were 51 seconds, $49^4/_5$, $47^2/_5$, $48^2/_5$, and 48.

The most recent eight of River Rush's nine grass races were in the *Form*. He'd made the lead in all but one—he brushed the gate at the start of a stakes race and got away 10th, then rallied for fourth—and his lead was never less than a length.

His half-mile fractions on the lead were $46^{1}/_{5}$, $45^{2}/_{5}$, $46^{1}/_{5}$ twice, $45^{3}/_{5}$, $44^{2}/_{5}$, and, in his last race, with blinkers removed, $48^{1}/_{5}$ on a soft course. He'd won that one-mile grass race at Saratoga, his second start following an $8^{1}/_{2}$-month layoff, by $3^{1}/_{2}$ lengths. In his first start back, a \$75,000 claimer, he had blazed a half in $44^{2}/_{5}$ and three-quarters in $1{:}08^{1}/_{5}$ before tiring to third, $4^{3}/_{4}$ lengths behind the winner, who covered the mile in $1{:}33^{4}/_{5}$.

River Rush had won 3 of 9 grass starts at odds of 5-1, 7.60-1 and, in his last start, a nonwinners-of-three allowance at 7.50-1.

He was moving up in allowance company to nonwinners of four, but so what? Aslaaf was the favorite and River Rush had already beaten him on grass at the same distance as today.

Wasn't it possible that Tap the Admiral would take back? If he did, River Rush would have his own way, probably at a square price. I picked River Rush, who went off the fourth betting choice at 7-2 under Richard Migliore. Windsor Castle was 3-1 making his grass debut. He had a good Tomlinson Rating of 310, but not as high as that of River Rush, who boasted the best Tomlinson of the field, 330, and had plenty of turf form showing in the PP's. Peak Dancer went off at 7-2, Tap the Admiral 8-1, and Montecastillo 15-1.

The race was over on the first turn. Tap the Admiral did take back and River Rush cruised on the lead, getting a first quarter in a pedestrian 25 seconds. Ball game. Migliore did a masterful job on the lead, and River Rush was alone after a half in $48^{2}/_{5}$. After three-quarters in 1:12, he had a $5^{1}/_{4}$-length lead. He cruised under the wire $1^{1}/_{4}$ lengths ahead of Aslaaf and paid \$9.60.

The pick six paid \$2,086!

It was quite a rush, thanks to River Rush, a selection I might not have made had I not spent a great deal of time handicapping his race. I spend a lot of time handicapping grass races. You should, too. Go for the green!

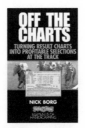